BRUSSELS

INSIGHT *City* GUIDES

Edited by Kristiane Müller
Translated by Jane Michael-Rushmer
Managing Editor: Dorothy Stannard

A P A

PUBLICATIONS

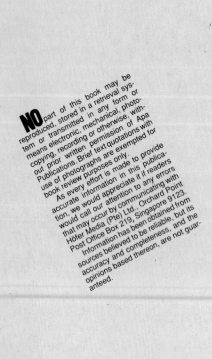
BRUSSELS

First Edition
© 1992 APA PUBLICATIONS (HK) LTD
Printed in Singapore by Höfer Press Pte. Ltd

ABOUT THIS BOOK

It is no accident of history that Brussels plays such a key role in Europe today; it has always done so. In the days when the Low Countries were in French hands, then in Spanish, then in Austrian, Brussels was always the chosen capital of "the Netherlands". Even since becoming the capital of the independent Kingdom of Belgium in 1830, the city has maintained its European identity. And, although the poets and thinkers, artists and merchants it once attracted have been largely superseded by the planners of the European Community and NATO, it remains a thriving place where not only Europeans but the world can feel at home. After all, no less than one in four of its inhabitants is a foreigner.

But there's more to Brussels than the EC and NATO. The city does, after all, possess what many consider to be the world's most beautiful market square, the Grand' Place. Another famous symbol of Brussels is the statue of Manneken Pis, which embodies the Brussels citizen's typical tendency to carp and his ungovernable spirit. It is in Brussels – which lies only a few kilometres north of the French linguistic boundary – that the clash between Belgium's contrasting cultures of the Walloons and Flemings can be most clearly seen. It is a conflict that manifests itself not least in the language rivalry. The visitor will immediately notice that signs and street names, as well as all city districts, are labelled in both Flemish and French.

Even if Flemish and French are the official languages, most people here actually speak French. And another aspect of the city with a decidedly French accent is the cuisine. Brussels is a gourmet's delight; the repertoire consists of much more than just the legendary "Moules et Frites". But Brussels doesn't only produce culinary delicacies; another speciality which has carried the city's name to all the corners of the world is Brussels lace, which continues to be produced here in the capital of Brabant, the capital of Belgium and the capital of Europe.

The Writers

It is partly the cuisine of the city that motivated **Kristiane Müller** to edit *CityGuide Brussels*. She likes to sample local specialities wherever she can, and has already done so for three other Apa guides: *The Rhine*, *Düsseldorf* and *Belgium*. For this book she explored Brussels and Brabant with **Eberhard Urban**, a calendar maker from Frankfurt. Here, he takes a look at some of the famous names to have been associated with the city – clergymen and philosophers, artists and writers, movers and shakers from Erasmus of Rotterdam and Karl Marx to Peter Paul Rubens and Pieter Brueghel the Elder. His daughter **Susanne Urban**, who studies politics and history in Frankfurt, provided the article about one of the darker chapters in Belgian history – the acquisition of the colony of the Congo.

Hartmut Dierks works as a journalist and radio producer in Northern Germany. Here he gives us an insight into what the long-serving king of Belgium, Baudouin I, actually does, in addition to describing the city's role as the headquarters of the European Community and other organisations. He also outlines what the city has to offer in terms of shopping and evening entertainment.

Nina Köster works as a freelance journalist in Hamburg. She is another experienced

Kristiane Müller *Susanne Urban* *Hartmut Dierks* *Nina Köster*

Apa contributor and edited *CityGuide: Cologne*. Here she describes the origins of Brussels, the fortunes of the city under Habsburg rule, the life of the emperor Charles V and the period after the 1830 revolution. She also describes the city's lacemaking tradition and examines why "Brussels is tops".

Kirsten Kehret from Frankfurt has also written for Apa before. For this book she wrote on the "Kingdom of Belgium".

The author and journalist **Rosine de Dijn** hails from Antwerp, though she has lived for almost 20 years in Cologne. She was responsible for tracing the fate of Jewish children during the war. **Joseph Lehnen**, a journalist from Brussels, looks at the development of the country after World War II. He also explores Brussels' fascinating Marolles district and describes some of the local personalities that have left their indelible mark on the city.

Gisela Decker teaches English and literature in Frankfurt. Here she reports on the problems of the continuing language dispute between the Flemings and the Walloons. **Helmut Müller-Kleinsorge**, who refers to himself as an "all-weather journalist", also looks beyond the boundaries of the city as such and explains why it is that the Belgians have only ever produced one sportsman of truly international standing, namely the cyclist Eddy Merckx.

Wolfgang Schmerfeld, who has also contributed to a number of Apa guides, looks at the way of life in Brussels' Upper City and examines what's on offer at some of the city's bustling markets. Every day is market day in Brussels. A journalist who reports a great deal about food and drink, Schmerfeld also samples what's on the menu in the city's best restaurants. It is not known whether he managed to taste all of the astonishing variety of beers available.

Few people know the Royal Greenhouses at Laeken better than local man **Edgar Goedleven**. He is director of the "society for the preservation of monuments and the landscape". The historian and author **Dr Barbara Beuys** provides a guide to the battlefield of Waterloo, reliving the events of Wellington's finest hour and Napoleon's final defeat.

The Photographers

The photographs are the work of a variety of specialists, including the portraits of Cologne photographer **Bodo Bondzio** and the best shots of another Apa old hand, **Wolfgang Fritz**, who explored Brussels and Brabant extensively. Further images were supplied by **Henning Christoph**, **Thomas Mayer** and **Jörn Sackermann** who maintain a photo agency in Essen. Last but not least comes **Ingeborg Knigge**, who has now lived in Brussels for some years. The picture selection was supervised by **Professor V. Barl.**

Special thanks go to **Madame Cécile Pierard** from the Vlaams Commissariaat-Generaal voor Toerisme and **Madame Annette Beautrix** from the Office de Promotion du Tourisme de la Communauté Française de Belgique, both based in Brussels. Thanks also to the Belgian Tourist Office in Düsseldorf as well as the journalist **Marion Schmitz-Reiners** in Antwerp who procured some important pictorial material.

The original German text was translated by **Jane Michael-Rushmer** and **Susan Sting**, under the supervision of **Tony Halliday**; the English edition was produced in Apa's London office by **Dorothy Stannard**.

Lehnen   *Schmerfeld*   *Stannard*

History and Culture

Preceding pages: the famous Grand Place.

Places

Maps

TRAVEL TIPS

**For detailed information
see page 225**

THE FOURFOLD CAPITAL

Opinions vary about Brussels. Matthew Arnold called it a "white sparkling, cheerful, wicked little place". Herman Melville, on the other hand, claimed "a more dull, humdrum place I never saw".

What isn't disputed is its key role in modern Europe. Thackeray's comment that it had "an absurd Lilliput look with it" belongs firmly to the 19th century. Today, about 1 million people live and work in the city. It is the capital of Belgium and Brabant and headquarters to thousands of EC and military personnel. Thanks to its high-technology industries, Brussels – the former weavers' town – is well equipped to march forward into the next millennium as a modern, cosmopolitan metropolis.

The city has a colourful history, and its fair share of legends. The man who planted Brussels at the centre of Europe is said to have been St Gaugerich; according to the story, he carried Brussels here as a seed in his bishop's mitre in the 6th century. In the course of time, both town and country were ruled by Burgundy, Spain, Austria, and France. Its inclusion in the Netherlands in the 19th century was only briefly tolerated. A performance of Auber's opera *Masianello* – in which Act IV contains the exhortation "No tyrants, no slavery; all power to the citizens!" – triggered the revolution which put Leopold of Saxe-Coburg on the throne as the first King of the Belgians.

Not to be forgotten are the darker chapters in Belgian history – the acquisition of the colony of the Congo under Leopold II and the German invasions during two world wars. A tribute to the struggle of the Belgian Resistance is included in this guide, as is an account of the rescue from the Nazis of hundreds of Jewish children.

Visitors enjoy getting to know all aspects of Brabant and its capital; there is plenty to see and experience here: the Grand' Place, the glittering Upper City, the historic Lower City, its top restaurants and humble snack bars, the colourful markets and the luxurious shopping arcades, the Heysel Park and the Atomium, the Botanical Garden, the Museums of Ancient and Modern Art, the Comic Museum, the Stock Exchange, the theatre, and the capital's surrounding countryside, from the idyllic towns of Leuven and Tervuren to historic Waterloo.

Preceding pages: richly-decorated and gilded facades recall the wealth of the city's merchants; the Atomium; the capital of Europe; celebrating – the favourite pastime of the people of Brussels. **Left**, the Catholic Church continues to wield its influence.

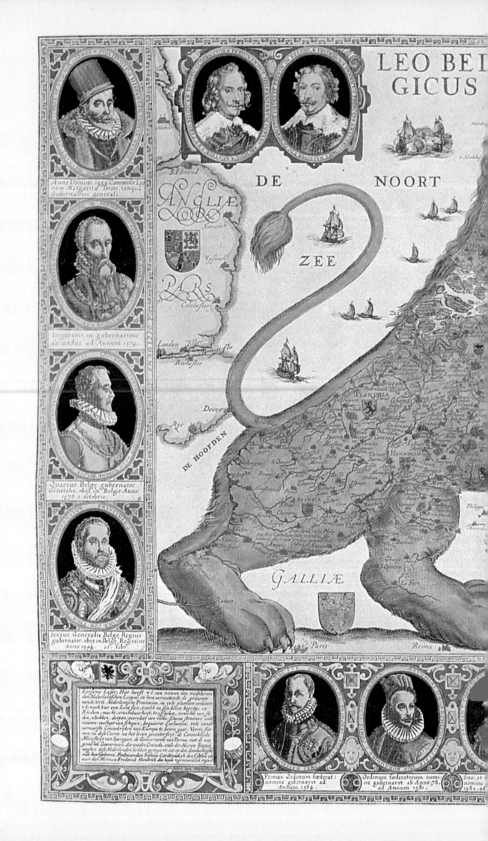

LEO BEL
GICUS

According to legend, it was St Gaugerich, Bishop of Cambrai – also known as St Gery – who was responsible for the founding of Brussels. It is said that he carried the seed of the city here in his mitre and planted it like a flower. At least, that is one version of the story. According to a more plausible version of events, the bishop fell ill here while travelling across his diocese and had a chapel built on one of the islands in the Senne. A settlement rapidly developed around the chapel. Opinions vary as to the exact date that this took place, but it is generally thought to have been some time between AD 580 and 695.

Brussels was first mentioned in records in the year 966, under the name *Bruocsella*, which means something like "The House in the Swamp." In 977 Charles of France, Duke of Lorraine, built a fortress here. Two years later he made it his residence. For this reason, 979 is regarded as the year in which the city was officially founded.

With the river – today completely built over – providing additional natural protection, craftsmen and merchants soon settled around the castle. The new town expanded rapidly when Count Lambert II of Leuven moved into a new fortress on the Coudenberg in 1041. In an unprecedented move, he ordered the building of a rampart to separate the classes of townsfolk. His knights and stewards and local merchants built their homes within its walls while the humble craftsmen and peasants were forced to remain outside. This strict segregation of the classes was to sow the seeds for many a future conflict.

The weaving industry: During the following century, Brussels profited from its location on the trading route between Cologne and Bruges and rose to prosperity and renown. Artefacts of worked gold and silver from

Brussels became desirable trading items. The town spread from the valley to the slopes of the surrounding hills.

During the 13th century the weaving industry flourished. Wool was imported from England and processed here. Nowhere else did the manufacture of cloth match the cloth-making industry of Belgium. Colourful fabrics from Flanders and finely-woven material from Brabant were in demand as far away as the Orient. The beneficiaries of this development, however, were the cloth mer-

chants rather than the weavers, dyers and fullers. The craftsmen were relegated to the position of humble employees, earning pitiable wages.

The worst examples of exploitation involved the Beguine communities, in which women lived and worked together as if in a convent but were not tied by lifelong vows. They sewed, wove and embroidered for the "Glory of God" – a privilege which benefited the cloth merchants rather than the women because it reduced still further the abysmally low wages of the industry. Some Beguine convents have survived until this day.

Preceding pages: Leo Belgicus. Left, the Cathedral of St Michael and St Gudula, the city's patron saints. Above, a recluse for women: the Beguine Convent.

The city soon began to express its burgeoning prosperity in fine building. In honour of St Michael and St Gudula, the town's twin patron saints, the construction of the Cathedral of St Michael was begun in 1225. The remarkable building with its twin towers was not completed until the 16th century, so it is not surprising that it should incorporate features of so many different architectural styles. It is known unofficially as "St Michael and Gudula's".

Class war: At the end of the 13th century the craftsmen revolted against the supremacy of the merchants and cloth manufacturers. They were tired of having to labour on behalf

of the privileged few whilst they themselves continued to live in poverty and without civic rights. They joined forces in an attempt to improve their lot.

Initially their efforts backfired, and their right to form a guild was made subject to the agreement of the town council. Their second offensive was more successful; in 1303, following the example of their fellow guildsmen in Bruges – who had ejected their French rulers in the "Battle of the Golden Spurs" – the oppressed masses of Brussels rose up openly against those in power and the patrician minority were forced to give way.

The guild of weavers, fullers and dyers was awarded the right of representation on the Town Council.

The peace following their hard-won victory was short-lived. In 1306 Duke Jean II, backed by the patricians' mounted troops, took up arms against the "Plebejer". The rebels were defeated in a bloody battle at Vilvorde; their leaders were buried alive before the city gates. From then on, craftsmen were forbidden to carry weapons and weavers and fullers, who had been at the forefront of the unrest, were subjected to a curfew and forbidden to leave their homes after nightfall. Nonetheless, the forces of change had been set in motion and the grim determination of the guildsmen enabled them to win progressively more civil rights.

To protect their city against foes from far and near, the upper classes of Brussels built a second enciente wall. It was 6 km (3¾ miles) long and enclosed 450 hectares (1,100 acres). Entry was via seven fortified gates and drawbridges. The position of the ramparts roughly corresponds to the ring of avenues encircling the city today.

By this time, Brussels was gradually eroding the position of Leuven as the capital of the Duchy of Brabant. In 1402 the foundation stone of a magnificent Town Hall was laid. Miraculously surviving the artillery bombardment by Louis XIV of France during the 17th century virtually unscathed, its 90-metre (200-ft) tower still dominates the market place today.

The building of the Town Hall coincided with the start of a new stage in the city's development. At the beginning of the 15th century the powerful Dukes of Burgundy assumed power in Brussels, a position they were to maintain until 1477. Their regency marked the beginning of an era of prosperity for the city. The local citizens – or at least, the wealthy upper classes – were able to enjoy life to the full.

The manufacture of artistically worked wall hangings replaced the cloth industry, which by this time was no longer able to compete with its English counterpart. Brussels tapestries became famous all over the world. Many of the redundant weavers were able to redirect their skills and make a livelihood in this sphere; those who could not left the city.

The Burgundian Court: In 1430 Philip the Good became the ruler of Brabant and Brussels became the favoured residential city in his powerful kingdom. As a result of a number of cleverly arranged marriages and fortuitious land acquisitions, by the middle of the 15th century his territories included Brabant, Flanders, Limburg, Holland-Zeeland, Hennegau, Namur and Luxemburg as well as Burgundy. Philip, like his son, Charles the Bold, who succeeded him in 1467, had a fondness for ostentation, luxury and elitism. To celebrate the occasion of his

its service. Jan van Eyck, for instance, painted the portrait of Philip's future wife, Princess Isabella of Portugal, and Rogier van der Weyden worked for many years as the official artist of Brussels.

The city became the arena for magnificent jousting tournaments and festivals, and an ambitious building programme was embarked upon. The Church of Notre-Dame-de-la-Chapelle, which had been destroyed by fire, was promptly rebuilt. The remarkable Church of Our Lady of the Victories was built at the behest and expense of the city crossbowmen, who decided to replace a smaller place of worship built in 1304. Pros-

marriage, he founded the Order of the Golden Fleece, a knightly order for the aristocracy of Europe.

The glittering lifestyle at the Burgundian court attracted large numbers of famous artists and craftsmen. Philip was the richest man in Europe and his court became a focal point of European civilisation and culture. Famous Flemish painters were employed in

Left, Philip III ("the Good"), Duke of Burgundy, amassed great luxury – and power. **Above**, weaving brought prosperity – at least until the revolt (painting by Isaac Clacsz, around 1600).

perous burghers surrounded the market square with dignified guildhalls reflecting the ruler's love of pomp.

The fall of the House of Burgundy was ultimately due to its over-ambitious aspirations. Charles the Bold's attempt to create an extensive, independent Kingdom of Burgundy, at the expense of his archrival, the King of France, including the province of Lorraine foundered in 1477 in the Battle of Nancy. Charles himself was killed in the battle. His body was discovered many days later, naked and bearing the marks of attack by wolves.

UNDER THE HABSBURGS

The death of Charles the Bold in 1477 brought to an ignominious end one of the great periods of European history. His daughter Mary's marriage to Maximilian I of Austria was the only thing which could save the Burgundian possessions in the Netherlands from French attack. There was, however, a heavy price to pay: the acceptance of the Habsburg yoke. When Mary died young following a nasty riding accident, the Netherlands sank into war and civil unrest. At one stage Maximilian himself was held prisoner in Bruges.

In 1494 Maximilian handed over the Netherlands to his 16-year-old son, Philip the Handsome. By virtue of his marriage in 1496 to the Spanish princess Joanna of Castile, Philip laid the foundations for what would in the future become the world empire of their son and heir, Charles V, born on 24 February 1500 in Ghent.

At the age of 15, Charles V took up residence in Coudenberg Castle. Although he spent little time in the Netherlands, travelling constantly in his capacity as King of Spain and Holy Roman Emperor (from 1519), he regarded Flanders and Brabant as his home throughout his life. In 1531 Brussels was declared capital of the Netherlands. It is to Charles that Brussels owes its cultural and political importance in 16th-century Europe. No other city within his vast empire profited more from Charles's reign.

Trade in luxury goods flourished. Brussels lace achieved world fame. Parisians in particular considered it fashionable to wear pillow lace from Brussels. Equally coveted were weapons forged by the city's smiths; Henry VIII of England tried in vain to persuade some of them to work for him. With the completion of the Willebroek Canal between Brussels and Antwerp in 1561, the city acquired a direct link to the North Sea.

Poets and philosophers, artists and merchants all revelled in the city's lively atmosphere. The great philosopher Erasmus of Rotterdam lived for a few months in Anderlecht. Returning home to Rotterdam, he looked back nostalgically on his visit. "Oh... if only Brabant were not so far away!" Pieter Brueghel the Elder, the most famous 16th-century artist in the entire Netherlands, left Antwerp in 1563 and settled in Brussels.

Science also flourished in the city. Charles V's personal physician, Andreas Vesalius, who was born in Brussels in 1514, was bold enough to disregard the taboos of the time and dissect human corpses in the course of his studies. His discoveries revolutionised medical practice and became the basis of modern anatomy.

Religious unrest: But dark clouds were already looming on the horizon. When Charles V abdicated in 1555, he was succeeded by his son, Philip II, who proceeded to rule the Netherlands ruthlessly from Spain. His father's means of preventing the forward march of the Reformation had been to have Calvinists beheaded or burned at the stake as heretics; Philip took even firmer action and sent in the Inquisition. When the religious struggle developed inexorably into a popular uprising against Spanish rule, the troops of the Duke of Alva set out for the Netherlands.

The duke established the "Bloody Council", intervening mercilessly and suppressing the revolt with great cruelty. In 1568 Count Egmont and Count Horn were executed on Brussels' market place for demanding more sovereignty for their country.

After Egmont's death – recorded for literary posterity by Johann Wolfgang von Goethe's drama – aristocratic leadership of the rebellion was assumed by Prince William I of Orange (William the Silent). A skilled negotiator and fundraiser, he succeeded in breathing new life into the struggle for civil rights and freedom of religious practice throughout the Netherlands and finally forced the Spanish to give way. In 1576

Left, a knight in shining armour: Charles V, German Emperor and King of Spain (copy by Peter Paul Rubens, 1603, after the original lost painting by Titian, 1548).

he entered Brussels at the head of a triumphal procession; and in 1579 he established the independence from Spain of the Seven United Provinces. But conflict continued. This time it was the turn of the Catholics to be persecuted.

Philip's desire to concentrate all power in himself led to a policy of repression, intrigue and a series of military campaigns. The ill-fated Armada which set sail from Spain in 1588 was to form part of an attempted invasion of England by a Spanish army from the Netherlands. Having previously sent the Duke of Parma, Alexander Farnese, to the Low Countries at the head of a large army,

sels, which remained capital of the Spanish Netherlands, returned to a peaceful existence. The economy boomed again, the gallows and scaffold disappeared, and courtly pomp prevailed once more.

Brussels' citizens rediscovered their taste for celebrations. At no other time were there so many processions and banquets as during the ensuing years. Peter Paul Rubens, the most famous baroque artist in Europe and, during his youth, Albert's court painter, captured the spirit of the era in his paintings.

The peace, however, was short-lived. In 1695 Brussels was drawn into the conflict between France and Spain which had flared

Philip had been able to force the rebellious southern states to capitulate one by one; in 1585 Brussels, too, was retaken by Farnese. In the meantime, however, the northern provinces had broken away from Spain and asserted their independence following the ceasefire of 1609. In the South, a mass exodus got under way; some 100,000 Flemings emigrated to the republic of the United Netherlands (the Netherlands of today).

In 1598 Philip transferred his power over the Spanish Netherlands to his daughter Isabella and her husband, Archduke Albert of Austria. During their reign life in Brus-

up at intervals throughout the century. Louis XIV's artillery bombarded the city for two days. Thousands of buildings were destroyed. The Grand' Place was reduced to rubble; only the tower of the Town Hall remained standing.

Within the space of a few years the citizens of Brussels completely rebuilt their city. The market place acquired its present character, which has won universal acclaim as an architectural masterpiece; and the harmonious fusion of Gothic, Renaissance and baroque elements has made the Grand' Place famous throughout the world.

The death of Charles II in 1701 marked the end of the Spanish branch of the Habsburg dynasty. After years of fighting, the Spanish possessions were divided between Austria and France. Then in 1714 the Spanish Netherlands were ceded to Austria. Brussels was torn apart by unrest caused by the new foreign rulers. The revolt was led by François Anneessens, the leader of the guilds. His execution in 1719, however, put an abrupt end to the uprising.

Under the Empress: A more settled era dawned in 1744, when Charles of Lorraine arrived in Brussels as governor on behalf of Empress Maria Theresia. He quickly set

fanned the smouldering resistance to Austrian rule. Although Joseph's attempts to curb the influence of the Church of Rome left most citizens apart from the Catholic clergy indifferent, he aroused unpopularity at every level with his range of administrative and judicial reforms.

In particular, his plans for a centrally-run German-speaking empire met with universal opposition. Encouraged by the revolutionary turn of events in France, the citizens of Brabant successfully revolted in 1789. They evicted the Austrians, and a United Belgium was proclaimed.

In 1792 the Austrians succeeded once

about improving the city. The Place Royale and the Forest of Soignes – the capital's green lung – both date from this period. The dignified style adopted under Charles's aegis is typified by the exquisite Place du Musée close to the Place Royale.

However, the over-hasty reforms of Maria Theresia's son, the Emperor Joseph II, who became sole regent of the Spanish possessions in 1780 following his mother's death,

Left, the city is dominated by the spire of the Town Hall. **Above**, a solid wall protected the citizens from the enemy outside.

more in winning back power, but just two years later they were forced to withdraw once and for all in the face of the French revolutionary army. Belgium now became French; and Brussels became the capital of the "Département de la Dyle".

The hopes cherished by its citizens – especially the poorer classes – in these new rulers were unfulfilled. A series of reforms was undertaken, but the misery of the masses scarcely improved. On the contrary: the Napoleonic Wars drained the city of its few remaining resources. Only the wealthy benefited in any way from the new regime.

In 1803 Napoleon himself visited Brussels for a reunion with Josephine. During his stay he attempted to ingratiate himself with the populace; the fountains gushed wine, and craftsmen were inundated with contracts. Nonetheless, few tears were shed in Brussels when Napoleon's empire came to a bloody end in 1815 on the battlefield of Waterloo, 18 km (11 miles) from the gates of the city.

Unification at last: At the Congress of Vienna (1814–15) the major powers decided to link Belgium with the neighbouring republic to form the United Kingdom of the Netherlands under William I of Orange. After more than two centuries of separation, the dream

of a single country finally came true – albeit only for 15 years. It was attended by a new flare-up of the old conflict between the Walloons and the Flemings, at the root of which lay the boundary between German and French spheres of influence, which divided the land in two. Brussels and The Hague were nominated joint capitals, but the northern half of the country, economically the stronger, set the tone. The constitution received no majority vote in the South, but was put into force by virtue of a trick.

William introduced Dutch as the official language in both halves of the country. Much

to the annoyance of the citizens, even in Brussels itself – for many years a French-speaking city – he ruled that Flemish was to be spoken in the schools and courts, and by all official bodies. Unrest was also provoked by the King's interference in the training of priests and the curriculum. Catholics and liberals alike felt themselves badly treated.

The slogan for the revolt against the loss of Belgium's autonomy first went up on the evening of 25 August 1830, during a performance of Auber's opera *Masianello* (*La Muette de Portici*) in the city opera house, the Théâtre de la Monnaie. The audience became restless during the aria *Sacred love of our Fatherland.* "Far better to die than to live a wretched life in slavery and shame! Away with the yoke before which we tremble; away with the foreigner who laughs at our torment!" The words expressed precisely the feelings of the citizens of Brussels under the rule of William and the Dutch.

The finale of Act III heightened tensions in the theatre: "Bring your weapons! Bring your torches! Courage! We shall fight now for the victory of our cause!" And during Act IV, as the cry went up, "No, no more tyranny! No more slavery! Power henceforth to the citizens!", the audience rose from their seats and stormed on to the streets, where a workers' demonstration was taking place. Together, the insurgents stormed the Palais de Justice. The revolution was triggered.

The troops of the Netherlands army were successfully beaten back. On 25 September 1830 a provisional government was established; it declared the independence of Belgium on 4 October. Brussels became the capital of the new kingdom; the throne was offered to Leopold of Saxe-Coburg (1790–1865), who at this time was living at the English court and who entered Brussels in triumph in July 1831. He married one of the daughters of Louis Philippe of France. Leopold ruled the country strictly according to the constitution. He managed to safeguard and strengthen Belgium's neutrality.

Left, the 1830 uprising brought Belgium liberation and independence. Right, Charles V abdicated the throne in 1555 in favour of his son Philip (a 16th-century etching by Hogenberg).

EMPEROR CHARLES V

Charles V, Holy Roman Emperor and King of Spain lived in the saddle of a fast horse or on the creaking deck of a sailing ship. His territories and responsibilities were vast. Despite his sickly constitution, the last emperor of the Middle Ages made nine journeys to Germany, seven to Italy, six to Spain, four to France, two to England and two to Africa.

Flanders and Brabant were the nearest thing to home that Charles ever knew. He was born on 20 February 1500 in Ghent, the son of Philip the Handsome, King of Castile, and Joanna the Mad. His childhood was spent in Mechelen, but it was in

Emperor's crown. In 1522 Charles returned to strengthen his hold on Spain, which was torn apart by rebellion.

He had no chance to settle down. The Spanish and Habsburg empire he had inherited extended across Europe from Spain and the Netherlands to Austria and the Kingdom of Naples, stretching across the Atlantic Ocean to Spanish America. Time and again he was forced to take up arms – to put down his archrival, François I of France or to quash the infidels (Turks and Protestants) within and without his realm.

In the final analysis, he failed on both these counts. By the end of his life he had managed to prevent neither the schism within the Christian church nor the fragmentation of his empire. Charles's fortunes waxed and waned as King

Brussels that he was declared of age, being nominated Duke of Brabant and King of Spain (as Charles I) in 1516. He returned again and again to his native land; and at heart he remained a Netherlander all his life. He shared with his compatriots a love of good food, riotous feasting and fine art. As an old man he referred to the Netherlands in a letter to his son Philip as "Our Father Burgundy".

And yet, he never had the chance to settle there. His life of travelling began when he was only 17. After the death of his grandfather, Ferdinand of Aragon, he sailed to Spain in order to take up the reins of government there. But, three years later, in the summer of 1520, before he had a chance to win over the proud southerners to his cause, he had to hurry to Germany to receive the Holy Roman

Henry VIII of England and the popes transferred their allegiance between his cause and that of François I and back again.

In 1553, old, sick and disillusioned after a lifetime of almost continuous war, he returned to the Netherlands. It was here that he made his last public appearance in October 1555. In a moving speech before the assembled estates of the 17 provinces in the Great Hall of his castle in Brussels, Charles V renounced the throne of the Netherlands in favour of his son Philip. At the beginning of 1556 he also relinquished the Spanish crown; and shortly after that he abdicated as Holy Roman Emperor in favour of his brother Ferdinand. Divested of power, he left the Netherlands for ever, retiring to San Geronimo de Yuste in Spain, where he died in 1558.

THE BATTLE OF WATERLOO

About 10 km (6 miles) south of the Belgian capital lies Waterloo, where Napoleon, following his period of exile on Elba, attempted to return to the political arena of Europe. It was here in June, 1815, in an area of countryside just 2 km square, that 45,000 men died in agony or were seriously crippled and 15,000 horses were slaughtered.

From half-past two during the night of 15 June 1815, the French army could be seen marching northwards in two columns – a total of 125,000 men and 25,000 horses. The next day, at noon, Napoleon, mounted on his dainty grey, rode through Charleroi. Leaving the town behind him, he rode on to a rise where the road forked left towards Brussels and right towards Fleurus. Here the Emperor came to a halt. Back on the road, the endlessly winding procession was veiled in dust; the tramping of thousands of soldiers mingled with the rhythmical beating of drums, the shrill blasts of bugles and the echoing cries of *"Vive l'Empereur!"*

Battle tactics: A short time later, Napoleon explained his war strategy to his field marshals and commanders. The English soldiers, under the command of the Duke of Wellington, had stationed themselves around Brussels; the Prussian troops, under Field Marshal Blücher, were approaching from the Rhine. It was essential to French success that these two armies should be prevented from joining forces.

It was not until 26 February 1815 that Napoleon had been able to leave his place of exile of the island of Elba. But he didn't waste much time in re-establishing his power. On 20 March he had entered Paris in triumph. Within five days, an alliance had been formed by Austria, England, Prussia and Russia with the aim of waging war against him.

On Friday 16 June 1815, Marshal Blücher set up his command post in the windmill at Brye. Only a few kilometres to the south as the crow flies Napoleon had installed himself in a windmill near Fleurus, from which point he could observe the troop movements of his opponent through a telescope. At 3 p.m. he gave the signal to attack.

The Prussian army had lined up a force of 84,000 men and 216 cannon, and were dug in at Ligny; they hoped that Wellington's troops would reach them during the course of the afternoon. Napoleon had 67,500 men and 164 cannon.

Ligny was soon engulfed in a sea of flames under the carefully aimed gunfire of the French. The Prussians waited in vain for reinforcements from the English. By 10 o'clock that night it was clear that the French would emerge from the bloodbath victorious and Prussia, having lost the battle but not the war, beat an ordered retreat. That same night they marched off in a northerly direction with the intention of joining the English in the final struggle against Napoleon. Almost 20,000 dead and wounded remained on the field of battle.

Napoleon failed the next day to reinforce the advantage he had gained at the battle of Ligny. Wellington and his troops, who had left Brussels the previous night, took up battle positions on the hill known as Mont St.-Jean on the road between Brussels and Charleroi. Their plan was to ward off the French army until Blücher arrived. Wellington himself established his headquarters three kilometres to the north, in the old posting station of the village of Waterloo. During the afternoon of 17 June there was a sudden thunderstorm.

Napoleon reached the Belle Alliance inn, 9 km (5 miles) south of Waterloo on the Brussels road, shortly after 6 p.m.. He watched Wellington's troops setting up camp across the valley on the Mont St-Jean, only 1.5 km away, then took up quarters himself in the dairy farm La Caillou.

The rain looked as if it would never cease. The cavalry soldiers sat huddled in their saddles trying to snatch some sleep. The foot

Preceding pages: a modern re-enactment of the Battle of Waterloo. **Left,** a more contemporary view of the decisive battle.

soldiers searched in vain for dry patches in the trampled fields of corn. The camp fires had to be stoked continually with wood. They produced clouds of acrid smoke, but very little warmth. It had been a wasted day, a day for reflection.

The protagonists: The three leading players in the battle of Waterloo were no strangers to each other. For 20 years, Europe had acted as a stage for their posturings. Napoleon Bonaparte, a native of Corsica, was the most famous of the three. He had become consul, emperor, ruler of the continent and beneficiary of the Great Revolution of 1789. But Arthur Wellesley, since 1814 First Duke of Wellington, and Gebhard Leberecht Blücher, a Pomeranian landowner and field marshal, were both revered military men.

Wellington, a tall, slim Irishman, was a typical product of the British aristocracy. Cool, almost phlegmatic, he regarded soldiering merely as a job, not a matter for emotional involvement. He rarely wore a uniform; his tailor was considered one of the finest in England. He had been commissioned in 1787, and from 1796 to 1805 had served as a soldier and administrator in India. In 1808 the British government had sent him to Portugal to support the local citizens' guerrilla war against the Napoleonic forces of occupation. In defeating the French, he had allowed their forces to withdraw, a concession for which he was court-martialled but later exonerated. In 1812 he had marched into Madrid, driving Napoleon's forces back into France; two years later, he had reached Toulouse.

What drove Blücher on to the battlefield was hatred; his hatred of Napoleon and his destructive power. The longer Napoleon's rule lasted, and the more oppressive it became, the more Blücher's view was shared by his compatriots. With every battle which Napoleon won, and with every corner of Europe he seized, the more Prussia yearned for freedom and unity.

The Germans proved apt pupils when it came to learning the lessons of the French Revolution. The twin ideas of nationhood and democracy were born together. During the struggle against Napoleon, a pan-German patriotism arose for the first time,

spreading across the frontiers of the many individual German states.

There was a basic difference in the motives of the English and the Prussians. The English were determined to defy Napoleon, but their enmity remained basically dispassionate: they already lived with a confident national identity. However, Napoleon's territorial aspirations had destroyed Prussia, the one state on which German hopes of national unity were based, and the Prussians wanted their revenge. Shrill voices of protest were to be heard from the intellectual élite, whose violent resistance to Napoleon echoed the missionary-like fervour of the

French revolutionaries. When, in 1813, the French tyrant had been defeated near Leipzig by an alliance between Prussian and Russian forces, with the assistance of Sweden, the nationalist movement in Germany – which had been gaining steady support – had become full of hope.

But the diplomats at the Congress of Vienna in 1814 were divided as to the best way of resolving the most pressing problems in Europe. The majority remained determined to reinstate the feudal conditions of 1789 and to prevent the rise of a powerful Germany. The Congress of Vienna attempted to set out the framework for the restoration of order in post-revolutionary Europe, but for the Germans it signalled the beginning of a long period of frustration, of the failure of national democratic hopes. Blücher, by this time 73 years old, shouted to the soldiers as they set off westwards from Berlin in June 1815, "Now we soldiers can put right the diplomats' blunders!"

The campaign to defeat Napoleon represented a combined strategy by the Allied Coalition – the seventh formed against France between 1792 and 1815. A total of five armies was involved: an Anglo-Dutch force under Wellington and Blücher's Prussian regiments were to meet near Brussels and converge on France; the Austrians under Karl Philipp zu Schwarzenberg were to operate along the Rhine, with the Russians led by Barclay de Tolly in reserve; and an Austro-Italian army commanded by Johann Maria Frimont were to block a retreat from northern Italy.

During that June of 1815, the English and Prussian forces spearheaded the attack. Refusing to be discouraged by the defeat at

Ligny on 16 June, during which Blücher was wounded, the Prussians broke camp at Wavern at dawn on 18 June to continue their westward march. Blücher was in good spirits. He was confident that once they had joined forces with the English army, his soldiers would easily defeat Napoleon.

Napoleon and his troops also rose early that Sunday. The breakfast table was laid before 5 a.m. But, as fate would have it, bad rain impaired visibility, and the attack – planned for 9 a.m. – was delayed. The gun crews could hardly move the cannon on the muddy ground even with teams of 15 men and 12 horses per gun. But, despite such

unpromising conditions, Napoleon was sure that victory would be his: "Gentlemen, if you carry out my orders well, we shall sleep tonight in Brussels," he said.

Napoleon's defeat: At 11.30, from his command post south of the Belle Alliance inn, the emperor gave the signal to attack. The English troops were engulfed in the fire from 120 French cannon. Opposite, in his headquarters at Mont St-Jean, Wellington took shelter under an elm tree, from where he could direct his army.

In the valley between Mont St-Jean and the Belle Alliance lay the ancient manor of

Left, a smile from a girl dressed as a French sutler. **Above**, into battle with music and wine.

Hougoumont to the west and the farmstead La Haie Sainte to the east, on the road to Brussels; both were occupied by English troops. It was evident that if the French wanted to storm the Mont St-Jean they would need to take both strongholds first.

The attack on Hougoumont started shortly after 11 a.m. At 5 p.m. the French gave up the attempt. Piled up in front of the perimeter wall was a gruesome heap of corpses – almost 3,000 French soldiers lost their lives in the assault. In the meantime, at 1 p.m., Napoleon had ordered his men to attack the centre of the valley. He had already been informed that the Prussians were approach-

ing, but it did not alter his plan.

The French infantry charged down into the valley in columns of 4,800 men in 24 rows of 200 soldiers each. The English forces waited behind the embrasures of La Haie Sainte or behind the hills. A deadly rain of cannon fire engulfed the manor; to the amazement of the French, thousands of English soldiers suddenly rose up from the crest of the hill and fired their muskets.

The French, even more than their opponents, fought as if in a drunken frenzy. Some of their columns did actually manage to reach the top of the eminence, but the task of killing the enemy became progressively more difficult as the growing mountains of dead soldiers and horses hampered their advance. At 6.30 p.m. the French Tricolour was hoisted above La Haie Sainte. Wellington's front at the heart of the Mont St-Jean wavered. He had no more reserves. Hopes for the arrival of Blücher or nightfall was the only comfort he could offer his generals when they demanded fresh supplies.

But Napoleon, too, had only one more reserve battalion when, at about 7.30 p.m., the first brigades of Prussians reached the battlefield. The emperor sent his personal guard charging down the hill of Belle Alliance. The well-aimed fire of the English marksmen hit them fatally at short range. By 8.30 p.m., Blücher and his entire army had arrived. Shortly afterwards there was no holding the French; they knew they faced defeat. The battle cry went up "Run for your life!" as the Prussians and British careered down the hillside after the fleeing soldiers.

Victory and repercussions: At 9.30 p.m., Wellington and Blücher embraced each other in the courtyard of the Belle Alliance inn. The Prussian band played "God Save the King" and *"Grosser Gott, wir loben Dich"*. News of the French defeat reached Brussels at about 10 o'clock. Four days afterwards, Napoleon dictated his second document of abdication in Paris. In Wellington's words, the outcome of the battle had been "the nearest run thing you ever saw in your life."

It is Wellington who in most British minds was the key figure in the the victory at Waterloo; but in Germany Blücher became an equally popular hero and a symbol of German aspirations. These aspirations were thwarted at the Congress of Vienna, and for the Germans 1815 signalled the beginning of a long period of frustration, of the failure of national democratic hopes, which would be repeated in the Revolution of 1848.

On 18 June 1990, the 175th anniversary of the battle was celebrated in colourful costumes on the battlefield of Waterloo. Visitors travelled to witness the occasion from England, France and Germany.

The English infantry (left) lives to fight another day, to the displeasure of Napoleon (right).

42

THE KINGDOM OF BELGIUM

After the battle of Waterloo in 1815, the country which would later be known as Belgium once more found its fate in the hands of foreign powers. The members of the "Holy Alliance" – Austria, Britain, Russia, Prussia, France and the papacy – linked Belgium with the Netherlands to form the "United Netherlands". The union took no account of the historical, political and economic differences between the two halves of this uneasy partnership.

Dissatisfaction with this arrangement quickly took root, with the Belgians seeing themselves as victims of discrimination. Catholics, liberals, supporters of the French connection and conservatives all united with the common aim of ridding their land of the rule of the Dutch House of Orange. When a number of petitions sent to the foreign rulers brought about no improvement, social and national tensions increased.

National independence: France became Belgium's role-model. In France itself, the July Revolution of 1830 aimed to revive the ideals of the 1789 French Revolution. For the Belgians this was to prove the signal to rise up against the House of Orange. In August 1830 the War of Independence began in Brussels, actively supported by the French government.

The 4 October of that year went down in the annals of Belgian history. On this day, Belgium officially declared itself to be an independent country. The provisional government demanded instant recognition of the new state by other European governments. A few months later on 26 July 1831, during the London Conference, the European Great Powers confirmed Belgium's independence and guaranteed its neutrality.

This acceptance of the new nation's autonomy marked the first step along the road towards true independence. As the next step, the newly-created parliamentary monarchy

needed a suitable king. In their search for an appropriate sovereign, the political leaders of the country agreed upon Leopold of Saxe-Coburg. By virtue of his blood ties with the English monarchy (he was the uncle of Queen Victoria), his education, his diplomatic skills and his interest in military matters, Leopold united all the qualities considered to be desirable prerequisites of a representative royal sovereign.

In 1831, the national congress voted

Leopold of Saxe-Coburg king, and 21 July was proclaimed a day of national rejoicing.

In 1832, Leopold I married Louise, a daughter of King Louis Philippe of France – an act which strengthened the friendly links between the two countries.

Leopold I's principal successes lay in the improvement his reign saw in relations between Belgium and the neighbouring Netherlands and the foundations that were laid for the industrialisation of the country. However, despite such measures, from 1840 an undercurrent of restlessness could be detected beneath the apparently calm surface

Left, the Belgian flag is aired for the national holiday. **Above**, the first king of the Belgians was a German: Leopold I of Saxe-Coburg-Gotha.

and workers began to rebel against their appalling living conditions. Leopold I was unable to live up to his task as mediator and unifier of the Flemings and the Walloons and against the background of the language dispute, initially regarded as a secondary problem, violence repeatedly broke out. On his death, in 1865, Leopold bequeathed a range of social problems to the son who succeeded him, Leopold II.

Private colony: The new king had various aims, principally characterised by his own personal interests rather than those of the nation as a whole. First, he attempted to boost the national economy by bringing his

tioned in 1885 by 14 nations at the Berlin Congo Conference, under the chairmanship of Bismarck. In return, Leopold agreed to allow unrestricted trade and freedom of navigation within the Congo basin. Belgium's economic upswing profited still further from this exploitation of the colony. Meanwhile, in England and Belgium, opposition to this private colony was growing, and in 1908 Leopold found himself obliged to subordinate his sovereignty over the Congo to the Belgian parliament.

Leopold, a man who had repeatedly managed to assert his personal will against the liberal powers of parliament, died one year

influence to bear on Belgian financial policy, and then, having achieved this, he set about realising his long-cherished dream of colonial power.

The king's intermediary in the African Congo was an Englishman, Sir Henry Morton Stanley. Through the offices of Stanley and by pursuing a policy of murder, deception and colonialism of the worst type imaginable Leopold II gained control of the entire Congo basin. The region, half the size of Western Europe, in effect became his private property.

Leopold II's coup in the Congo was sanc-

later. The next king, Albert I, was his nephew. In 1914 German troops marched into Belgium at the beginning of World War I and Leopold II declared war. Belgium was defeated later that same year; but at the Treaty of Versailles at the end of the war Belgium gained the German-speaking territories of Eupen and Malmedy.

Albert I died near Namur during a mountain walking trip in 1934. His son was crowned Leopold III at the height of the Great Depression. He had married Princess Astrid of Sweden in 1926 and the royal couple had three children: a daughter

Josephine Charlotte (the current Archduchess of Luxembourg) and two sons, Baudouin and Albert, who made their political debuts after World War II.

The German invasion: In the face of the increasing threat from Germany, the king was able to have Belgium reinstated as a neutral country in 1936. Only a few months after the beginning of World War II, German troops invaded Belgium. Leopold III capitulated in the name of his country on 10 May 1940. Although the government fled to London, the king remained at home. Until 1944 he was interned by the forces of occupation in Laeken Castle; then, as the Allied army

and handed over the throne to his son, Baudouin, then aged 20. The new king was crowned on 17 July 1951.

One of Baudouin's most pressing official duties was to supervise the decolonisation of the Congo. Before that, however, there were private matters to attend to: in September 1960 he became engaged to a Spanish noblewoman and trained nurse, Dona Fabiola de Mora y Aragon.

Whilst the engagement celebrations were taking place in Brussels, in the Congo Belgian troops were firing on a population which – despite international protest – had been thrust into independence without any

advanced, he was moved to Germany. He remained there whilst Belgium was liberated, his brother, Prince Charles, becoming temporary regent.

When Leopold III returned it was not possible to quash all rumours of his collaboration with the Germans, but a referendum as to whether he should continue to reign voted in his favour. In 1950, however, he abdicated

Far left, Leopold II was notorious for his exploits with the dancer Cleo. **Left**, Leopold II in a more official pose. **Above**, King Baudouin remains the longest-serving king in Europe.

preparation. The royal couple were married in December 1960.

Future hope: The marriage is childless, so the present heir to the throne is the king's eldest nephew, the son of Baudouin's brother Albert and his wife, Paola. Prince Philippe is being prepared for his future role in the traditional manner: he is already a colonel in the Belgian army and has studied political sciences. In addition, he has had ample practice at dealing with the media. Baudouin, however, has no known plans to abdicate and the Prince may have ahead of him many years of waiting in the wings.

THE BELGIAN CONGO

For many years Belgium kept out of the race to acquire colonies. Leopold I, who became the first King of Belgium in 1831, refused to be involved in an official state colonial policy. After his death in 1865, however, his son, Leopold II, made up for lost time.

Sir Henry Morton Stanley (1841–1904), the British explorer and journalist, provided the king with the expertise for such a venture. Stanley's first expedition to the River Congo concluded that the river's wide channel made it an ideal trading route. In 1878, Leopold II commissioned the explorer to undertake a second trip to the Congo. Following the instructions issued by the Belgian monarch, Stanley came to "agreements" with several of the native tribes .

The basis of these contracts was that the Africans would receive fabric and similar items in return for granting the white intruders the usufruct on their land. The wording was such that the terms could be interpreted as "purchase". In this way, by 1884 Leopold II had gained possession of almost the entire area. He named it the "Congo Free State".

The 19th-century colonial powers soon began to demand a formal agreement on the Congo State. The "Congo Conference" was held in Berlin between November 1884 and February 1885. Belgian authority over the Congo was recognised – with the proviso that henceforth in perpetuity there should be freedom of trade within the country.

At the instigation of Leopold II, the Berlin Conference also passed a resolution repudiating the slave trade. In reality, things were very different. Within Africa slavery was at its peak. Natives were unscrupulously sold as cheap labour and porters, or press-ganged as soldiers. Whippings and murder were daily occurrences. Between 1889 and 1890 the "Anti-Slavery Conference" was held in Brussels; once more, lip service was paid to the noble aims of colonialism.

From 1890 the Socialists and progressive Liberals protested with increasing frequency against the King's colonial policy. In the meantime, the Congolese themselves took up the fight for their own freedom. Between 1895 and 1897 riots were brutally quashed.

In 1908 the criticism openly voiced in Europe concerning the King's authoritarian system of exploitation forced the Belgian government to transfer the monarch's power over the new Belgian Congo to the state.

When Leopold II died in 1909 his nephew, Albert I, became king of Belgium and the Belgian Congo. Between 1912 and 1918, the determined resistance of the oppressed Congolese led to further unrest. Following the arrest of ringleader Simon Kimbanga, the leader of the African National Church and a Congo resident (he was imprisoned until his death in 1959) there was a general strike. The ruling powers replied with a machine-gun salvo from the "Force Publique" and the internment of freedom fighters in so-called "improvement camps".

After the war the Congo experienced an economic boom, and the outbreak of World War II overshadowed the problem of independence. After 1945 the unrest flared up anew. King Baudouin and the majority of Belgians were disinclined to relinquish the colony, whose minerals, rubber, palm oil and ivory boosted national prosperity.

However, unrest could not be contained. The revolt which erupted after the First African Peoples' Conference in 1958 finally led to the Belgian government's precipitate agreement to independence on 30 June 1960. Inter-tribal conflict subsequently broke out in the newly-independent state and the breakaway of the rich mining province of Katanga (now Shaba) led to fresh conflict. The superior attitude of the Belgians who had remained led to a desperate rebellion on the part of the Congolese. Once more, Belgian soldiers fired their guns at the native population. The unrest led to the first Congo Crisis. In 1971 the state, still tottering, assumed the name of the Republic of Zaire.

Bruxelles-Laeken   La Tour Japonaise

The history of Brussels after the Revolution reflects that of Belgium as a whole. Brussels is the seat not only of the King, but also of both government and parliament. The history of the country is determined from Brussels. Since Belgium became independent, Brussels has also served as the starting point for the country's rapid economic growth.

The years following Belgium's declaration of independence in 1831 were characterised by a gradual overthrow of the foreign domination it had so long endured. The industrial revolution began with the construction of the railway line between Brussels and Mechelen, the first on the continent.

The rail network became steadily denser as the exploitation of the coal mines in the South and the development of the iron and steel industry in the area around Liège raised Belgium to a position amongst the principal industrial nations. The process was supported by a flourishing textile industry centred upon Ghent and Kortrijk.

Furthermore, in 1863 Leopold II was able to buy back from the Netherlands the right to levy customs duties on the River Scheldt, a loss which had severely hampered the expansion of Antwerp. The arms industry was a further source of financial profit. The country's industrialists used their head start in heavy industry to gain a foothold in new export markets.

Prosperity at a price: But not everybody benefited from the boom. Wages were low and working hours long. Female and child labour were commonplace. Social security, industrial safety standards and free Sundays were a long way off the political agenda.

Brussels achieved the dubious honour of having the highest infant mortality rate of all European capitals. The working classes lived in indescribable misery in damp, cramped apartments; their diet consisted

largely of cabbage, potatoes and bread. Their wretched existence could be summed up in one word: the Marolles. This was the district in the city centre where the poor and the oppressed had lived together for centuries. It was here, too, that the first workers' associations were formed.

As far as the outside world was concerned, Belgium and Brussels enjoyed a reputation for progressiveness. The country's freedom of speech and freedom of the press were often upheld as examples of what might be achieved in other countries. Brussels became an asylum for persecuted socialists from all over Europe. Karl Marx sought refuge here in 1845. In 1848, when the Paris Revolution was on everyone's lips, he and Friedrich Engels published their joint *Communist Manifesto*. This, however, stretched the liberal attitude of the city fathers too far, and Marx was expelled from the country a few months later.

His ideas, however, did not go unheeded by the citizens of Brussels and at the turn of the century they led to bitter fighting which

Left, Nippon in Laeken: a Japanese pagoda for the king (coloured postcard from around 1900). **Above**, Brussels' lacemaking industry once employed thousands of women.

eventually led to the introduction of universal suffrage and the right to strike.

Colonial power: In the meantime, Belgium had taken its place amongst the world's colonial powers. In 1878, for lack of public interest, King Leopold II had purchased the Congo out of his own private fortune. His one-man enterprise proceeded to flourish. A regime of forced labour and reign by terror in the colony filled his coffers, profiting Belgium in general and the capital in particular.

The king made over part of his income from his colony to the state, and Brussels itself was treated to a facelift. Leopold had a number of magnificent avenues constructed

Belgium, despite the latter's neutrality. For almost four years pitiless trench warfare was fought between the Germans on one side and the English, French and Belgians on the other. Hundreds of thousands laid down their lives on the battlefield. By the end, Flanders was devastated and the town of Ypres had been razed to the ground.

The city of Brussels was spared during the actual hostilities, but was the object of attempts at political occupation on the part of the Germans.

The city courageously continued its policy of passive resistance. At the head of the movement against the forces of occupation

and various fine buildings erected. The Palais des Colonies was built in the suburb of Tervuren.

The import of copper, uranium, diamonds, rubber, cotton and tin increased the general prosperity of the Belgian people. But it was at a heavy price. The merciless exploitation of the Congo, which brought death to hundreds of thousands of natives – through exhaustion, hunger, violence or merely the whim of the mercenary troops – is one of the blackest episodes in Belgian history (*see chapter on the Belgian Congo, page 49*).

In August 1914, German troops invaded

was the mayor, Adolphe Max. Refusing to reveal the names of unemployed workers destined for forced labour in Germany, he was arrested and deported.

King Albert I acquired a glorious reputation during World War I. He had become regent in 1909, and personally led the Belgian army as well as encouraging the country's citizens to resist the foreign invaders. In the autumn of 1918 the country lay in ruins, but at last the trench war was over. In November there was an armistice.

Immediately after the end of the war, the population was rewarded by a number of reforms. Belgium introduced universal male suffrage (though women were not given the vote until 1948) and the right to strike. The economy, badly damaged by the war, was slow to recover.

When the Allies failed to enforce the high reparations that the Treaty of Versailles had levied on Germany, hopes of compensation for the devastation wreaked by the war went unfulfilled. During the Great Depression, unemployment rose rapidly. Here, as in other cities across the continent of Europe, Fascists profited from the general unrest.

On 10 May 1940 German troops marched into Belgium once more. Their offensive

Collaboration and resistance: The Belgian Pierlot-Spaak government refused to capitulate and continued the fight from its London exile. Nonetheless, there was widespread collaboration with the occupying forces. Various right-wing groups declared their open sympathies with Hitler's regime.

On the other side stood the communists, socialists and Christians, who fought actively against the Germans. Many unemployed Belgians joined the Underground because they were afraid of being transported to labour camps.

A Jewish resistance group was also formed. It succeeded in saving 20,000 Bel-

continued unabated until they reached Dunkirk. Unlike his father, who had stood at the head of the resistance movement against the German invaders during World War I, King Leopold III was a great disappointment to his people during war. Leopold's request for a ceasefire on 27 May 1940 served as a prelude to the country's rapid acceptance of German occupation.

Left, German field kitchen on the Grand' Place (World War I). **Above**, young members of the Resistance fought as a "secret army" against the Germans (1944).

gian Jews from Hitler's concentration camps by organising their flight abroad or by hiding them in the homes of non-Jews.

Following the landing of the Allied troops in Normandy, Belgium was liberated in September 1944. Collaborators were brought to trial throughout the land. A total of 57,000 were sentenced; 241 of them were executed. Following a number of bloody riots, Leopold III was forced by the Walloons and the citizens of Brussels to abdicate. He was succeeded on 31 July 1950 by his son, Baudouin. With this, Belgium entered a new era of prosperity.

WHAT HAPPENED TO BELGIAN JEWS?

There are few people who do not know the poignant story of Anne Frank (1929–45), the daughter of a Jewish businessman from Frankfurt, who along with her family fled to Amsterdam early in the Hitler regime. In 1942 she and her family went into hiding. With the help of Gentile friends, they managed to survive for over two years in a secret annex in a warehouse. Then, in 1944, they were betrayed to the Gestapo by Dutch informers and transported to concentration camps in Germany. Anne's father alone survived; her mother died in Auschwitz in 1944, and she and her sister in Bergen-Belsen in 1945.

Returning to Holland after the war, Anne's father found the diary she had kept during her years in hiding. *Diary of a Young Girl*, recording the events of her life during World War II, was published in 1947 and quickly became a classic of its kind. It serves as a memorial to the millions of Jews exterminated in the Nazi Holocaust.

In Belgium, a total of 2,700 Jewish children survived the persecution of the Nazi era. Their escape was thanks to the relentless efforts of a unique underground organisation that hid the children under false names in convents, boarding schools and private families.

But inevitably rescue came at a price to the children. The children had to live under the enormous strain of an assumed identity, a burden later replaced by feelings of guilt associated with being one of the "lucky" ones who escaped.

Now the generation of those who helped them is dwindling one by one. Many members of the underground rescue operation lost their lives at the time, or have died in the intervening years. Most of those who remain are now about 80 years old. Some of them have written accounts of the period of history through which they lived; none of them can free themselves from its shadow.

After the war and its aftermath, the generation of children they saved withdrew into a sort of emotional no man's land. Even today, so many years on, few of them are willing to talk about their years in hiding. This is an account of what happened in Belgium.

From 1 June 1942, Belgian Jews were required to wear the yellow Star of David. When they were called upon to volunteer for the labour camps in the early summer of 1942, many of them actually did so, believing this was their safest course of action. This led to thousands going unwittingly to their death. In the 100 days between August 4 1942 and 31 October 1942, more than 17,000 Belgian Jews were deported from the Flemish town of Mechelen alone. In the two-year period between October 1942 and September 1944 (Brussels was liberated by the Allies on 4 September) the Germans captured 8,000 Jews, less than half the number in that 100-day period in Mechelen. The reason for this was that, from October 1942, those remaining realised the outcome of surrendering. By then, they knew that their only hope of survival lay in flight or going underground and began to organise themselves accordingly.

Their principal aim was to save their children. Adults were in a position to arrange a life on the run, but the question of what they could do with their children was difficult. In this time of desperate need, an organisation of Jews and non-Jews – Belgian resistance fighters, social workers and idealists – joined forces to do whatever they could.

Organisation and co-ordination were vital to their success, but so was absolute secrecy. Maurice and Estera Heiber, a Jewish couple whose child also had to be hidden, set up an illegal coordination centre. Yvonne Rospa, a Jewish social worker and dedicated anti-racist, set out with a group of Belgian supporters to find accommodation and hideouts for the children who were at risk. Under the fictitious name of Madame Pascal, Estera Heiber could be found each morning in the flat of a Belgian opera singer. Here she could be consulted, could receive and pass on information, provide money for accommodation and distribute food ration cards.

The helpers were faced with a gargantuan task, not least how best to persuade loving parents that it was better for all concerned if they agreed to separate from their children. Parents had to accept the fact that they would receive no details of the name and address of the prospective foster parents. The separation of family members in such dangerous circumstances was heart-rending, but knowledge and information represented an additional risk of discovery.

Yvonne Jospa says that not all Belgians were prepared to help, but she refuses to judge those who failed to do so. Some were too afraid; others were unconcerned. She says that assistance came from isolated individuals from every social class. Those who agreed to take a Jewish child into their families were well aware of the risks involved and prepared to face them. The child had to remain as inconspicuous as possible, adopting the customs of the host family, attending the local state or confessional school with the other children in the

dren unscarred. Those children who survived refer only occasionally to their years spent in hiding. The parents on the other hand, especially those who were actively involved, find it easier to convey their experiences. They were able to join the resistance movement, whereas their children were helpless in the face of their fate.

Andrée Geulen, a former Belgian partisan married to a Jew, has six grandchildren. She lives in Brussels. She knows from the annual meetings with "her children", those she helped rescue, just how sensitive these Jews are today. Now aged between 45 and 55, they have made their homes all over the world.

"It is amazing," she says, "to discover that only now, more than 45 years later, are some of my

family and going to church. They had to pray and eat exactly as the family did.

False passports were issued with the help of Belgian officials. Names were changed to disguise Jewish origins – Apfelbaum, for example, became Appelmans – so that a ration card could be claimed. Without one, survival in wartime Belgium was impossible.

The tragedy of being separated from their parents, of having to live with the permanent anxiety of an assumed identity and with the ever-present fear of being discovered, did not leave these chil-

Left, Jewish children murdered by the Nazis in World War II. <u>Above</u>, many Jewish girls were hidden by Catholic schools; they survived the Holocaust.

protégés willing to permit others to see just how deep these unhealed wounds go. Only now have they begun to speak hesitatingly about their repressed, deep-seated fears. How can we possibly comprehend the feelings of a six-year-old girl snatched away from the bosom of her family and burdened with the inhuman knowledge that she must never reveal that her real name is Rachel, must never betray the fact that she is Jewish, for to do so would mean death?

"I knew personally the little girl called Rachel. Throughout the war she was known as Monique. Today she is almost 50 and admits she never answered when called by her assumed name. People tended to think she was retarded, but – as she recently told me in tears – 'I just didn't really know who I was'."

Brussels After World War II

The best clue to understanding present-day life in the Brussels metropolitan area can be found by examining the pattern of its development over the years. The city centre roughly corresponds to the working-class districts of the 19th century. (Even now they are inhabited largely by the poor and by immigrant guest workers.) The social housing programmes of the inter-war years determined the rest of the town's social structure. The garden cities built during the 1920s for the burgeoning middle classes, for example, lie in a green belt around the centre.

The centre and the surrounding districts dating from the 19th century comprise about 75 percent older houses, most of which are in a dilapidated condition and usually divided into privately owned flats, mostly extremely small. Around this core lies a zone containing somewhat better flats; and in an outer circle lie the luxurious villa districts.

By the 1960s and '70s the exodus from the city centre was already under way; the nouveaux riches had begun to settle on the periphery of town.

As has happened elsewhere in European cities, during the 1980s this trend was reversed. Once more, a number of people, particularly the young, began to seek accommodation in the heart of the city. Reduced purchasing power, increasing unemployment and rising interest rates all contributed to this development, but so did a desire to escape the monotony of characterless suburbia. It seems as if the second generation of suburban dwellers (now aged between 20 and 40) are anxious to live in the heart of the city again, breathing new life into old buildings and adapting it to suit their own lifestyles.

If the capital of Belgium wants to realise its ambitions as the European city of the future, many changes will have to take place. In some areas this process is already under

<u>Left</u>, the beauty of the facades around the Grand' Place is enhanced still further by these brightly-coloured standards.

way. Brussels is a popular target for investment, and new jobs are being created all the time. Environment-friendly industries, development and research institutes and the service industries form the basis of this trend. But the city still lacks an adequate international transport infrastructure and sufficiently flexible links to regional, national and European official bodies.

A great deal is currently being done to alleviate these chronic problems. The Regional Development Authority in Brussels has already created four scientific industrial centres, each of which is partly administered by one of the four universities. Three are

TGV railway lines will pass nearby, linking Paris with Amsterdam and London with Cologne. This improved network will bring the so-called Capital of Europe within just a few hours' travel of the other major cities on the continent.

There are still numerous opportunities for expansion within the service industry sector. Large firms are tending to leave this sphere (office-cleaning, courier services, sales, marketing and legal and management consultancy) to medium-sized concerns. The mass of unemployed, unqualified young people, women and foreigners provides an inexhaustible reservoir of labour.

situated in the vicinity of the principal university hospitals. The fourth zone is located in Belgium's so-called "Silicon Valley", near the European Headquarters of NATO on the road leading to the international airport at Zeventem.

The decision to move the centres of academic learning to the city outskirts, near the industrial areas, demonstrates a carefully planned overall strategy: they are all easily accessible by motorway and underground. Brussels also lies on a canal which links it to Antwerp harbour, one of the largest ports in Europe. By the mid-1990s the high-speed

Accommodation crisis: Most people in Brussels live in rented flats, since few are able to raise the capital required for house purchase. Nonetheless, keeping rents affordable and rented properties available is a problem.The situation in the centre of the city is particularly critical: the "original" residents of the old city centre cannot afford to buy a home, but are excluded on income grounds from government-owned accommodation. Elements of the communities in the metropolitan area are anxious to attract capital-intensive industries and new residents with high purchasing power. Unfortunately such projects can mostly only succeed at the expense of the city's long-standing residents, who have to move out to make way for the new money.

Despite efforts by conservationists whose aim is to preserve the many historic buildings in the Marolles district for indigent future generations, the number of individuals or – in many cases – property companies in the process of buying up the dilapidated, in many cases uninhabited, buildings is increasing. Sometimes they are able to purchase an entire street and transform it into private luxury flats and elegant offices. As a consequence property prices are rising

facilities and cultural events attempts to keep pace with other developments.

Culture plus: The wide variety of cultural and artistic opportunities available in the city ranges from the Opera – the Théâtre de la Monnaie – to the almost 100 museums, many of them beautifully restored, and the exhibition halls. Regular events are staged in the Palais des Beaux-Arts, the Botanique, the Halles de Schaerbeek and the Ancienne Belgique. Festivals of drama, music and film are frequently staged.

Above all, the city lives for – and from – its trades fairs, exchanges and congresses. The modern way of life has produced new trade

sharply, and experts have predicted that development similar to that found in Washington can be expected. The Art Nouveau houses of the area are particularly coveted; for the man-in-the-street, however, they are exorbitantly expensive.

The present trend is quite clearly luxury-oriented; the city's new residents are mostly high earners. Grandiose hotels are mushrooming on all sides, and the range of sports

and cultural centres standing side by side with the old.

Last but not least, Brussels is an international metropolis in which various ethnic groups form their own cultural associations. For example, in some districts North Africans – mostly Moroccans – form a Muslim majority. Freedom of worship for all is guaranteed by law.

The numerous foreign restaurants and shops resulting from the rich cultural mix form an integral part of the city's character; the *Matongué* from Zaire at the Porte de Namur, the Chinese restaurants behind the

Left, where is the king? A solitary guard protects the palace. **Above**, a summer stroll through the shady Mont des Arts.

Stock Exchange, the Turkish establishments in the Chaussée de Haecht, the Maghrebi places in Saint-Gilles, and the Vietnamese eateries near the University in Ixelles. There are French and Italian restaurants on virtually every corner.

Whilst on the subject of restaurants and shops, it is worth mentioning the upmarket, yuppie haunts in the Rue Dansaert, the famous shops around Sainte-Cathérine, Saint-Géry, the luxury stores between the Porte de Namur, the Porte Louise and the Avenue Louise, the antique shops around the Sablons and – increasingly – those in the historic Marolles district.

skirts. One of the largest shopping and entertainment centres can be found on the Heysel estate in the Northwest (Brupark, Océade and Mini-Europe).

Brussels is, however, first and foremost a political switchboard. It is not only the capital of Belgium, but also – since the most recent constitutional reforms and the federalisation of the state – the capital of the Flemish half of the country, of the French community and of the Brussels region. It is expected that increasing numbers of private firms will settle in the vicinity of the administrative capital in order to ensure a more effective lobby in the chambers of political

Big business: Formerly, most businesses were located on the upper side of the North-South axis. Today, the centre of gravity has shifted more from the Place Rogier to the Place de Brouckère and beyond, in the direction of the Stock Exchange. Increasing numbers of business people are attracted to the Canal district, where new shops, leisure centres and comfortable, upmarket flats are being built.

Since the early years of this century there have been department stores and shopping galleries in the city centre. During the past few years, others have opened on the out-

power. On a European level, lobbying of this kind has been going on for many years – and not only since Brussels declared its ambition of becoming the capital of Europe.

Should the European Parliament one day settle exclusively in Brussels, it will be able to take immediate possession of a new parliamentary building for almost 1,000 representatives. This is already under construction and completion is expected within the next few years. Brussels will also have to absorb and integrate between 10,000 and 15,000 new Eurocrats. In addition there would be more embassies, banks, news agencies, representatives of international companies, associations and organisations, shopping centres, cafés and restaurants.

There is still a shortage of office accommodation and housing, but in the various ministries officials are already poring over proposals for balanced new zoning plans.

The city's business district extends from the North Station (Manhattan Centre, CNN), the Rue de la Loi (Parliament, the ministries) across the Quartier Léopold (site of the new European Parliament) and the Avenue Cortenberg to the E5 motorway (Silicon Valley, NATO), the Boulevard du Souverain and the Avenue de la Woluwé.

thus provide the main pool of unskilled labour in the city) forces them to the fringe of society, whilst other minorities – for example, the British, American, Scandinavians and Japanese – enjoy a higher social status and hence have experienced no problems with integration.

Recent studies indicate that discrimination against ethnic minorities – particularly regarding housing and jobs – must be brought to an end before it leads to serious racial problems.

Old rivalries: Finally, mention should be made of the tiresome language rivalry between Flemish and French speakers in the

No history of recent developments in Brussels would be complete without some reference to the problems of the city's Maghrebis, Turks and Black Africans. Although it would be an exaggeration to speak of ghetto-like developments in the various districts, some quarters certainly contain strong concentrations of these ethnic minorities. Their socio-economic status (they tend to belong to the weakest social groups and

Left, Belgium's motorways are so well-lit that they can be discerned from the moon. **Above**, enjoying ice-cream on the Grand' Place.

capital – the fires of which are frequently fanned by politicians and students of language. In spite of its bilingual status, Brussels is 85 percent Francophone.

Since the creation of the Region of Brussels, which has its own government, the Flemish minority has complained of difficulty in maintaining its identity and asserting itself in the face of French competition. That said, individuality is the cornerstone of the Belgian personality: Flemish speakers won't yield to the French-speaking majority without a fight – very often literally, as the violent demonstrations of the 1960s showed.

WHAT DOES THE KING DO?

King Baudouin of Belgium, now in his sixties, is the longest reigning monarch in Europe: he came to the throne in 1951, after the abdication of his father, and recently celebrated his 40th anniversary. That is the most remarkable fact available on the subject of the current King of the Belgians. He is an uncontroversial figure who fulfils his duties diligently and takes his role as the representative of his country very seriously .

The royal couple's official residence is the Palace of Laeken, situated in the northern outskirts of Brussels. A black, red and gold striped flag fluttering from the palace roof indicates that they are at home. The official office and audience rooms are in the Palais Royal in the centre of Brussels. Here Baudouin conducts most of his state work, receiving overseas ambassadors accredited to his court, as well as representatives of the various European Community bodies and foreign firms.

The rights and duties of the King of Belgium were laid down by the country's constitution of 1831. A number of modifications have been made to the clauses of that first constitution, but those referring to the sovereign have remained unchanged.

According to Article 65, the king is responsible for nominating and dismissing his prime ministers. In practice, of course, the choice lies in the hands of the political parties and the king has no real power of his own. However, every day King Baudouin is required to sign a large number of documents and makes full use of his right to be informed concerning all matters of state. He frequently summons governmental ministers, representatives of parties, trades unions and other important organisations to his presence, sometimes successively in the course of a single day.

Article 63 of the constitution states that the king's person is sacrosanct. Article 64 rules that all documents signed by the king also require the signature of a minister to make them valid (the minister bears sole responsibility for the content). In addition to attending to paperwork, King Baudouin represents the state on all occasions, including on an international basis. He frequently sends an envoy to the various celebrations amongst the aristocracy of Europe.

King Baudouin's principal interest lies in his country's continued industrial progress, and in particular in the development of new technologies. He is a regular and welcome guest in research centres and factories across the country. If you wish to see the King Baudouin in the flesh, your best chance is to visit the city towards the last week in July. On 21 July, the national holiday, he traditionally takes part in a huge military parade held in honour of the nomination of Prince Leopold as the first King of Belgium in 1831.

King Baudouin and Queen Fabiola often receive guests in their private palace at Laeken, greeting them in the royal glasshouses. Once a year they invite the general public to view the greenhouses (*see the chapter on The Glass City, page 197*).

The royal couple are great fans of classical music and frequently attend musical events in Brussels. Queen Fabiola is actively involved in many charitable organisations; she is, for example, the patron of the National Association for Handicapped Children. Her duties regularly include visits to hospitals and social centres.

King Baudouin and Queen Fabiola have no children of their own, but they have made preparations for the succession. Their eldest nephew, Philippe, son of Baudouin's brother Albert, is being groomed to follow in the footsteps of his uncle.

In an age which has seen the birth of so many new republics, monarchy seems secure in Belgium. The fervently royalist people can rest assured that they won't have to remove the little crowns which they so proudly mount on their car numberplates.

Inseparable for 25 years: King Baudouin and Queen Fabiola celebrate their Silver Wedding at their country seat in Ciergon. Baudouin remains the longest-serving king in Europe.

Brussels is widely considered to be the most cosmopolitan city in Europe. Its reputation in this respect is based primarily on the presence of the various EC organisations.

Over the centuries, the city and its inhabitants were ruled by a succession of foreign powers. Forces from all over the continent succeeded in occupying the city; Burgundy gave way to Spain, and France to the Netherlands, until in 1830 the Walloons and Flemings launched a revolution for independence. By and large, the Belgians are not particularly patriotic; they are more concerned about the freedom of the individual. They are proud of their country's reputation for freedom of speech and the freedom of the individual.

The attitude of the statue of Manneken Pis, known to the genuine Brussels citizen as Menneke Pis, embodies something of the citizens' independent spirit and tendency to complain. The determination of the various ethnic groups to fight for respect for their different cultures is demonstrated not least in the frequently mentioned language rivalry.

It is in Brussels – which lies only a few kilometres north of the French linguistic boundary – that the clash between the contrasting cultures of the Walloons and Flemings is most clearly evident. One result is that all signs and street names, as well as all city districts, are labelled in both Flemish and French, although Belgium actually has a third official language – German.

It may be that the centuries of foreign rule account for the remarkably low level of xenophobia. Brussels today has a population of approximately 1 million; every fourth person is not a native Belgian. Even the city's geographical position is interesting, for it lies at the heart of Western Europe. If you were to draw two diagonal lines across the continent, from Scotland to Greece and from Spain to Denmark, you would discover that Brussels lies where the two axes cross.

The prime reason behind Brussels' internationalism is undoubtedly the presence of the three principal supranational organisations: the European Commission, the Council of Ministers of the European Community, and NATO.

Cradle of the Common Market: In March 1957 the three associations – the European Coal and Steel Community, Euratom and the European Community – joined together to

form the European Economic Community. Brussels was the obvious choice as permanent headquarters, since in 1956 the negotiations which formed the basis of the founding treaties of the European Economic Community and the European Atomic Authority had taken place here. Apart from the city's central location and good transport links with the rest of Europe, other advantages included its wealth of office space for the vast numbers of officials.

At the time, Brussels was preparing for the 1958 World Exhibition. Taking advantage of the opportunity, Brussels was able to

Left, subjects enjoy a late-afternoon beer outside the "King's House". **Above**, a place to sit and watch.

make a successful bid to be the site of the European Community administration.

Initially the offices of the departments stationed in Brussels were scattered across several districts of town. Since 1967 the present EC building has been located in the Palais Berlaymont at the eastern end of the Rue de la Loi, which stretches from the city centre to the Palais du Cinquantenaire.

In 1967 the Community consisted of only six members. Its gradual expansion to 12 member countries and the subsequent influx of their representatives increased the cosmopolitan nature of the host city.

North Atlantic manoeuvres: In 1966, the is represented here by no fewer than three embassies. Ambassadors from some 100 countries are accredited to the royal court and most countries have diplomatic representation at the EC and NATO as well. Politicians and businessmen from every corner of the earth flock to Brussels to present their interests to the European organisations. Altogether there are some 800 branches of worldwide trading organisations, European centres and an endless list of international company offices.

Brussels is truly international on the hotel and restaurant scene too, so every visitor is bound to feel at home. Many European offi-

French president Charles de Gaulle forced France's withdrawal from the North Atlantic Treaty Organization and expelled all NATO commands from the country. Consequently NATO moved its military headquarters to Belgium, to the vicinity of Mons; the administrative arm (the NATO Council, the Military Committee and the international staff) was transferred to Brussels. The result was that the city became home to thousands of foreigners employed in the service of the EC and NATO alone.

In addition, Brussels is the residence of some 200 ambassadors, since each country cials are conspicuous by the EUR numberplates on their cars.

The diplomats and international officials receive a number of privileges as well as expatriate allowances and tax advantages. This has a direct influence on the city's high prices and rents. Thanks to its bureaucracy, Brussels is ranked amongst the world's 10 most expensive cities. That said, and in spite of the flood of arrivals from all over the world, the city of Brussels is one of the few metropolises in Europe where flats are still available to rent.

Virtually all nations can claim a community of some sort in Brussels. They each consist of an infrastructure of churches and schools. Apart from the international schools, the so-called European Schools, there are specific schools for the German, French, Netherlands, Japanese, British and American communities – especially for the children of those families whose stay in Brussels is only temporary.

Guest workers form the biggest single body of foreign workers. Traditionally they comprised large numbers of Spaniards; now, in the wake of rising living standards in Spain and the tendency of its poorer classes to stay put, they include increasing numbers

area, in particular following the closure of the coal mines in the French-speaking region. The flight from the land has resulted in a steady increase in urban unemployment.

On the other hand, the direct result of the city's rapid expansion was a corresponding flight from the city to the outskirts and the surrounding villages on the part of old-established families. The outlying districts are favoured above all by the members of the international working community. During the past 30 years some 100,000 people have moved out of the city. These population movements have completely altered the city's character.

of Maghrebians, Turks and Black Africans. African students, businessmen and dissidents from the states of Ruanda and Burundi (which were previously mandated territories under the control of the Belgian League of Nations) and Zaire (the former Belgian Congo) also form an important racial minority in the city.

In addition, Brussels has recently received a steady migration from the surrounding

Nostalgic note: Many members of the city's old guard regret the passing of the lifestyle they enjoyed prior to 1958 and Brussels' transformation. The rapid international development of the capital has inevitably destroyed a large part of the city's attractive provincial nature. By and large, the citizens of Brussels accept the endless flood of newcomers with traditional Belgian nonchalance, but some social commentators maintain that unless measures are taken to avert the problem the high unemployment figures will cause resentment among the city's indigenous population.

Left, a difficult choice: shopping at the Sunday "Exotic" Market at the Southern Station. **Above**, the city attracts visitors from all over the world.

THE LANGUAGE PROBLEM

The citizens of Belgium speak either Walloon – a form of French – or Flemish, a Netherlands dialect. However, as anyone trying to research the matter will quickly discover, the most recent figures on the percentage of the population belonging to each linguistic group are those dating from the Language Census of 1947.

Since then, the Flemish, finding themselves to be increasingly losing ground to the French speakers, have sought to prevent any formal tally less they should highlight their demise. Even traditionally Flemish-speaking areas – for example, the scientific zone of the city – have seen an influx of French-speaking residents and workers. Casual observers may sense the deep feelings underlying the use of the two languages.

The Belgians do not make life any easier for the student of language who wishes to write down both the cultivated and colloquial forms of the language, not to mention standard and dialect forms. The very term "Flemish" is lacking in precision as a description of a language spoken for the past 1,000 years north of a linguistic boundary roughly running from Aachen to north of Lille. Flemish is actually a mixture of Flemish dialects and standard Dutch. Walloon, on the other hand is none other than French with a number of Walloon idiosyncrasies.

Flemish has never really developed an independent written language of its own. Instead, it uses standard Dutch, enriched by a number of Belgian characteristics. This form is also the spoken language used by the media, the Church and in schools, although both teachers and pupils revert to the dialect form after hours.

The long-standing quarrel between the two linguistic groups arose because of the chronological shift in the settlement of the territory of the *Belgae*. German peasants came from the North, whilst settlers from the Romance countries bordering the Moselle

and the Mediterranean made their homes primarily in the remote regions of the Ardennes, which remained undeveloped for many years.

No formal boundary was ever drawn between the two groups; their different lifestyles were adjuncts to their specifically Belgian political culture and mentality. Maybe they even needed to develop an eccentricity of this nature in order to assert their own individual character between the

powerful civilisations of the French on the one side and the Dutch on the other.

The relationship between the two languages was always a painful one; even today, it is tinged by an element of distrust. The Flemish are afraid of being swallowed up by French in its capacity as a world language; the Walloons look disparagingly upon Flemish – a language which sounds barbaric to their ears, and which has virtually no international application.

The linguistic battle is accompanied by mutual feelings of envy, particularly economically; nowadays, for example, in view

Left, a drum roll for the Walloons. Above, a Flemish farmer's wife confronts the police.

of the fundamental crisis in the coal and steel industry, the Walloons in the South consider themselves at a disadvantage compared to the Flemish North, where Antwerp is the centre of a petrochemical boom. Maybe it is a particular strength of the Belgians to be able to survive despite this imbalance – an ability acquired during many centuries of foreign rule.

Historical evidence: The reasons why linguistic identity should play such an important role in Belgium can be traced to the historical development of the country. When the first modern nation arose within the boundaries of the present-day Benelux

starkly with the more rural, overwhelmingly Catholic South. Not all Flemings became citizens of the hard-fought "Republic of the United Netherlands". The frontier remained some 50 km (31 miles) north of Antwerp; south of this border, what would later become Belgium started to develop.

Belgium was still far from independent, however, as it formed part of the Habsburg empire. The language which enjoyed the higher prestige – especially during the Age of Enlightenment – was still French. When, in 1794, post-revolutionary French troops began to conquer Belgium for France and a rigid centralised government as well as a

States under the Dukes of Burgundy, French – the language of the court – became the symbol of power and social success. Simultaneously, however, the flourishing cloth trade with England enabled the Flemish provinces of Flanders and Brabant to win high economic status.

When, during the 16th century, the Netherlands (including present-day Belgium) revolted against the Spanish Habsburgs, a clear north-south division within the Dutch-speaking area was already evident. The predominantly urban North, devoutly Calvinist in the wake of the Reformation, contrasted

compulsorily introduced "Religion of Reason" took over, the most impassioned resistance fighters were the peasants from Flanders. The Flemish legacy stood them in good stead against France on the battlefield.

At the Congress of Vienna in 1815 Belgium was annexed as part of the newly-created Kingdom of the Netherlands under William I, who introduced Dutch as the official written language. It transpired, however, that the Flemings had developed their own identity at last. Even they found the language forced upon them boorish – *boerentaal* – and regarded their new masters as heretics. The border established 50 km before Antwerp divided a population which had diverged linguistically and culturally. Catholic Flemings and French-speaking Liberals united in revolt against the rulers of the United Netherlands. In October 1830 a temporary government proclaimed the newly-formed state of Belgium. From this point onwards controlling the linguistic power struggle in the country was nothing less than a balancing act.

The Belgian Constitution of 1831, created in the prevailing spirit of liberalism, calls for a strict principal of neutrality regarding the linguistic education of the nation's children.

the language used by the man in the street. This was the situation when *The Lion of Flanders*, a novel by Hendrik Conscience (1812–83), was published in 1838. The book, still counted amongst the works of world literature, fired the imagination of the Flemings. From then on the Flemings began to demand the *taalvrijheid*, the right not to be forced to use French in their dealings with official bodies.

The urgency of these demands was underlined in a gruesome manner during the trial of two Flemings living in the French-speaking region. The men, Coecke and Goethals, were falsely convicted of murder in 1865

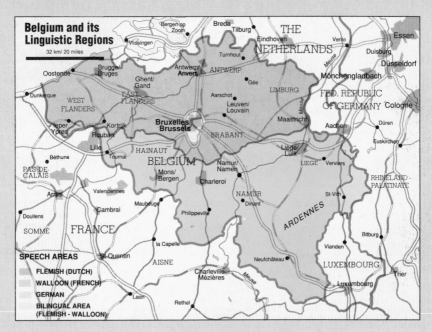

School attendance was not made compulsory. This clause tended to work to the disadvantage of the Flemings. Their children were mostly instructed in the less well-equipped confessional schools while the more prosperous private schools introduced French as the teaching language.

French also became the language used in public administration, and continued to be regarded as the language of the refined classes. Flemish had the reputation of being

Left, clash of symbols: "Put that flag away, or I'll come and tear it down!"

because they were unable to follow the proceedings in French and were hence not in a position to defend themselves. In 1898 both languages were declared of equal official status. No boundaries were laid down to define the areas in which each should be considered predominant.

The divide widens: The language dispute has become even more acute during this century. On two occasions, German troops invaded Belgian territory despite its declared neutrality. The subsequent occupation exacerbated the internal conflict between Flemings and Walloons. The majority of Belgians remained anti-German, but one Flemish group, the "Activists", campaigned for an independent state as a German protectorate; during World War I, the group collaborated with the forces of occupation.

In 1917, two separate linguistic regions were determined within Belgium. Each had its own ministries in Brussels and Namur. Only a mass demonstration in Brussels on 11 February 1918 prevented total separation. After World War I, everything Flemish was anathema and was despised as being anti-Belgian. In its external policies, Belgium moved closer to France.

During the 1920s the language dispute

continued primarily within the walls of universities. The argument became particularly heated in Ghent. Justified claims for a separate Flemish institute of higher education, realised during World War I, were shelved after the war. There was frequent unrest among the Flemish speakers.

During the 1930s, the nationalist spectrum became polarised in accordance with the spirit of the times. Laws governing the use of language in administrative circles, and the insistence on the use of the local language as the official language in courts and classrooms, made Belgium a state with two lin-

guistically homogeneous regions with equal rights. A strongly centralist principle continued to dominate; most leading officials in Brussels were either Walloons or non Flemish-speaking citizens. The validity of the French speakers' claims of "cultural superiority" was too obvious to be ignored.

World War II completely destroyed the status quo once more. This time there were collaborators not only amongst the Flemings (in fact, this time most Flemish associations resisted the German temptation). Walloon monarchists under the leadership of Leon Degrelle dreamed of Belgium belonging to a fascist corporate state. When the war was over, each language group ostracised the other in attempts to find a better concept for peaceful coexistence.

Violent protest: Since July 1966 the governing principle has been one of strict monolinguality in predetermined regions (Brussels, which is bilingual, and a small number of linguistic enclaves enjoy special status). The Flemings were forthright in asserting their claims. They insisted, for example, that in the Flemish seaside resorts with an international clientele, French notices should appear only beside those which are also translated into other foreign languages – as an indication that French, too, was "foreign". And they were not afraid to use violence: their repeated interruption of French church services and funerals during the 1960s resulted in a series of television films of furious, irreverent Flemings that shocked the world and shook the popularly perceived image of Belgian gentility.

Less controversial are the surprising statistics, which indicate that many schools in the Flemish-speaking regions offer French teaching of such a high standard that parents whose homes lie south of the language border send their children to them.

It is fair to say that the Flemings tend to speak better French than the Walloons speak Flemish, although the latter language has equal status. It is also clear that English is making rapid progress as a language of wider communication.

<u>Left</u>, King Baudouin – a king for uniformed Walloons. <u>Right</u>, a picture of harmony.

To list all the important men and women associated with Brussels would fill an entire volume of *Who's Who:* the city is full of memorials to dukes, emperors and governors. The following account does not therefore pretend to mention all the politicians, soldiers, saints and artists that have lived in, died in or visited Brussels but it includes those that are remembered most affectionately by citizens.

A passing reference seems adequate in the case of Julius Caesar and all the other conquerors from the Dark Ages, for the history of Brussels proper begins in about AD 580 with St Gaugerich, also known as St Géry or St Goorik depending on which language you are using, who founded the city.

Other holy men and women associated with the city include St Michael and St Gudula (*see page 28*) and St Alène, daughter of the Lord of Dilbeek. Her baptism in the Church of St Denis in Forest so enraged her father that he beat her to death. According to legend, numerous miracles occurred at her grave as a consequence, whereupon her father converted to Christianity and Alène was canonised.

Later, the city was stage for many more quarrels concerning the one true faith. In 1921, Erasmus of Rotterdam, the famous scholar and humanist who preached tolerance during the great Wars of Religion, lived in the district of Anderlecht: the Erasmus House at Rue du Chapitre 31 has been converted into a museum in his honour.

Foreign blood: Over the course of Belgium's turbulent history the city lay in the power of a succession of rulers from many lands. Even the first king of Belgium, Leopold I, was not a native of the country, and when he ascended the throne in 1831 he travelled to Brussels from his home in London. His wife Louise was the daughter of

King Louis Philippe of France. Later members of the aristocracy also included a good proportion of foreigners, including Elisabeth Gabriele Valerie Marie, the daughter of a Bavarian duke, who married King Albert I of Belgium in 1900 and came from Possenhofen near Munich; and Princess Astrid, who married King Leopold III in 1926 and was of Swedish extraction. The current Queen, Dona Fabiola de Mora y Aragon, who married King Baudouin in 1960, is a

Spanish noblewoman.

Napoleon first visited Brussels in 1803. Twelve years later he was the reason for the arrival of another great soldier in the city, Arthur Wellesley, better known as the Duke of Wellington. Born in Dublin, Wellesley had risen to fame on the battlefields of the Iberian peninsula. He had hastened to the Belgian capital in order to join forces with the Prussians against Napoleon in the historic battle of Waterloo.

Another man who changed the world came to Brussels armed only with his sharp wits. Just as Erasmus influenced the thinking

Left, this picture by Pieter Brueghel the Elder depicts the struggle between enjoyment and piety. **Right**, *The Man in the Bowler Hat* by René Magritte.

of his age, so this newcomer would turn out to be one of the greatest philosophers of the capitalist era. His name was Karl Marx. Since 1843 Marx had lived in Paris, but in 1945, banished from the French capital at the instigation of the Prussian government, he moved to Belgium to live in exile with his wife and family.

Some of Marx's most important writings were produced in Brussels, including *The Poverty of Philosophy*. In collaboration with his friend and fellow-campaigner Friedrich Engels, this was followed by *The Holy Family* (not a religious work, as one might assume from the title, but a criticism of

Hegelian idealism), *The German Ideology* and finally *The Communist Manifesto*. Publication of the latter led to expulsion from Belgium too; Marx subsequently moved via Paris to Cologne.

Europe's best sculptors and artists were employed to adorn Brussels. The achievements of the master masons and architects are preserved for posterity in the city's buildings. Brussels' most famous landmark is undoubtedly the Town Hall on the Grand' Place. The left wing and the lower section of the tower were built between 1401 and 1420 under the supervision of Jacob van Thiemen

and Jan Bornay. Between 1449 and 1455 the tower was completed by Jan van Ruysbroeck. It soars to a height of 91 metres (291 ft) above the market place. From 1515, work continued on the King's House (opposite the Town Hall), also known as the Bread House and later the residence of royal officials. The mastermind behind the project was Anthonis II Kelderman, a member of the illustrious family of master builders.

The Grand' Place has been the setting for a number of historic incidents. Egmont and Horn, two counts who strove to win sovereignty for the Netherlands in the 16th century, died at the hand of the executioner on the Grand' Place in front of the Maison du Roi in 1568 – thereby gaining eternal fame. The French Marshal de Villeroy found notoriety here when, in 1695, he and his troops bombarded the Lower City on behalf of King Louis XIV. The Grand' Place suffered considerable damage during the attack.

Another Frenchmen, Barnabé Guimard, came to Brussels with more benign intentions. A master builder, he was responsible for the church of St James on the Coudenberg (whose construction began in 1776) and the Palace of the Council of Brabant (1778–83), which later became the Parliament building.

The new age of the bourgeoisie demanded a new architecture different from that of the age of feudalism. Contemporary and historic-style buildings stood side by side. The greenhouse in the Botanical Garden, constructed in 1826 by Tilman-Frans Suys, was a spectacular example of the new style. Together with Charles Vanderstraeten, the same architect created a neoclassical palais for the Prince of Orange between 1823 and 1829; today it is known as the Palais des Académies.

First-ever shopping mall: Another innovation popular in Europe at the time was the erection of covered shopping centres to serve the elegant wives of the continent's growing class of prosperous businessmen. The first such gallery was constructed in Brussels. The foundation stone was laid for Jean-Pierre Chuisensaer's Galeries Saint-Hubert in 1846.

The star architect of Brussels' bourgeoisie

was undoubtedly Joseph Poelaert (1817–79). Together with Winand Janssens he designed the Church of St Catherine in Laeken in the neo-Gothic style which came to represent the Age of the Bourgeoisie; the same architect employed the style again in the Palais de Justice, the largest monumental building of the 19th century. The terraced gardens around the Pillar of Congress were also the work of Poelaert, as was the rebuilding of the Théâtre Royal de la Monnaie.

At the behest of the local citizens, Leo Sluys designed the Stock Exchange in 1871 as a sort of temple of capitalism. One in the army of sculptors who came from Paris to

Hero of Art Nouveau: Horta (1861–1947) had studied in Ghent, Paris and Brussels. He was promoted to a professorial chair in 1912 and between 1927 and 1931 assumed the directorship of the Académie des Beaux-Arts in Brussels. Together with van de Velde and Hankar, Horta is regarded as one of the leading exponents of Art Nouveau architecture in Belgium. He constructed trend-setting apartment houses and hotels of stone and cast iron. One such building which has been maintained and restored to its original charm is the house of the cloth merchant Waucquez, since 1989 the home of the Comic Museum. Influenced by a trip to

decorate the sacred halls of Mammon with fine statues was Auguste Rodin.

The city's palaces were not built on the instructions of the ruling bourgeoisie alone. The working classes were gaining in influence and had a so-called People's House erected between 1897 and 1899. The trades unions commissioned their Maison du Peuple from an architect who sympathised with their political views – Victor Horta.

<u>Left</u>, a woodcut from *The Ages of Life* by Frans Masereel (1889–1972). <u>Above</u>, inside the Museum of Classical Art.

America, Horta returned in his later buildings to a conventional neoclassical style; representative of this period are the Palais des Beaux-Arts (1922–28) and the Main Station (1936–41). A museum devoted to this famous architect can be found in the Rue Américaine at number 23–25.

Another famous architect of the time was Henry Clemens van de Velde (1863–1957). A proponent of Art Nouveau, which was just beginning to make its mark, van de Velde had begun his career as an artist. In 1890 he turned his attention to architecture, becoming director of the Academy of Art in

Weimar and opening a college of architecture in Brussels in 1926. Van de Velde was an open critic of the practice of imitating styles from the past. He campaigned for an approach in harmony with the purpose and materials of the building.

This approach was also endorsed by Auguste Perret (1874–1954), who was the first architect to make a point of using reinforced concrete. One of his pupils achieved even greater fame than he did; his name was Le Corbusier.

The Austrian architect Josef Hoffmann left his mark on the countenance of Brussels in the form of his Villa Stoclet. Rectangular forms predominate here, as in virtually all his buildings; as a result, he was nicknamed *Quadradl-Hoffmann* – "Hoffmann the Square".

A number of contemporary architects have also produced noteworthy buildings, including André Waterkeyn, the architect of the Atomium, and De Westel, the creator of the European Community headquarters. Between 1963 and 1969 De Westel followed an irregular cross-shaped ground plan in his design for the Palais Berlaymont.

The great painters: Across the centuries, Brussels was always a forum of European trade. As trade flourished, the arts blossomed. It is therefore not surprising that panel painting was invented here. Painting was restricted to walls or books until, at the beginning of the 15th century, the brothers Jan and Hubert van Eyck developed the technique of painting pictures on wooden or canvas panels. This panel painting spread from Flanders to all the corners of the earth. The artists themselves were held in high esteem; they received commissions from home and abroad, and were elected official city painters.

Another of the city's official painters was Rogier van der Weyden (1400–64), a pupil of Robert Campin, the Master of Flémalle. Van der Weyden became the official artist of Brussels and influenced the work of Goes, Bouts and Memling. Hugo van der Goes (1400–82) became a master craftsman in Ghent. Dieric Bouts (1415–75) had great influence on early wood-cut book illustration and achieved fame as a portrait painter.

Hans Memling (1433–94), an immigrant, was an innovator in the Flemish school. His journeys along the Main and the Rhine took him to Cologne, where he probably learned his skills in the studio of Stefan Lochner. He completed his training under Rogier van der Weyden in Brussels and later became in many respects the personification of the spirit of Bruges.

An entire family also achieved artistic fame in Brussels: the Brueghels. Pieter Brueghel the Elder (1525/30–1569) – "Peasant" Brueghel – was the father of two sons who both became painters. Pieter Brueghel the Younger (*circa* 1564–1638) was known

as "Hell" Brueghel because of the scenes of devils he portrayed; his brother, Jan Brueghel the Elder (1568–1625) was nicknamed "Velvet" or "Flower" Brueghel. He became court painter to the Spanish governor and executed a number of works in collaboration with his friend Rubens; as Jan Brueghel's nickname indicates, he always painted the flower arrangements.

Peter Paul Rubens (1577–1640) was born in Siegen in Germany. An artist and freedom fighter, he was a remarkably self-confident individual who frequently served hostile sovereigns. In a great many respects, Rubens epitomises the baroque Age with its characteristic pendulum swings between universal reason and limitless exuberance. The herald of the power and glory of heaven on earth, Rubens became the court painter in Brussels in 1609.

This was a position also held by David Tennier the Younger (1610–90), the son and pupil of Tennier the Elder. Under the influence of Brouwer and Rubens, he banned all scenes of popular life from his canvases. His contemporary Lucas Fayd'herbe (1617–97) was a pupil of Rubens and worked as a sculptor and architect in Brussels.

After this Golden Age had waned, many

ting, thereby spreading revolutionary consciousness.

After the 1789 Revolution, David became a member of the National Convention, the Committee of Public Safety and the Popular Education Committee. When Robespierre was overthrown he fell from favour and spent two periods in prison. However, Napoleon's rise to power revived his fortunes; the famous soldier supported David and made him his "First Painter". David fled to Brussels in 1816 following the emperor's defeat; there he exerted a profound influence over the new generation of young artists, in particular J.F. Navez. David's influence is also

years elapsed before the oppressed Belgians once more ascended the peaks of artistic creativity. The revival of Belgian painting was instigated by a revolutionary who sought asylum in Brussels: Jacques-Louis David (1748–1825). A leading representative of the Classical movement and a Jacobin, David liked to portray the civic virtues of republicanism in an antique set-

Left, part of a whole district had to be demolished to make way for the gigantic Palace of Justice, (around 1900). **Above**, the splendid St Hubert Arcade.

evident in the works of Gustave Wappers, N. de Kayser, Louis Gallait, Edouard Bièfve and L. Leys; it even extended to the paintings of Ferdinand Pauwels at the end of the 19th century.

Art in the Modern Age: Famous during his own time and then forgotten, only to be subsequently celebrated as a forerunner of the symbolist and surrealist schools was Antoine J. Wiertz (1806–65). His influence – his works depict cruelty and beauty – is honoured by a special museum in Brussels.

Another trendsetter who pointed the way towards radically new artistic horizons was

Guillaume Vogels (1836–96); he influenced Rops and Ensor and was one of the co-founders of the artistic association known as "XX" (Les Vingts). Félicien Rops (1833–96) achieved notoriety on account of his erotic fantasies.

Les Vingts itself played a notable role on the European art scene. It staged important exhibitions and invited famous artists from all over the world. Vincent van Gogh was a guest in Brussels for a short time between October 1880 and April 1881, when he studied art at the Academy.

Other artists in Belgium at this time were influenced by naturalism. Constantin Meunier (1831–1905) became famous for his sculpture of a man carrying a heavy load as well as his paintings of people at work. The works of Charles de Groux (1825–70) illustrate similar themes.

Other naturalist painters were Jan Stobbaerts (1839–1914), who rebelled against the doctrines of his established fellow-artists in Antwerp and moved to Brussels in 1885, and Léon Frédéric (1856–1940), the most popular Belgian painter during the 1920s, who painted mainly peasants and workers.

Alfred William Finch (1854–1930) studied with Ensor at the Brussels Academy and also belonged to Les Vingts. Another member was Theo van Rysselberghe (1862–1926), who also studied in Brussels and became one of the leading Belgian Impressionists.

James Ensor (1860–1949), a virtual contemporary, is regarded as marking the beginning of the modern period. A friend of Khnopff and the protégé of Rops, Ensor remained a loner. His painting *Christ's Entry into Brussels* shocked public and critics alike. His expressive pictures remained largely unappreciated until the 1920s.

Another member of Les Vingts was Fernand Khnopff (1858–1921), a Symbolist without whose work Belgian imaginative painting would have been much poorer. Other representatives of the "Reality of Fantasy" are Degouve de Nunques (1867–1935) and Jean Delville (1867–1953), who studied and later taught in Brussels.

The most famous visionary of all was René Magritte (1898–1967), who was often mistakenly regarded as a Surrealist. He was trained in Brussels and travelled to France, Britain and Germany, staying in Paris for three years between 1927 and 1930. When he returned to Brussels he painted a number of murals for Belgian public buildings.

Another artist, Paul Delvaux (born 1897), destroyed all the paintings from his first creative period after witnessing the anatomical peepshow of the Spitzner Museum at the Brussels Fair. Naked bodies and skeletons peopled his works from that time on, and he became influenced by Magritte.

Also influenced by Magritte was Félix Labisse (born 1905) whose visionary paintings are characterised by nude figures often in iridescent shades of blue. Labisse was also influenced by Ensor and Delvaux.

Gaston Bogaert (born 1918) first came to Brussels as an actor. He then became an advertising designer for the Belgian airline Sabena. His first exhibition of paintings displayed in a Brussels gallery in 1965 place him as another member of the Brussels visionary school.

Contemporary art in Brussels does not consist only of the abstract, as the work of Pierre Alechinsky (born 1927), Marcel Broodthaers (1924–76) and John C.F. Delogne (born in Uccle in 1933) makes clear. And artistic contributions of another kind are supplied by the artists who have transformed the underground railway stations into a whole new gallery of contemporary art.

Literature and music: Many men of letters also passed through Brussels across the years. Rousseau and Voltaire stayed in the Palais d'Egmont. Victor Hugo often paid visits to his friend Juliette Drouot, who lived in Brussels' Galeries des Princes. Colette and Cocteau were both members of the Royal Academy of French Language and Literature in Brussels.

Of the many Belgian writers, only a handful actually lived in their country's capital. Amongst them was the popular writer Charles Théodore Henri de Coster (1827–79), who lived in Brussels from early childhood. His important prose epic *Tyll Ulenspiegel und Lamme Goedzak* made use of the Flemish narrative tradition, creating a national epic tale; de Coster also established the contemporary francophone literary tradition in Belgium.

Hermann Teirlinck, born in 1879, the year in which de Coster died, was another of the city's leading literary figures. A poet and playwright who is regarded as instigating the renaissance of the Flemish theatre, Teirlinck also taught languages at the royal court. He died in 1967; his house on the city outskirts at Uwenberg 13 has been transformed into a commemorative museum.

The writer Ernest André Jozef Claes (1885–1968) chose the peseudonym G. van Hasselt for the realist tales and novels for

temps (1820–81), occupied the professorial chair at the Brussels conservatory from 1871. The director of the *Conservatoire* was François Auguste Gevaert (1828–1908), a versatile composer, conductor, music scholar and patron of the music of Bach.

Another important supporter of the Bach renaissance in Brussels was Edgar Tinel (1854–1912), a composer of church music and organ works who became director of the *Conservatoire* in 1909.

A more modern composer was Paul Gilson (1865–1942), a member of the contemporary Flemish school. He was also the Inspector of Musical Education in Belgium.

The Entry of Christ into Brussels by James Ensor (1888).

which he was to become famous.

The Queen Elisabeth of Belgium Music Competition, established in 1937, has provided the stepping stone to success for many of the country's musicians, including its very first winter, David Oistrakh.

Another violinist who was amongst the friends of Queen Elisabeth, a member of the Bavarian Wittelsbach dynasty, was Albert Einstein.

A professional violinist, Henri Vieux–

Marcel Poot (born 1901), a neoclassical composer and director of the *Conservatoire,* achieved international fame. So, too, did Henri Pousseur (born 1929); he studied in Brussels and Liège and composed electronic music in series.

Recently, Brussels has made a name for itself on the popular music scene. The singer Dani Klein and the double-bass player Dirk Schoufs met in one of the city's bars. The jazz duo *Vaya con Dios* is also famous beyond the city boundaries, its European tours proving that in this sphere, too, Brussels can compete with the best.

THE COMIC MUSEUM

If you want a museum that absorbs children for hours and offers something for adults too, head for the Comic Museum, occupying the house at Rue des Sables 20/Zandstraat. Allow plenty of time for your visit (the museum is open to the public every day except Monday, from 10 a.m. until 6 p.m) and take your time over the hands-on exhibits; whoever completes first – you or the kids – can take advantage of the reading room, comfortably strewn with cushions and comics.

This treasure-chest of picture stories is a gem in itself, because the building in which it is housed is

Rémi) first introduced them to the newspaper-reading public in 1929. They are his most popular cartoon characters, followed by the twin detectives Thomson and Thompson, Captain Haddock and the absent-minded Professor Calculus. For 60 years their adventures have entranced the whole world in every imaginable language. The museum contains sketches, drawings, relief plates and many other items.

Incredible though it may seem, the lovely Horta-designed building was at one stage poised for demolition. The *Magazins Waucquet* had closed its doors in 1970 and the building was threatened by the same fate that befell many other buildings in the city centre, including the "House of the People", mentioned in every account of the city's

a prime example of Flemish Art Nouveau architecture. Known as the Magazins Waucquez, it was built in 1906 for a fabric merchant named Waucquez by the famous Belgian architect Victor Horta, who lived from 1861 to 1947 (*see preceding chapter, page 77.*)

In those days, customers to the fabric shop entered through a fine portal and then mounted the sweeping staircase. Today these same stairs serve as the launching pad for the red-and-white checked rocket which Tintin and Snowy used to reach "Destination Moon" long before the Americans managed it.

Tintin – who outflanks even Manneken Pis in fame – and his faithful terrier are omnipresent in the museum. Their artist-creator Hergé (Georges

architecture. The capital of Europe needed more space to house its increasing numbers of politicians and businessmen. The demolition was short-sighted and ruthless. No account was taken of the loss to Brussels' cultural heritage.

However, Horta's Magazins Waucquez was saved from the same fate. Artists and architects managed to persuade the Belgian Minister of Housing and Construction that the house in the Rue des Sables should be saved and restored. The ingenious idea of turning it into a comic museum was widely supported by Brussels' citizens. The plan was to create a symbiosis between Art Nouveau and the "Ninth Art" – that of cartoon drawing. King Baudouin and Queen Fabiola added their support for the project; it was in their presence that the new museum was at long last inaugurated in the autumn of 1989.

The treasures of Belgian comic art were thus preserved for posterity. The indiscriminate and reckless sale of comic books, magazines, drawings and printing plates was stopped in its tracks. Previously, early printing plates of Hergé and Morris cartoons were sold to collectors abroad for about £10,000 each.

The museum is not just a home for Tintin and Snowy and their many fans, as a brief tour of the exhibition rooms indicates. It is entertaining and educational, and a place for meeting well-loved friends from your past – whichever generation you belong to.

On the ground floor, to the right, lies the

cartoon films are made, including sketches and drawings at every stage of development.

Ascending the staircase, the visitor passes Tintin's rocket and arrives at the first floor. Here, the auditorium of the King Baudouin Foundation is reserved for special events.

Also on the first floor is the Museum of the Imagination, the place to meet all those old friends. In the room dedicated to the journal *Spirou* visitors find the cunning bellboy himself, and in the Vandersteen Room you will find Professor Barabas's time machine.

In the room housing the Jacques Martin collection you can experience a thunderstorm by night in ancient Rome, and in the Tillieux Room you will find Jeff Jordan's favourite saloon. Entering

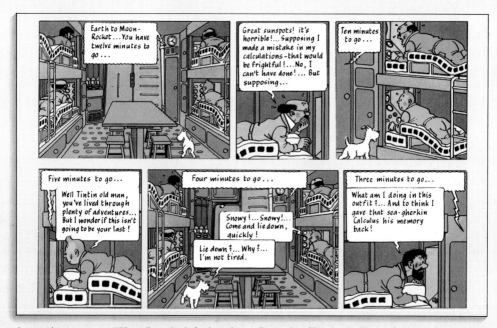

brasserie-restaurant, "Horta"; to the left, there is a bookshop named Slumberland after the Art Nouveau comic strip about Little Nemo. Also on this floor is a permanent exhibition commemorating the life and work of architect Victor Horta, and two libraries – one for leisurely reading and the other for more serious study.

On the mezzanine floor, the visitor enters the Saint-Roch Treasure House, where original manuscripts are preserved. Also here are a cinema, a video library, and an exhibition explaining how

Left, the *Adventures of Tintin* spread to outer space in *Destination Moon*, first published in 1953. **Above**, no turning back for Tintin, Snowy and crew.

Gaston's office in the Franquin room, it seems as if Marsupilami cannot be far away; and in the Hubinon Room you can stand on the aircraft carrier next to Buck Danny. In the Morris room you encounter the shadow which shoots faster than Lucky Luke.

That is only a sample of the experiences in store at the museum. In addition, prepare to meet Jacobs' Blake and Mortimer, Roba's Boule & Bill, and Peyo's Smurfs.

There seems no end to the range of comic figures created by Belgian artists. Quite apart from the established artists who have now become classics, there is a steady stream of new talent in the country. Belgium boasts more comic characters than anywhere else in the world.

A PEN PUSHER'S PARADISE

Brussels' new nickname, "The Office Desk of Europe", couldn't be more appropriate. If one thing symbolises the city better than the exquisite white pillow lace that adorned the rich and powerful in the 16th century it's the large number of rich and powerful bureaucrats – the army of ministers, senior diplomats and influential industrialists – that populate the city today.

The people inside Brussels' committee rooms and offices manipulate the fates of millions: the committees of the EC determine everything from member states' agricultural policy to their currency exchange rates, and the North Atlantic Treaty Organization helps determine world security and defence. And it isn't just the EC and NATO that account for the preponderence of top-ranking official bodies and organisations; more than 1,000 other international associations and over 1,300 multinational industrial concerns have headquarters here.

Rise and fall: American companies were the first – during the 1960s – to discover the many advantages of Brussels' location. The city lies at the geographic heart of Western Europe and even in those early days it seemed set to become the focal point of the Western bloc. Furthermore the city was particularly attractive for its low wages, the tax advantages it offered foreigners, and an apparently inexhaustible supply of inexpensive flats and offices. One famous American concern after another set up branch offices in the secret capital of Europe.

Then, as the 1970s waned and the 1980s dawned, the unexpected happened. The flow of foreign investment capital from across the Atlantic suddenly dried up. Many American firms decided to leave the city; the fall of the dollar, the vastly inflated wage and social security costs and rapidly escalating prices for houses and flats had suddenly made Brussels an expensive, and therefore unfavourable, place in which to work.

Today, however, Brussels is experiencing

The alternative way of getting to the post office.

another boom. As before, investors from America are well ahead of their competitors in Europe, the Far East and Canada. In 1988 Brussels contained offices of 671 US concerns, and smaller numbers from the United Kingdom (174), France (170), Germany (162), Japan (84), Switzerland (80), Italy (75), Spain (35), Denmark (18), Canada (17) and Norway (12). One of the most interesting developments in recent years is the growing number of Swedish investors who are pouring large sums of money into the city.

There are several reasons for this change in investment behaviour. In 1982, the Brussels government alarmed at the departure of

moval of internal trade barriers, has also contributed to the improvement in Brussels' position in recent years.

Property prices provide first-hand evidence that Brussels is a popular investment choice. During the past decade, office rents in Brussels have increased two-and-a-half-fold. In Frankfurt, by comparison – another European city which is popular with investors – commercial rents only doubled. However, prices in Brussels still lie approximately 20 percent below Frankfurt levels, making it a more favourable choice. Furthermore, rents in general in the Belgian capital are still very low compared with those in

so many American firms and struggling with the reality of a general economic crisis, took pre-emptive action. It prescribed a drastic cure for the entire country. Wage increases were linked to the inflation rate, social welfare payments were reduced and foreign investors offered further tax incentives in addition to the existing favourable conditions: foreign employees of international firms with a branch in Belgium, for example, need only declare 50 percent of their income for tax purposes.

The progress towards European unity, best illustrated by the proposals for the re-

metropolises such as London, Paris, Madrid, New York and Tokyo. It is therefore not surprising that in an international survey of office running costs prepared by the London-based firm Jones Lang Wootton Brussels came out favourably.

In order to ensure that relatively inexpensive rents continue to attract foreign companies to Brussels, it will be necessary to create a further 1.5 million sq. metres (16 million sq. ft) of office space by the year 2000. No one in Brussels doubts that these new offices will soon be occupied by companies. The European Community alone is guaranteed to take over much of this additional space.

Brussels would also like to strengthen its position as a financial centre. There is already a formidable foreign presence; 61 of the 86 foreign financial institutions with branches in Belgium have dependencies here. The Belgian Stock Exchange, on the other hand – founded in 1801 – still occupies only a subordinate position.

Fair competition: Brussels has proved most successful as a centre for trade fairs and congresses. Three modern complexes in the heart of the town have made the Belgian capital the third-largest conference city in the world, after London and Paris.

and Horesca – an international hotel fair – in November. In this respect the city can look back over a 500-year tradition. And it is not so many years since the 1958 International World Exhibition aroused widespread attention. It also provided Brussels with one of its most futuristic and famous landmarks – the Atomium.

The strong presence of political institutions, international associations and multinational companies has made Brussels into a cosmopolitan city. According to census figures, one in four out of the Belgian capital's 1 million-plus residents was born abroad. The European Community and NATO alone

With a 75-hectare (185-acre) trade-fair site including 12 hectares (30 acres) covered by buildings, Brussels is the leading trades fair centre in Europe. Throughout the year, businessmen flock in their thousands to participate in such important events as the Leather Goods Fair in January, the Euroba trades fair for bakers, chocolatiers and confectioners, the International Trade Fair in March, the car accessories fair Autotechnica in April, and the International Furniture Fair

Left, "Elvis Pompilio hats suit me best." **Above**, the trade fair site by night.

account for some 20,000 foreign diplomats and officials.

Many countries have three diplomatic representatives: one at the Belgian court, one at the EC and one at NATO. It is estimated that 100,000 of the foreigners living in Brussels are here on account of the international organisations and industrial headquarters. Some 150,000 represent the guest worker and overseas population to be found in any large city.

In spite of the steady increase in the service industries sector, Brussels is still an important industrial centre. The range of products manufactured is as varied as the people who live here: lace and carpets, chocolate and beer, plastics and pharmaceuticals, computers and cars. Traditional items and high-technology goods all have their place. Good transport links guarantee that manufactured articles can be shipped without delay to any destination in the world.

Brussels is an important European railway junction; it also lies in the centre of a well-developed motorway network and has air links with overseas, Asian and African markets. The Willebroek Canal, constructed during the 16th century and widened at the beginning of the 20th, provides the city with

free will. The Belgians had cunningly decided to allow the import of automobiles only in the case of foreign manufacturers who already had an assembly plant in the country. That Volkswagen is able to profit handsomely from this arrangement can be deduced from the fact that during the next 5 years the company is planning to invest BFr 15–20 billion in the expansion of their Brussels plant.

Of course, the citizens of Brussels benefit from the arrangement too; they can claim the highest per capita vehicle production in Europe, despite the fact that they have no automobile company of their own. Each year,

direct access to the North Sea.

The largest industrial employer in Brussels is, surprisingly enough, not a Belgian concern. The German car manufacturers Volkswagen has their world headquarters in Wolfsburg, but in the factory in Forest – one of the 19 communities forming the Brussels metropolitan area – over 6,000 workers assemble Passat and Golf cars. In 1988, 186,000 vehicles rolled off the production lines – a total of 6.5 percent of the company's entire output.

When Volkswagen set up in Brussels in 1948, they did not do so entirely of their own

more than 1 million cars from a variety of European manufacturers roll off the assembly lines in Brussels, Antwerp and Ghent.

Sweet sensation: Belgium is well known for its chocolate and the long-established Brussels confectionery firm Godiva has an excellent reputation all over the world. For the sweet-toothed the trademark picture of a young lady on a horse represents the ultimate in exclusive chocolates. The company produces 3,000 tonnes of chocolate each year.

Established in Brussels in 1926, Godiva acquired the royal seal of approval in 1968; as official court supplier, it continues to enjoy an advantage over its many competitors. Today the company operates on a worldwide basis.

In addition to Volkswagen, another long-established foreign company in Brussels is the US technology firm IBM, which celebrated its 50th anniversary in the Belgian capital in 1986. Another high-technology concern is Honeywell Bull, which has been in production in Belgium since 1948 and which chose Brussels as its European headquarters in 1969.

A relative newcomer to Brussels is the firm Alfa-Laval, which intends to make the city its bio-technology centre. It has set up a

Together with the "Banque de Belgique", founded in 1835, this financial giant determined the country's economic development and was responsible for maintaining over many years Belgium's dominant position in the smelting of non-ferrous metals based on the rich copper, cobalt and zinc deposits in the southern Belgian Congo.

In other spheres, too, the Belgians enjoyed a distinct head start. In 1835 the first railway line on the continent was built between Brussels and Mechelen. During the 19th century, there was scarcely a railway construction project in Europe, Mexico, Russia or China in which the Société Générale de Banque

factory in Evere, the Silicon Valley of Belgium, where other high-technology firms such as Digital Equipment, Wang and Texas Instruments already have premises.

Brussels can demonstrate a long tradition of innovative technology. Under William I, who ruled the Netherlands and Belgium for a short while as the kingdom of the "United Netherlands", the "Société Générale de Banque" was founded in Brussels in 1822.

Left, handmade Belgian chocolates. **Above**, business people congregate in the Ravenstein Gallery.

was not involved.

Nowadays it is the task of the Brussels Regional Development Company (SDRB) to persuade high-technology companies to establish themselves in the area. Their success rate to date is noteworthy: the company has attracted 50 forward-looking concerns providing the citizens of Brussels with a total of 7,000 jobs.

It is fair to assume that Brussels, which first established a prominent position for itself as a cloth manufacturing and trading centre, will be well equipped to survive the transition to the next millennium.

BRUSSELS LACE

Brussels lace is famous the world over. Developed during the mid-19th century and initially used to adorn the shirt collars and cuffs of the nobility, Brussels lace was soon being used extensively. At one point it was fashionable to wear gowns made entirely of the precious fabric.

Brussels lace was particularly sought after at the royal courts in Paris and London. Queen Elizabeth I of England reputedly owned 3,000 lace dresses; it is said that Empress Eugénie years of age. During the 17th century, 22,000 women and girls worked as lace makers; during the 19th century, the total reached 50,000. In Brussels alone, the capital of lace production, the figure was some 10,000.

Brussels lace was unsurpassable as regards both the fineness of the thread and the beauty of the motifs. The capital's churches and museums are full of examples of the delicate work produced. A particularly fine specimen of the lace maker's art can be found in the Royal Museum of Art and History: a bedspread which Albert I and his wife Isabella received as a present upon the occasion of

of France owned a lace gown which 600 women had toiled over for 10 months using a total of 90,000 bobbins.

By the second half of the 16th century, women throughout Belgium were engaged in the craft and lace was being exported to prosperous families all over Europe. At the end of the century there was scarcely a young girl, even in the most rural areas, who was not employed by the lace merchants.

The labour intensive industry posed unforeseen problems, namely a shortage of serving maids in the homes of the wealthy. Eventually a decree was passed prohibiting the manufacture of lace by girls of more than 12 Albert's elevation to Duke of Brabant.

Other masterpieces include the Virgin Mary's veil, on display in the church of Notre-Dame-du-Sablon, and a lace bedspread, carefully preserved in the Museum of Costumes and Lace, which belonged to Emperor Charles VI. The bedspread is decorated with the imperial eagle, symbolising the pomp and circumstance of monarchy.

The production of large covers and entire robes was only made possible when the technique of lace-making moved away from the use of a single continuous thread towards knotting. Until this point it had only been possible to produce small pieces of lace, the size of which was determined by the length of the thread wound on to the bobbin. The technique of joining together individual motifs to produce a single large piece revolutionised the industry. This method permitted the creation of large-scale items with highly imaginative patterns within a relatively short time.

Following this method of production many women produced the same motif time and time again, often over a period of several years. The creative aspect of the craft was thus gradually lost in a sort of mass production. Other workers were allotted the task of joining the individual pieces together.

lution lace-making in Belgium was in decline. The craft experienced a brief renaissance during the 19th century but was never able to regain its previous fashionableness or degree of skill.

Today, the craft attracts only a modest following in its country of origin. Very few women possess the requisite skills. Two schools, in Mons and Binche, train young women in what was once a world-famous art. Unfortunately, nowadays too few Belgian women want to learn the intricacies of lace-making to satisfy the rapidly increasing demands for hand-made lace. Much of that on

None of the lace makers ever became famous or rich. Their reward for their arduous work was determined by the lace merchants, few of whom were generous; the lace makers were often forced to work in badly-lit, damp cellars where the thread would be less likely to break.

Until well into the 18th century, Brussels lace remained a popular symbol of luxury for the rich. Inevitably, however, fashions changed and by the time of the French Revo-

sale in Brussels today was actually made in China. The Asian product is considerably cheaper but inferior in quality.

One of the largest lace merchants in Brussels is the Manufacture Belge de Dentelles, whose shop can be found at 6-8 Galerie de la Reine. A wide variety of antique and modern lace is on sale.Those who prefer simply to look at fine Belgian lace should visit the Museum of Costumes and Lace just behind the Town Hall at 6, Rue de la Violette. There is also an excellent lace collection in the Royal Museum of Art and History in the Parc du Cinquantenaire; the entrance will be found in the Avenue des Nerviens.

Left, *The Lacemaker* by Jan Vermeer van Delt (1665). <u>**Above**</u>, **even expert lacemakers can't produce more than a few inches a day.**

Eddy Merckx, the legendary racing cyclist of the 1960s and '70s, is probably the only Belgian sportsman whose name is familiar to non-Belgians. At various stages in his career, Merckx won every major international cycling race, gaining the coveted Tour de France trophy no less than five times.

All in all, however, Brussels does not play an important role on the international sporting scene and Merckx is the only world-calibre athlete that the country can boast. Even so most Belgians enjoy participating in one or more sporting activities and support their national teams with enthusiasm.

Brussels sports fans are particularly well catered for, with a choice of six stadiums, three horse-racing tracks and several ice rinks. There are top-ranking football teams such as R.S.C. Anderlecht, and an internationally famous light athletics meeting (Ivo van Damme Memorial).

Since 1985 Brussels has been haunted by the curse of Heysel stadium. This was when hooligan supporters of the British national champions, Liverpool, staged a brutal riot during the European Cup Final against Juventus Turin. The tragic episode cost 39 Juventus fans' lives and resulted in British clubs being banned from European tournaments. The event had a profound effect on the city; it had very little to do with the everyday sporting reality – active or passive – of the average Brussels man-in-the-street.

A nation on its bike: Cycling is without doubt the favourite national sport. It holds a place in the national soul comparable to that of baseball in America, cricket in England, bullfighting in Spain, or ice hockey in the Soviet Union and Canada. Cynics maintain that its popularity represents an escape from the boredom of a Belgian Sunday. Indeed, hardly a day goes by on which there is no cycling race somewhere or other, and they are always supported by thousands of enthusiastic spectators; a classic cycling race from

Liège to Bastogne and back, for instance, will be lined by throngs of spectators all along the route.

But it isn't just the cycling that people come to see. A rally is also a social event. Friends meet, drink a beer together, become carried away by the speed at which the cyclists race past, and enjoy listening to the results on the radio later on. In addition, cycling events are invariably attended by fairs and other attractions appealing to

younger family members.

Speculation as to why this enthusiasm for cycling should have grown up in Belgium usually cites the topography of the land. One ideal precondition is without doubt the flatness of the countryside. Except in the hilly eastern provinces, Belgium – like the Netherlands – makes the bicycle the most convenient and inexpensive mode of transport. Children organise impromptu races on the way to school, and farmers' wives use their ancient bone-shakers to reach the nearest village. When national heroes such as grocer's son Eddy Merckx make headline news

Left and above, billiards is a popular pastime, as is cycling – here at the Zandpoortvest in Mechelen.

in the international press, their success fires the enthusiasm of the aspiring youth. The popularity of the sport has little to do with the prospect of monetary gain; apart from the trophies, the prizes are not usually very significant. In a small country like Belgium, the few top sportsmen become role models to a far greater extent than elsewhere.

The Belgians are a convivial people; they love their families and enjoy celebrating with friends. A Belgian who participates actively in some form of sport will naturally tend to belong to a club. For Flemings and Walloons alike the latter performs the role of a second family, a second home.

frequent events; many take place through the streets of towns, with all speed limits temporarily lifted (be warned: barriers to protect the spectators are seldom erected). Tens of thousands flock to the race from Spa to Francorchamps, hoping to witness as many hazardous thrills as possible. Celebrations know no bounds when a compatriot wins, and heavy disappointment descends if a Belgian entry is eliminated early on in the race. However, competing is considered the most important thing.

Bar billiards: Brussels citizens with more limited sporting ability tend to retire to the city's bars to indulge in a game of billiards,

An example of this sociability can be found in the cycling club at Plombières, in the three-country triangle between Aachen, Maastricht and Liège. Although the lively club has had no active cycling members for years, it still continues to organise a "Grand Prix of Plombières" each autumn. The winner is usually from the Netherlands. A crate of beer is the prize for the fastest circuit, and the winner is rewarded with a trophy and a certificate.

Sport in Belgium has a great deal to do with spectacle. The louder and more colourful the event, the better. Motor races are

a favourite evening pastime. The professional standards reached by some of these players are documented by the string of world championship titles won by the nation's experts.

Apart from cycling, football and billiards, the other sports enjoying popularity in Belgium include tennis and golf – both as fashionable here as elsewhere on the continent. Cross-country skiing is practised in the winter in the hills of the Ardennes; and during the summer months, sailing and surfing are both popular pastimes on the English Channel coast between Knokke and De Panne.

Rugby is played mainly in the French-speaking provinces, where it is a favourite spectator sport.

Top sportsmen have a difficult time in a small country. Belgium has produced few world-class athletes, although it has established a winning tradition in a number of disciplines. Gold medals or unexpected success produce a spirit of national euphoria. In the 1986 World Football Championship in Mexico, the Belgian team reached the semifinals. Nobody slept during the victory night; celebrations lasted until well into the small hours. Apart from that, however, things are quiet on the higher sporting plane.

century ago. The archers attempt to shoot down the containers; if they succeed in their aim, the cages shatter in mid-air; the rats fall to the ground and lie there stunned until their throats are slit. The local newspaper, *Het Nieuwsblad*, which always sponsors the event, maintains that this is a more humane death than poisoning.

Twice a week between 15 October and 1 May (on Tuesday and Saturday), a hunt takes place in the Vielsalm region. It is a full-blooded mounted chase in which a stag is pursued by hounds and horsemen to the bitter end. The hunt can last as long as 10 hours. The host of the event is Baron Eric

Rat catching: The combination of sports and spectacles has a long tradition in the country. Every August in the village of Zaffelare, near Ghent, an archery contest is held – a sporting event, but with the spirit of a funfair. The chief aspect of the contest is somewhat gruesome. The targets are not the normal ones used in archery, but cages full of rats which are suspended at a height of 27 metres (86 ft). The event marks a plague of rats that descended on the village over a

Left, Belgium is ideal for cycling. **Above**, the less energetic try their hand at minigolf.

Jansen, whose guests for the occasion are drawn from the aristocracy and the highest echelons of industry. After the killing, the hunting party recovers at an exclusive champagne reception.

Public outcry at blood sports of this nature is vociferous in Belgian. Protest is also directed against a substantial number of birdcatchers, who are wont to describe theselves as animal lovers and sportsmen. Each year in the late autumn and early winter, almost 1 million migratory birds are caught; they end up in the country's aviaries and cooking pots.

PLACES

The best way to get acquainted with Brussels is to put on your most comfortable shoes and walk. Start with the the Rue Royale in the Upper City, a route which leads past the parliament building and across the municipal park as far as the magnificent square in front of the museum. The most imposing building in the entire city, the monumental Palais de Justice, can be approached via the Rue de la Régence or the Rue aux Laines. At its feet nestles the Marolles, an historic district where you will find, squeezed side by side, the chic, the original and the extremely poor.

If you like wandering through colourful markets, collecting bric-à-brac, books, fake antiques or exotic spices, you will be pleased to discover that every day is market day in Brussels. Belgium's capital is a maze of shopping arcades where you will find genuine Brussels lace, French *haute couture* and precious jewels alongside postcards and souvenirs.

Brussels is also the place for gourmets. You can eat better here than almost anywhere else in the world. The best place to head for is the Ilôt Sacré, where the restaurants lie cheek by jowl. Try more than mussels and chips (a Brussels speciality); the variety of restaurants is as wide as the price range. Beer drinkers in particular are spoiled for choice, because some 200 kinds of ale are available. The Petite Rue des Bouchers is aptly known as the "Stomach of Brussels".

The Lower City contains the city's most famous sites. Passing through a maze of little side streets, you will reach one of the loveliest city squares in Europe: the Grand' Place (Grote Markt), graced by baroque, Gothic and Renaissance architecture. Nearby you will find Manneken Pis, the best dressed statue in the world. His outfits – he has well over 300 – change according to the season.

Later on during your visit you may like to make an excursion from the Château Royal to the Palais du Cinquantenaire, or visit the Atomium on the Heysel plateau. You can round off your visit to Brussels with a trip to the university town of Leuven or the village of Waterloo, where Napoleon made his final stand.

Preceding pages: bowler hats are not just a preserve of the English; a Maypole celebration takes place in the city in August; Brussels contains a host of noble restaurants; modern art is displayed in a number of galleries. **Left**, taking in the sights.

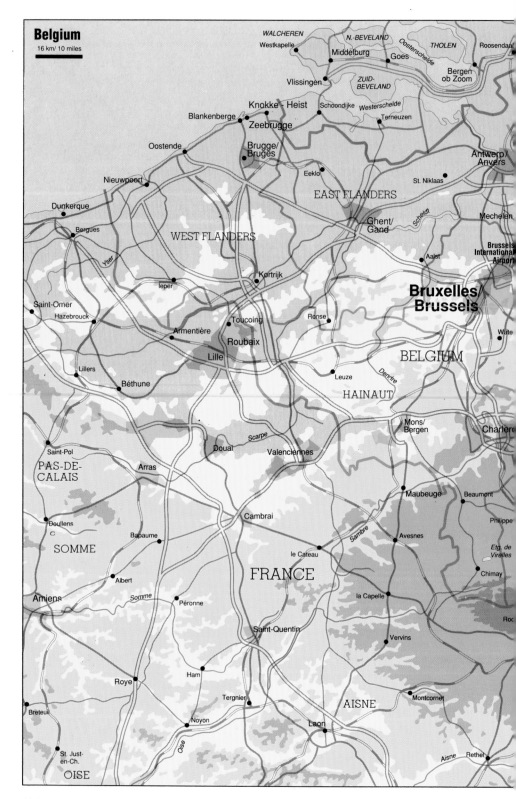

Belgium

16 km/ 10 miles

WALCHEREN

N.-BEVELAND

THOLEN

Westkapelle

Roosendaal

Middelburg

Goes

Bergen
ob Zoom

Vlissingen

ZUID-
BEVELAND

Knokke - Heist

Schoondijke

Westerschelde

Blankenberge

Zeebrugge

Terneuzen

Oostende

Brugge/
Bruges

Antwerp/
Anvers

Nieuwpoort

Eeklo

St. Niklaas

Mechelen

Dunkerque

EAST FLANDERS

Bergues

Scheldt

Ghent/
Gand

Brussels
International
Airport

Yser

WEST FLANDERS

Aalst

Saint-Omer

Ieper

Kortrijk

Bruxelles/
Brussels

Hazebrouck

Ronse

Wate

Armentière

Toucoing

BELGIUM

Lillers

Roubaix

Lille

Leuze

Dendre

Béthune

HAINAUT

Mons/
Bergen

Charler

Saint-Pol

Scarpe

PAS-DE-
CALAIS

Arras

Doual

Valenciennes

Maubeuge

Beaumont

Doullens

Cambrai

Philippe

SOMME

Bapaume

Sambre

Avesnes

Etg. de
Virelles

Albert

le Cateau

Chimay

Amiens

Somme

Péronne

la Capelle

Roc

Saint-Quentin

Vervins

Roye

Ham

Breteuil

Tergnier

AISNE

Montcornet

Noyon

Laon

St. Just-
en-Ch.

Oise

Aisne

Rethel

OISE

107

Hammebrug

Hamme

Maalbeek

Bever

Hanveld

Ring 0

Tangebe

Kobbegem

Autoroute A 12

Rasselhoek

Strombeek-Bever

Koningslo

Wemmel

Palais
du Centenaire
Eeuwfeestwijk

Neder
Heembeek

Relegem

Heysel/Heizel

Schaliënhof

Pavillon Chinées
(Chinese Pavilion)

Atomium

Château Royal
(Royal Palace)

Zellik

BOIS DU LAERBEEK
LAARBEEKBOS

Avenue

Autoroute E 40

Ring 0

Laeken

Jette

Helmet

Ganshoren

Port
(Haven)

Groot Bijgaarden

PARC ELISABETH
ELISABETH PARK

Gare
du Nord

Koekelberg

Ossegem

St. Joost-Ten-Node
St. Josse-Ten-Nood

Dilbeek

Pl. de
Broukère

Grand' Place
(Grote Markt)

Bruxelles/
Brussels

Moortebeek

Chaussee de Ninove

Gare
Central

Itterbeek

Bon Air

Maison
d'Erasme
(Erasmushuis)

Gare
du Midi

Neerpede

la Petite Ile/
klein Eiland

Vlasendael/
Vlazendaal

Het Rad
la Roue

PARC
DUDEN
DUDENPARK

Abbaye
de la Cambre
(Abdij ter Kameren)

Université
Libre de
Bruxelles

Ring 0

Canal de Charleroi

BOIS
DE LA
CAMBRE

Boondae
Boondaa

Langeveld

Rattendaal

Klein Bijgaarden

TER
KAMERENBC

Zuunbeek

Neerstalle

PARK VON
WOLVENDAEL

Observatoire
(Observatory)

Grote
Bempt

Stalle

St. Job/
St. -Job

Drogenbos

Zenne

Calevoet/
Kalevoet

Ruisbroek

St.-Pieters-
Leeuw

Institut
Pasteur

N.D.-de la Paix /
O.L.V van de Krede

Greater Brussels

1600 m/ 1,0 miles

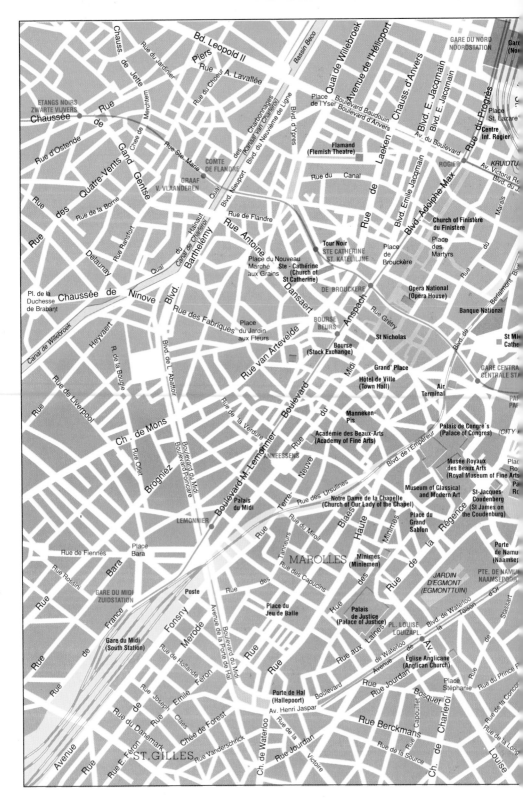

SCHAARBEEK

Blvd. General Wahis

Chazal

Av. Ernest Cambier

Avenue Rogier

Avenue Rogier

Paul Deschanel

Rue de la Poste

Rue de la Poste

Avenue Gen. Eisenhower

Rue Dupont

Haecht

Pl. de la Reine

Ste - Marie (St Mary's Church)

Josaphat

Rue de la

Rue Royale

Place des Bienfaiteurs

Rue Paul Devigne

ST.-JOST

Chaussée

Rue

de

Rue de la Limite

Avenue

Consolation

Rue Artan

Grande

Rue François

Bossaerts

Place de la Patrie

Place Col Bremer

JIN NIQUE NICAL EN)

Église de Jésu (Church of Jesus Christ)

du

Moulin

Place Col Bremer

Rue au

Rue Artan

Rue

Dailly

Avenue Bois

Chaussée de Louvain

BOTANIQUE KRUIDTUIN

Av. Galilée

Boulevard

Rue de la Commune

Place Houwaert

ST.-JOSSE

Verbist

Place Dailly

Rue

Mahillon

Bischoffsheim

Astronomie

Rue Scailquin

R. de la Ferme

Chaussée de Louvain

Rue John Waterloo

Rue de Pavie

Rue du Noyer

Avenue

Léon Victor

Hugo

Cirque Royal

Congrès

Rue des Eglises

Rue

des Eburons

Av. de la Brabançonne

Rue van Campenhout

de Louvain MADOU

s de la Nation ament Building)

Boulevard du Régent

Avenue des Arts

Rue des Deux Eglises

Square Marie-Louise

Square

Ambiorix

Rue des Patriotes

Franklin

Place de Jambline de Meux

de la Loi

âtre Parc

ARTS-LOI KUNST-WET

Rue Stévin

Rue

Joseph II

Rue Archimède

de

Cortenbergh

Rue du Noyer

Hobbema

C DE XELLES

Commerce

Rue de la Science

MAELBEEK MAALBEEK

EC Parliament Building

Rue

Stévin

Mosquée (Mosque)

Rue

Av. de la Renaissance

Rue des Arts

St-Joseph

Palais d'Assche

Rue de la Loi

Avenue

SCHUMAN

PARC DU CINQUANTENAIRE

Palais des Académies (Palace of the Academies)

Rue Belliard

Rue

de

Rue Montoyer

Froissart

Avenue

LUXEMBOURG LUXEMBURG

Gare du Quartier Léopold

PARC LEOPOLD

Rue Belliard

(JUBILEE PARK)

Champ de Mars

Rue du

Avenue des Nerviens

Rue

Rue du Cornet

Chaussée St. Pierre

Chaussée

St. Pierre Place St. Pierre

aussée de Wavre

St-Boniface St-Bonifaas (St Boniface Church)

Viaduc

Trone

Gray

Chaussée

Louis

Rue

ETTERBEEK

Rue Champ du Roi

ELLES/ SENE

Maison Communale d'Ixelles

Rue du Sans-Souci

Pl. R. Blyckaerts

Rue du Sceptre

de

Théulx

de Wavre

d'Auderghem

Rue Malibran

Av. de la Couronne

Rue du Vivier

Rue

Rue Ph. Baucq

Ch. d'Ixelles

de la Croix

Rue du Collège

Brussels City Centre

400 m / 0.25 miles

The most attractive route through the Upper City starts at the junction of the Boulevard du Jardin Botanique/Kruid-tuinlaan and the Rue Royale/Koningin-straat. Here, in times gone by, stood the city gate on the road leading from Brussels to Leuven.

Turning from the Boulevard du Jardin Botanique into the Rue Royale in the direction of the city centre, you will pass in front of the glass pavilions of the **Botanical Garden** (Jardin Botanique National de Belgique/Nationale Plantentuin van Belgie).

The park, which contains a fine collection of exotic flora, was completed in 1830. The large iron-framed greenhouse was constructed in 1826. In 1944, when the Botanical Garden outgrew its original site, it was transferred to the park of the Domaine Bouchot, on the northern side of the city. Since 1984 the former glasshouses have been converted and now house a well-stocked library as well as a cinema, several theatres and a number of exhibition halls belonging to the Centre Culturel de la Communauté Française (the French Community Cultural Centre).

One of the capital's oldest hotels is the Pullman Astoria. Built in 1909, it also stands on the Rue Royale. Directly opposite, the small but well-known Confisery Mary, confectioners by appointment to the Belgian royal family, is an ideal place to stock up on sweets and snacks for the trek across the city.

Continuing in the direction of the **Place Royale/Koningsplein**, the visitor should skirt around the right-hand side of the district surrounding the church of Notre-Dame-de-la-Neige (Our Lady of the Snow). Almost all the houses in this area were destroyed and rebuilt with fine contemporary facades during the course of the 19th century.

The Schaerbeek entrance to the Botanical Gardens.

Most of the streets originally converged on open spaces, which later developed into squares; the focal point of such a square is usually a monument to a famous past citizen.

If you glance to the right from the Place Royale you will catch a glimpse of the **Column of Congress** (Colonne du Congrès/Kongreszuil). This was erected between 1850 and 1859 in accordance with plans drawn up by Joseph Poelaert, one of the country's most famous architects. The monument commemorates the founding of the Belgian state in 1830; important dates and the names of the men and women who were instrumental in the Revolution are inscribed in golden letters.

A statue of the first king of Belgium, Leopold I, of the house of Saxe-Coburg-Gotha, occupies pride of place at the top of the column; it was the work of the sculptor Guillaume Geefs. On the pedestal at the monarch's feet sit four female figures representing the fundamental civic rights which until 1830 had

been denied: freedom of education, freedom of worship, freedom of the press and freedom of assembly.

At the base of the column, the ever-lasting flame burns on the grave of an unknown Belgian soldier in remembrance of all those who died during the two world wars. It used to be possible to reach a platform affording a magnificent view of the city by means of a spiral staircase inside the monument. Nowadays the column is a favourite setting for fashion shoots.

To the east, the Place Royale is blocked off by a wall, above which there is a fine view of the Lower City. On the horizon the slim tower of the Town Hall soars skywards above the Grand' Place/Grote Markt. The foreground is dominated by ministry buildings, the National Bank, the Philips Tower and – to the far left – the massive St Michael's Cathedral, which stands on the boundary between the Upper and Lower City.

Also near the square lie the offices and printing works of *Le Soir*, one of the

Trams still run in Brussels.

capital's most popular newspapers.

Standing slightly back from the Rue Royale is the cathedral, which is dedicated to the city's twin patron saints, St Gudula and St Michael. Constructed between the 13th and 15th centuries, the cathedral is basically Gothic in style, although the chapels surrounding the main edifice were added during the 16th and 17th centuries. It boasts some particularly fine 16th and 17th-century stained-glass windows, including fine portraits of Charles V and Isabella of Portugal in the North transept and King Louis II of Hungary and his wife, Marie, Charles V's sister, in the South transept; both were modelled on sketches by the celebrated artist Bernaert von Orley. Also of note are the carved wooden pulpit by H. Verbruggen illustrating the Last Judgment, and a number of paintings from the school of Rubens.

Returning to the Rue Royale, the visitor should turn into the Rue de la Loi/Wetstraat. After a few paces he will find himself in front of the **Parliament Building** (Palais de la Nation/Paleis der Natie). The twin chambers of the representative bodies of the Belgian people, the House of Deputies and the Senate, meet here behind a neoclassical facade. The surrounding buildings house various ministries.

These *palazzi* were originally constructed for the Supreme Council of the Duchy of Brabant; at one stage, the courts of justice also sat here. The entire complex was rebuilt during the 1880s following a fire.

Royal connections: Lying opposite the Lower House is the **City Park** (Parc de Bruxelles/Park van Brussel), a model of geometricity. As long ago as the 14th century it served as the royal hunting grounds; the present formal layout dates from 1776–80.

The central path leads straight to the **Royal Palace** (Palais du Roi/Paleis van de Koning). Although the Royal Family no longer resides here, the building houses the Royal Chancellery and a number of audience rooms and offices.

Waiting in vain; the king no longer lives in the palace in the city.

When the Royal standard flutters from the roof, it is an indication that the King is present.

In earlier times the site of the present palace was occupied by the Ducal castle. The building was destroyed by fire during the cold winter of 1731. There was virtually no water available to extinguish the inferno because everything was frozen. An attempt was made to quench the flames with beer, but it was to no avail and the seat of the Dukes of Brabant was burned to the ground. During the 19th century Leopold II had the castle rebuilt in the style of Louis XVI. Then, at the beginning of the 20th century, it was remodelled and extended once again.

The **Royal Park Theatre** (Théâtre Royal du Parc/Koninklijk Parktheater) can be reached via the Rue de la Loi. Opposite the Royal Palace, but still within the gardens, stands a bust of the legendary Russian Tsar, **Peter the Great**. According to the story he went out for a breath of fresh air in the palace grounds after a sumptuous banquet in the Old Castle, and didn't live to return. The bronze likeness marks the spot where his excesses finally got the better of him.

East of the Palace Square – to the right of the place of royal indisposition – stands the **Palace of the Academies** (Palais des Académies/Academien-paleis). The building was originally planned as the residence of the Prince of Orange; it was completed in 1829 in the style of the Italian Renaissance.

Barely 50 years later, the palazzo became the headquarters of the Academy, which was founded by the Empress Maria-Theresia. Today it houses the Academy of Sciences, the Academy of Literature and Fine Arts and the Academy of Medical Sciences.

Continuing past the Palace for a few minutes, visitors find themselves back in the Rue Royale. Turning to the left, they will reach once more the periphery of the **Place Royale/Koningsplein**, built during the 18th century on the

In the Parc de Bruxelles: three men and a dog.

summit of the Coudenberg hill. Constructed in the style of Louis XVI, it still retains the elegant proportions which characterise many of the sections of the city rebuilt at the end of the 18th century by Charles of Lorraine.

Of particular note are the classical facades of the houses lining the square. Behind a pillared portico with a flat gable recalling the entrance to a Roman temple is hidden the **Royal Chapel of St James on the Coudenberg**, dating from the 18th century. Surveying the scene from the middle of the Place Royale is the statue of **Godfrey of Bouillon**, the famous crusader who with 20,000 soldiers joined the First Crusade in 1096 with the intention of recapturing Jerusalem from the Saracens. He was duly elected ruler of Jerusalem in 1099, but died after a reign of only a year.

Originally standing sentinel here was a statue of Charles of Lorraine, upon whose orders the square was constructed. When metal was in short sup-

ply during the French Revolution, the bronze statue was unceremoniously melted down.

Continuing northwards along the Rue Royale for a short distance, the visitor will soon arrive at the **Palace of Fine Arts** (Palais des Beaux-Arts/Paleis voor Schone Kunsten). Lying between the Rue Royale and the Rue Ravenstein/ Ravensteinstraat, it contains a number of assembly halls for banquets, exhibitions and concerts. The building was completed in 1928 in accordance with plans drawn up by Victor Horta.

Before turning his attention to the Grand Sablon, the visitor should take a look at one of the loveliest churches in the city, the **Church of Our Lady of the Chapel** (Eglise Notre-Dame-de-la-Chapelle/Kapellekerk), which is situated on the corner of the Boulevard de L'Empereur/Keizerslaan.

The architecture demonstrates characteristics of various epochs: it was begun in the 12th century, but the main nave dates from the 15th century and the

Relaxing opposite the Church of Notre-Dame-du-Sablon.

existing tower from the 18th century. Apart from a lovely wooden statue of St Margaret of Antioch dating from 1520 the church contains the tombs of Pieter Brueghel the Elder – whose black marble monument is surmounted by a copy of a Rubens original of Christ handing over the keys of heaven to St Peter – and Anneessens (the Anneessens Tower, a remnant of the old city wall, stands on the Rue de Rollebeek/Rollebeekstraat).

Museums and modern art: From this point the route continues across the Place du Petit Sablon/Kleine Zavel to the **Instrument Museum** (Musée Instrumentale), containing over 5,000 exhibits: Bronze-age musical instruments, simple Indian flutes, a collection of handsome wind instruments and a number of other unique items from various periods.

A few metres further on lies the **Museum of Modern Art** (Musée d'Art Moderne/Museum voor Moderne Kunst), although it cannot actually be seen by passers by since the galleries are stacked up to eight floors underground.

Charles of Lorraine laid the foundations of the collection, which includes French and Belgian paintings and drawings and sculpture of the 19th and 20th centuries. Many of the artists whose works are to be seen here enjoy international fame. among them Stevens, de Baekeleer, Dubois, Khnopff, David, Coubet, Gauguin, Delacroix, Corot, Ensor, Delvaux, Dali and Magritte.

Opposite the museum lies the former **Palace of the Counts of Flanders**, today the office of the Auditor-General. To the right of **St James** stands a bank headquarters; to the left is a section of the Foreign Ministry and the **Congo Library** – economics and theology side by side in perfect harmony, so to speak.

Turning right into the Rue du Musée/Museumstraat, the visitor will soon find himself facing the magnificent square of the **Place du Musée**, dominated by the pleasingly-proportioned facade of the former residence of Charles of Lorraine. A statue of him surveys the palace

Affairs of the heart.

from a pedestal across the square. Forming part of the extensive complex, which includes the museums of ancient and modern art, is the **Royal Library of Albert I**.

Since their complete restoration in 1984, the **Royal Galleries of Art** (Musées Royaux des Beaux-Arts de Belgique/Koninklijke Musea voor Schone Kunsten van Belgie) have been considered to be amongst the most important collections in the world.

Apart from the Museum of Modern Art described above the complex also houses the **Museum of Ancient Art**, which contains works from the 15th, 16th, 17th and 18th centuries. Among the masterpieces displayed are paintings by Brueghel, Rubens, Jordaens, Tintoretto, Tiepolo, Bosch, Hals and Rembrandt.

The **Royal Library of Albert I** (Albertinum) contains the reconstructed studies of Emile Verhaeren and Michael de Ghelderode. The **Museum of Books** (Musée du Livre et Cabinet des Donations) displays valuable printed works and manuscripts, some of them gifts of prominent families. The **Museum of Sound** houses an interesting collection of audiovisual recordings, including almost 6,000 famous voices. Also worth visiting is the **Museum of Printing**, which includes typefaces, lithographic equipment, bookbinding and typesetting apparatus from the 19th and 20th centuries.

On view in the Albertinum are the private apartments of Charles of Lorraine, as well as woodcuttings and etchings in the **Prints Collection** (Chalcographie). The Albertinum was created in its present form during the middle of this century, in memory of King Albert I.

On the **Mont des Arts** near the Museum of Ancient Art and the Albertinum stand the **Palace of Congress** and the **Palace of Dynasty**, both contemporary buildings of the 20th century. The Palace of Dynasty, which lies behind the Royal Palace, contains an exhibition

At the local greengrocer's.

documenting the history of the Belgian Royal Family.

The Mont des Arts is an extensive complex lying between the Place de l'Albertine/Albertinaplein and the Place Royale/Koningsplein. It was constructed during the 1950s in accordance with plans drawn up by a team of architects, Ghobert, Houvoux and Van Steenberghen.

Returning to the Place Royale, the tour continues along the Rue de la Régence/Regentschapstraat. After a short distance the visitor will reach the **Zavelkerk**, also known as the Eglise du Sablon. The church's full name is the Eglise Notre-Dame-des-Victoires (the Church of our Lady of the Victories). It was erected and magnificently decorated by the archers of Brussels during the 15th and 16th centuries. Of particular interest are the chandelier, the murals in the choir and the carved wooden pulpit (1697) as well as the tombs of Count Lamoral and Count Thurn and the Taxis family chapel. The Eglise du Sablon is considered to be one of the finest examples of high Gothic architecture still standing. The main entrance to the church lies on the far side, on the Place du Grand Sablon/Grote Zavel.

The centre of the square is dominated by the **Fountain of Minerva**, a present from the Earl of Aylesbury in recognition of the asylum granted to him by Brussels during his exile from England.

Surrounding the Place du Grand Sablon are antique shops and a number of excellent restaurants. The Sablon District as a whole is dominated by the antique trade.

Returning to the Rue de la Régence, visitors should cross the street to reach the Place du Petit Sablon/Kleine Zavel. The small, well-tended park in the centre is surrounded by attractive wrought-iron railings; it is distinguished by a set of 48 bronze statues, each representing a guild or craftsmen's association. The first bears the features of Henry Beyaert, the master builder whose bust is also to be seen on the Belgian 100-franc note. Dominating the ensemble is a group of statues at the centre of the park; it depicts the two counts Egmont and Horn, the twin heroes of the uprising against the bloodthirsty Duke of Alva during the 16th century. The two noblemen are surrounded by famous humanists such as Dedenée, Mercator and Van Orley.

Forming the background to the square is the **Palais Egmont**, built during the 16th century and remodelled along classical lines during the 18th century. Among its famous residents were Louis XV and Voltaire. Today it is the home of the Foreign Ministry. It was here that Denmark, Great Britain and Ireland signed the Treaty of Accession to the European Community in 1972.

Symbol of power: Continue the tour either by returning to the Rue de la Régence or by taking the Rue aux Laines/Wolstraat, which passes in front of the Palais Egmont. Both streets lead to the magnificent **Palace of Justice** (Palais de Justice), whose enormous

The Porte de Hal, one of the old city gates.

120

bulk dominates the whole district. A large section of the Marolles, the oldest part of Brussels had to be demolished to make way for its construction. The hill on which the palais stands used to be the site where public hangings were carried out in the city.

The architect, Joseph Poelaert, was commissioned to design a monument to the Belgian constitution. In other words, it was intended that the building should be larger than any other sacred or military edifice in the city. In the end, his project developed into a complex of gigantic proportions which symbolised Belgium's rise to industrial and colonial power in the world.

The dome is 104 metres (333 ft) high; the total floor area comprises 25,000 sq. metres (30,000 sq. yards). The palais includes 27 audience chambers and 245 smaller rooms. Then there are numerous offices, and of course the prisoners' cells. The entrance hall alone measures 3,600 sq. metres (4,300 sq. yards). The Palais de Justice was constructed between 1866 and 1883; unfortunately its creator did not live to see its completion, for he died in 1879. Poelaert chose to construct the palais in the eclectic manner; that is to say, he united virtually every architectural style into a synthesis of the arts. Even today, the result is counted among the most powerful buildings in the world.

At the feet of the Palais lies the **Marolles** district, the true heart of the city (described in greater detail in its own chapter). It was in the Marolles that the Brussels dialect evolved – a hotch-potch of Flemish, French and Spanish with a liberal sprinkling of Hebrew and German expressions.

South of the Marolles lie the remains of the city's medieval fortifications, the **Porte de Hale/Hallepoort**. The original masonry is untouched apart from some alterations carried out during the 19th century. The museum of the same name, the **Musée du Porte de Hale**, houses an exhibition depicting Belgian military history until the 18th century.

The Belgians eat their chips either with mayonnaise or mussels.

THE MAROLLES

An observer standing on the terrace on the west side of the Palais de Justice and surveying the town spread out before him may fail to spot the district closely stacked at his feet – the Marolles. To notice it, he must cast his gaze downwards and then look out towards the south. At the end of the 19th century a considerable section of the Marolles had to be demolished to make way for the massive Palais de Justice.

The district developed in the 17th century as a residential area for the craftsmen working on the palatial homes of the Upper City. It remained a thriving working class district until the 1870s when, with the paving over of the Senne, the wealthier artisans moved out to the city's suburbs. From then on the district declined, eventually becoming a refuge for the poor and every new wave of immigrants in the city.

The continued survival of the Marolles and its inhabitants is due purely to their dogged determination to hold on to their district; they have taken up a common and yet highly individual fight against their wretched living conditions and intruders alike. The traditional appearance of the entire district is perpetually threatened by urban redevelopment and property speculation. An even more insidious enemy, however, is the deterioration of the fabric of the buildings, for the inhabitants have no funds available for essential repairs. Many of the historic builings are crumbling; some are literally falling down.

The Marolles seem condemned to economic ruin for the modern metropolis has deprived the small businesses and shops of their livings.

The district has no clearly defined boundaries; it suffices to note that it lies beneath the Palais de Justice, from the Boulevard de Waterloo, the Porte de Hal, the Boulevard du Midi and the Avenue de Stalingrad as far as the Chapelle des Brigittines on the edge of the aristocratic Grand Sablon district. The principal through roads, running side by side from one end of the Marolles to the other, are the Rue Haute and the Rue Blaes.

The district's inhabitants, some 10,000 in all, lead lives largely independent of the outside world. The daily round and the passing of the seasons have retained their original significance here. Traditionally, the Marolles was a district through which one passed rather than a place where one stayed, and a clear boundary exists between life in the Marolles and the rest of the city, despite the periodic incursions of outsiders.

The original inhabitants are gradually dying or moving away and being replaced by a variety of newcomers. Maghrebis and other immigrants from Mediterranean countries make up half the present population. Most share one characteristic with the original residents: poverty.

However, as the members of the various action groups for the preservation of the Marolles are well aware, in recent years property developers have acquired ambitions in the area. The community of immigrants and indigenous Marolles residents has been joined by a high-earning, fashionable crowd, and independent traders and shop owners have jumped on the bandwagon with a succession of boutiques, jewellers, galleries and restaurants. As they penetrate ever deeper into the district they are gradually eroding its true countenance.

And yet, the drab little snack bars are still

found on almost every street and for certain at every crossroads, hawking mussels, watery stews, soggy chips and thin draught beer. Also typical are the large, dilapidated tenement blocks containing council flats. One of the city's largest hospitals, the Saint-Pierre, also lies within the Marolles – as does the former fire brigade barracks at the Place du Jeu de Balle, where a series of shops – mostly art galleries and antiquarian booksellers – have set up next to expensive modern houses.

Early each morning the cafés surrounding the Vieux Marché opposite the Fire Station attract their first customers; as many of these

flats of the prosperous Grand Sablon. Here, the contrasts are too marked for comfort.

In some corners, however, the visitor will notice successful attempts at restoration. The numerous action groups are attempting to breathe fresh life into the district and encourage the residents to renovate their homes. Public funds, however, are only available sporadically, for the authorities prefer to place their trust in property sharks and international building firms. For many years they allocated no money at all for the rebuilding of this socially deprived district, finding it easier and more lucrative to encourage private in-

establishments are open until the small hours, some of them – logically enough – do not bother to close at all. They are typical of cafés of this type to be found all over the world: each has its own individual character and its own type of clientèle.

The outsider may well react with incomprehension or consternation at such evident despair, particularly in the La Samaritaine district lying cheek by jowl with art galleries, antique shops, gourmet restaurants and luxury

Left, hanging out the washing in the Marolles. **Above**, fortunate tenants live in the front courtyard; the poorest have to live in the back.

vestment by collaborating with builders and property dealers. Private investment, however, is not a realistic proposition in the Marolles, for the deprivation of its inhabitants is so severe that they are unable to finance any restoration work themselves.

The only real chance for the survival of the traditional countenance of the Marolles lies in the collective organisation of its residents, in negotiations with a clearly-defined third party, and in the abandoning by the municipal authorities of their paternalistic approach to the problems. It remains to be seen whether the individualists who live here will be able to adapt to a workable planning concept.

THE "OTHER" UPPER CITY: PLACE LOUISE

Of course, it would be inaccurate to maintain that there were two Upper Cities existing side by side in Brussels. On the other hand, the contrast between this upper city and the poor Marolles district or even the grand but more austere Rue Royale is marked.

The complex of streets in question extends on a southwesterly tangent from the Louise underground station to the Luxembourg, thus forming a boundary to the inner city. The city side is demarcated by the **Boulevard Waterloo/Waterloolaan**; opposite lies the **Avenue de la Toison d'Or/Guldenvlieslaan**. Each side of the dual carriageway has its own name. The boulevard and the Avenue Louise/Louizalaan, together with some of the surrounding lanes and passageways, represent the most exclusive district of Brussels, particularly for residential pur-

poses; the main thoroughfares were constructed around the middle of the 19th century to link the city centre with the Bois de la Cambre.

Life in this upper city is top-notch, as visitors soon realise. The whole place exudes a sense of luxury: shops are chic, residences are discreetly expensive, and the clothes and accessories worn by their wealthy inhabitants are by famous fashion designers. The Boulevard and the Avenue are catwalks as much as thoroughfares.

The most exclusive section of this district is centred on the **Place Louise**, where even the underground station is smart. Alighting from the train, visitors are treated to a blast of jazzed-up classical music. Artistic mosaics, stained glass, enamelwork and a tapestry all contribute to the carefully-tailored ambience of the place.

(Such artistic touches aren't confined to the station on Place Louise: in an effort to individualise the underground stations contemporary artists were

A view from the Upper City down to the Lower City.

124

brought in to assist in the planning of a number of the city's stations, including St-Guidon, Aumale, Jacques Brel, Gare de l'Ouest, Osseghem, Etangs Noirs, Comte de Flandre, Rogier, Botanique, Arts Loi, Luxembourg, Porte de Namur, Anneessens, Bourse, Parc, Mérode, Thieffry, Pétillon, Hankar, Herrmann Debroux, Montgomery, Joséphine-Charlotte, Gribaumont, Roodebeek and Vandervelde.)

The impression of exclusivity hits everyone emerging from the Louise underground station. Walking along the Waterloo side of the boulevard towards the **Porte de Namur/Naamsepoort**, visitors pass art galleries and jeweller's shops in between the chic boutiques of international designers: Yves Saint Laurent, Givenchy, Armani and Jil Sander among them.

Shortly before the Boulevard Waterloo becomes the Boulevard du Régent/Regentlaan, it crosses the **Rue du Pépin/Kernstraat**, a street which is fairly dead during the day but buzzing at night when its string of nightclubs – the best in Brussels – open their doors.

Beyond the Porte de Namur the district becomes somewhat more drab. The area is dominated by some of the large administrative headquarters, banks and insurance companies which have helped earn Brussels the nickname "The Office desk of Europe". Here, your best course of action is to turn round, cross the street, and stroll back along its other side, where the scene quickly becomes more attractive.

On this side the boulevard is known as the **Avenue de la Toison d'Or**. It is flanked by a number of extensive multi-storey shopping arcades. Some of them are surmounted by steel-framed glass domes and date from the 19th century. Originally such shopping malls – if such elegant arcades can be described by the same name as their modern counterparts – reflected the new confidence of the increasingly powerful bourgeoisie of 19th-century Brussels. They were an exciting new concept in retail trade.

One such arcade, bearing the name of the boulevard itself – **Galeries de la Toison d'Or** – lies just a few steps away. The shopping gallery also links the avenue with the Chaussée d'Ixelles/Elsense Steenweg. Beyond this, one reaches another arcade of shops, the **Galerie d'Ixelles**. Leaving this at the Chaussée de Wavre/Waverse Steenweg, the visitor will soon arrive at yet another shopping paradise, the **Galerie de la Porte de Namur**.

The range of goods on offer in these arcades is virtually unsurpassable: perfumeries, luxury boutiques and department stores are interspersed with restaurants and cafés, as well as chocolate and confectionery shops – expensive but worth it – and a variety of other small boutiques selling items from every corner of the earth.

Continuing along the Avenue de la Toison d'Or towards the Place Louise, you will come across a short flight of steps leading up to the **Church of the Carmelites**. The building contains no

Posh lantern on a posh facade in the posh Upper city.

ancient art to admire, but it is the setting for regular concerts of classical and church music played on a famous organ. The performances are frequently broadcast on Belgian radio or included in recordings.

Not far away is another gallery bearing the name of the square near which it stands: the **Galerie Louise** – a modern version of the celebrated Galeries St-Hubert. By walking through its complex network of corridors from one side to the other, you will soon reach the Avenue Louise, a lively street offering yet another profusion of shops selling luxury items.

If you choose to leave the arcade at the Place Stéphanie/Stefanieplein, you will have to retrace your steps for a short distance if you want to explore the **Rue Jourdan/Jourdanstraat**. The latter is characterised by a rapid succession of popular bars and restaurants, some of which remain open until the small hours of the morning. Be sure to stroll through the **Garden Stores Louise**, where el-egant shops are grouped round a pretty courtyard.

The Avenue Louise opens out into the **Bois de Cambre**. For many years the broad avenue leading away from the Place Stéphanie had a long strip of grass and trees in the middle; until 1957 its use was reserved exclusively for horse riding. Today, however, tram lines occupy the open space. The streets to the right and left of the Avenue Louise comprise what is considered to be the most expensive residential area in Brussels today.

Great escapes: One does not have to be an energetic walker to enjoy a short detour to the Cistercian **Abbaye de la Cambre/Ter-Kamerenabdij**. It isn't far and it is well worth exploring. To find it, go down the flight of steps behind Rue du Lac and through a little park as far as the Lakes of Ixelles/Elsene. According to one survey conducted in the city, this area is considered to be the very best address by Brussels' "top 10,000 residents".

Authentic originals in the Upper City.

Follow the signposts and you will soon reach the abbey, which lies in the middle of a park. The setting is idyllic: fish ponds shimmer amidst immaculately tended lawns. The garden terraces, which are laid out on five different levels, attract large numbers of visitors, both locals and out-of-towners, at weekends. The abbey itself, which was founded in the 12th century, has endured numerous tribulations during its long history. Today it houses a military academy and Brussels' College of Decorative Arts.

The Avenue Louise leads directly into the **Bois de Cambre/Ter-Kamerenbos**, the Forest of Brussels. The latter is best reached by tram or bus. With its elegant stands of birch trees, boating lakes, roller-skating rinks, restaurants and cafés it is a favourite leisure destination of local residents.

Keener walkers might like to try another popular escape lying to the east of the city: the **Forest of Soignes**, which extends into **Tervuren Park**. Formerly the preserve of charcoal burners and a favourite hunting ground of Emperor Charles V, today the woodland extends over 4,380 hectares (17 sq. miles) of hilly countryside and offers plenty of opportunities for water and land sports. Nestling in one of its valleys are the ruins of the ancient **Abbey of Groenendael**.

Also of interest hereabouts is the **Royal Museum of Central Africa (Musée Royal de l'Afrique du Centre/Museum voor Midden-Afrika**, with displays portraying Belgium's colonial past. It includes an exhibition which attempts the difficult task of explaining the historical development of Africa (*see also page 211 of the chapter "Around Brussels"*).

Situated on the edge of the Forest of Soignes is the fairy-tale **Rixenart Castle**, dating from the 17th century. Built of red brick in the style of the Renaissance, it houses a valuable collection of historic furniture, Gobelin tapestries and wall hangings from Beauvais.

The wealthy reside in houses such as these.

THE MARKETS

If you can't find a particular item on the market stalls of Brussels, it probably doesn't exist at all, for you can buy virtually anything here. Brussels' markets are some of the best places to find authentic local colour; and every day of the week is market day somewhere in the city.

One of the most interesting of the city's various markets is the **Antiques Market** which takes place every weekend (Saturday 9 a.m.–3 p.m.; Sunday 9 a.m.–1 p.m.) on the Place du Grand Sablon; you may even be lucky enough to find a bargain here, though you will probably have to search for it amongst a good deal of junk. In the Antiques Market, as elsewhere, the line between art and kitsch is a thin one.

Visitors should be wary of paying the asking price without question. Bartering with the stall holders is expected and considered to be part of the fun. Your best tactic if something catches your eye is to take a stroll around the square whilst you consider your purchasing strategy and the maximum amount you want to pay. Whatever the price you finally agree to, you can be quite sure that it will be less than you would pay in any one of the numerous antique shops found in the area.

Not many tourists come to Brussels to buy a horse. Nonetheless, a stroll to the **Horse Fair** on Place de la Duchesse de Brabant/Hertogin van Brabantplaats on Friday morning is entertaining even for those with little knowledge of horses or riding. (It takes place from 5 a.m.–noon). The powerful quadrupeds named after Brabant Province, also known as Pajottenland, are still used as draught horses on many farms in Belgium, so the fair still performs an important function. But it isn't just carthorses that change hands here; racehorses are also offered for sale.

One of the most interesting aspects of the market is the bargaining process. Even local residents may fail to understand a single word. Any visitor to Brussels who doesn't mind a horsey atmosphere should make a point of exploring the horse fair.

Any self-respecting town has a weekly market, but in terms of kaleidoscopic colour and multi-faceted variety few can compare with the market at the Gare du Midi (Southern Station). It resembles nothing as much as a superb supermarket in the open air; known as the **Exotic Market**, it takes place every Sunday morning.

The range of goods on offer is overwhelming. One can purchase clothes for every season of the year. Food of every kind is on sale here too, from fish to gâteaux. In between are mounds of exotic fruits, almonds and nuts, piles of pots and pans, pictures, jewellery, leather goods and books. The noise can be deafening: record and cassette traders turn the volume controls on their speakers to maximum while greengrocers and

Left, a gentleman of Brussels. Right, bargains galore at the flea market held on the Place du Grand Sablon.

ironmongers attempt to draw attention to his wares. Polyglot cries in Flemish, French and Dutch add to the babel of voices. As Jean Cocteau once maintained, "the city of Brussels is one big stage". The market is no exception.

Be sure also to explore the immediate vicinity of the market. The ever-expanding network of stalls has spilled beyond the spacious square itself and now extends into the surrounding side streets, where some of the best buys are to be found.

Some of the city's markets are more tranquil. One of these, the daily **Flower Market**, is held every day apart from Mondays and during the winter months on the Grand' Place/Grote Markt. The stallholders sit patiently as they wait for interested customers. Their buckets, pots and vases are always full of magnificent blooms. The function of the large umbrellas, in the traditional local colours of red and green, is not merely to provide protection from sun and rain. When they are tipped sideways at a right-angle

to the pavement it is a sign by the stallholders that business is bad on the Grand' Place.

On a few days each year the blooms and blossoms are not for sale at all, but form part of a magnificent display. On these occasions the city's gardeners and florists spread a gorgeous carpet of flowers right across the square. The best view of the spectacle is from a window of one of the surrounding houses.

Outside this special time, the flower market on the Grand' Place is open daily from 8 a.m. until 6 p.m.

Another relatively peaceful market is the **Bird Market**, where only the twittering of the birds disturbs the peace. Every Sunday from 7 a.m. to 2 p.m., breeders arrange their cages in front of the Grand' Place. The contents of these cages range from brightly-coloured songbirds to rather less conspicuous game.

Not that there isn't plenty of unhuman noise around. High-pitched twitterings are accompanied by the sonorous quack- **Two of a kind.**

ing of ducks, interspersed by the clucking of hens and the cooing of doves. In addition to the stall selling birds, you will find stalls selling all kind of bird paraphernalia: seed, nuts, medicines, toys, gadgets and cages of every variety and size.

Not every visitor to the bird market comes with the intention of purchasing. Many of the enthusiasts merely want to chat with the breeders or to discuss the merits of the latest bird seed for their pet canary or budgie. It is a place where experiences are exchanged and hobbies are nurtured.

Sunday best: Lovers of flea markets will want to visit the **Vieux Marché** on the Place du Jeu de Balle/Vossenplein. Here, in the very heart of the old Marolles district, stalls of some 20 traders or more can be found on any day of the week. The best day to visit, however, is on Sunday (7 a.m.–2 p.m., when the number often rises to 200).

Another Sunday market is to be found in the Rue Ropsy Chaudron/Ropsy-Chaudronstraat), where between 8 a.m. and 1 p.m. new and used cars are offered for sale. Car dealers can also be found in the Rue du Paruk/Paruckstraat; those operating here, however, are generally considered to offer fewer bargains.

Another favourite Sunday morning stroll takes the visitor to the Place de la Reine Astrid/Koningin Astridplein, where there is a market for records, paintings, secondhand-books, toys and jewellery. In recent years a number of food stalls have also started to appear on this site.

In addition to these regular markets, it is common to see clusters of stalls occupying the various squares dotted across the city. Some of these, however, vanish as quickly as they spring up, or disband without warning for weeks or even months at a time. When winter frosts set in, the number of people willing to man an open-air stall declines. Fair-weather traders don't bother to emerge again until Brussels is enjoying the first warm days of spring.

A paradise for browsers.

SHOPPING AND NIGHTLIFE

After a sightseeing tour of some of the principal buildings and sites of Brussels, a stroll through the city's shops makes an invigorating change. A leisurely shopping trip will grant the visitor a further insight into the way of life and culture of the capital's inhabitants, whether he decides to purchase typical souvenirs – Brussels lace or hand-made chocolates, for instance – or prefers to scour the city's antique shops in the hope of finding a more unusual gift or even a bargain to take home.

The metropolitan area includes a wide range of shopping districts. The heart of the city forms one vast shopping centre. Visitors can spend many happy hours perusing their wonderful shop window displays and even more spending money. Many shops offer arrangements for tax-free purchases provided that the goods supplied are for export only.

Where to shop: The main department stores are on a par with equivalent establishments in other European metropolises. The entire length of **Rue Neuve/Niewstraat** has been turned into a pedestrian zone, and contains a colourful array of elegant boutiques and speciality shops attracting customers from every corner of the globe.

Brussels proudly claims to possess more shopping arcades – in other words, covered shopping complexes – than any other city in Europe. Among the best-loved are the long-established **Galeries Saint-Hubert**, whose elegant classical facade is decorated by columns and a central Renaissance-style motif proclaiming *Omnibus omnia* – "everything for everyone" – as well as ultra-modern shopping centres such as **City 2** in the Rue Neuve.

Apart from housing a large number of small units, the lower level of City 2 has plenty of good cafés and bars where you can revive before resuming your expedition. A variety of fast food establishments span the gamut of international tastes: from Spanish tapas, Mexican tacos and Italian pasta to Chinese stir-fry dishes and hamburgers with typical Belgian chips.

The shopping centre's designers placed great emphasis on the visual appearance of the shopping complex; the architects strove to create a pleasant atmosphere in which shopping would be a pleasure rather than a chore. Surrounded by palm trees and fountains, a glass lift provides an attractive link between floors.

Even nobler in appearance are the Royal Arcades, which form part of the Galeries Saint-Hubert: the **Galerie du Roi**, the **Galerie de la Reine** and the **Galerie des Princes**. The elegant glass roofs are supported by a steel-framed vault; the shopping galleries, dating from 1847, house mainly luxury boutiques. Here you will find everything the well-heeled Brussels bureaucrat might need, from jewellery to Brussels lace, but don't expect it to be cheap.

A basement near the Grand' Place sells old engravings, maps and pictures.

No visitor should leave Brussels without sampling some of the capital's particular specialities. It is maintained that when it comes to making chocolates the Belgians are in a class of their own. And most travellers will be interested in the capital's world-famous lace, crystal and pewter ware.

Many little cafés are to be found lining the avenues of the inner city in the vicinity of the opera house and the Stock Exchange. In accordance with the French linguistic tradition, most so-called cafés here are actually more like pubs. Although coffee and cakes are not the main refreshments purveyed in them, they are not difficult to find if that's what you want. The city possesses excellent *pâtisseries*, and virtually every street corner has a stall selling the eternally popular waffles.

The Grand' Place/Grote Markt is where art lovers tend to head first; but music lovers, too, will find plenty to interest them here. In the **Rue du Midi/Zuidstraat** there are numerous music shops. Apart from new instruments, many hand-made, musicians can purchase excellent second-hand items or have a damaged instrument repaired. Philatelists will discover that this same street also contains a variety of specialist shops for stamp collecting.

The **Boulevard Anspach/Anspachlaan** in the neighbourhood of the Stock Exchange is a lively thoroughfare. Lining the section as far as the Place de Brouckère/De Brouckereplein is a succession of fashion boutiques, newsagents, chocolate shops and electrical stores.

The new galleries near the Grand' Place invite the visitor to browse at leisure. Even the tourist whose wallet is not particularly fat will find items to his taste and pocket here: jeans, leather goods, fashion items and jewellery, souvenirs and records. It is tempting to soak up the atmosphere of the galleries in the many little cafés, a number of which are fronted by a terrace. Particularly worth visiting are the **Galerie Agora,** the

Time for a snack.

Galerie du Centre and the **Galerie Saint-Honoré.**

The famous Grand' Place is always full of tourists, and as a consequence the neighbouring side streets are riddled with souvenir shops. If you want to purchase some genuine Brussels lace you are advised to avoid the shops here and make a short detour to the **Rue du Marché aux Herbes/Grasmarkt** which has a number of boutiques specialising in the craft.

Top shops: The district housing the most attractive luxury boutiques and jeweller's shops lies in the Upper Town. Here, along the **Boulevard Waterloo/Waterloolaan** and in the **Avenue Louise/Louizalaan** between the **Place Louise/Louizaplein** and the **Porte de Namur** you will find branches of every well-known French designer. A number of talented Belgian couturiers have established a reputation beyond their own national boundaries. The description "Made in Belgium" stands for quality and careful workmanship.

The shopping arcades in the Upper Town are also amongst the most elegant and expensive in the entire city. They include the **Galerie Espace Louise**, the **Galerie Louise** and the **Galeries de la Toison**.

Antique lovers should head for the district surrounding the **Place du Grand Sablon**. An antique market is held here on Saturdays and Sundays. It's a lively and picturesque affair, the stalls set against the backdrop of the square's attractive historic facades. It's worth having a good rummage through the goods on sale. Rare stamps, weapons and crystalware are amongst the many items which can be found.

Unlike in some countries, in Belgium the word "antique" is not synonymous with "old junk". A distinction is made between antique dealers, interior decorators and secondhand furniture dealers. Antique dealers belong to a special organisation, the *Chambre des Antiquaires*. By virtue of his membership in the association, an antique dealer guar-

Chips with everything.

antees the authenticity of the items he sells. It is customary for such a dealer to place a large sign bearing the message "Chambre des Antiquaires" in his shop window.

The so-called "interior decorators" do not deal exclusively in antiques. They see themselves as merchants of period furniture, offering for purchase examples of every imaginable period. The secondhand furniture salesmen are really flea market traders. They attempt to sell anything and everything which looks as if it is old and well-used. Their shops and stalls can be found above all on the Marché aux Puces, the flea market in the Marolles district.

Also worth a look on the Place du Grand Sablon is the **Sablon Shopping Garden**; it's the longest art gallery in Belgium.

Since business hours for shops are not controlled by law, the visitor will come across many shops open late into the evening. On Fridays all shops and supermarkets are open until 8 or 9 p.m.; on the remaining weekdays they are open until 6 or 7 p.m.. In addition, most bakers, butchers and small retailers open their shops on Sunday mornings.

Brussels is the ideal place for those who enjoy strolling through markets. In spite of the large number of chic boutique-type shops the citizens of Brussels love finding a bargain and you will come across clusters of stalls at almost every turn. The preceding chapter of this book deals with this aspect of the city's everyday life.

Time to boogie: In the city's nightlife, too, a clear distinction is drawn between the Upper and the Lower City. The differences are most obvious in the style and prices found in the various bars and discotheques. Whereas in the Lower City casual dress is the order of the day, a tie and jacket are essential prerequisites for an evening's entertainment in the Upper City. You will also find establishments in the Upper Town are a lot more expensive.

Brussels offers its visitors every im-

Done out with *kitsch*: the fashionable Café Roberta.

aginable possibility for night time entertainment: bars with dancing, bistros, music clubs in which live jazz and rock are played, and a variety of taverns and night clubs.

Members only: A typical phenomenon on the Brussels night scene is the city's many private clubs. The preponderance of these establishments came about as a result of a law restricting the sale of alcohol. Passed during the aftermath of World War I, it prohibited the sale of high-proof alcoholic drinks in public places whilst continuing to permit their consumption in private premises. A solution to the problem was found in the transformation of the numerous bars into private clubs accessible only to members. In order to obtain an "invitation" from the landlord it was necessary to buy membership on an annual basis; the fee charged in most cases, however, remained low.

Getting in to some of these clubs and discotheques can be difficult if you are not a member. Many only grant new-

comers entry when they are accompanied by a sponsor who is already a member. In some, however, it is possible to obtain membership for just one evening. Membership books are usually kept near the entrance door.

There is a variety of possibilities for an evening tour of the city's pubs and clubs; but since a venue can lose its popularity as quickly as it was gained – in other words, almost overnight – only those generally regarded as classic establishments and a handful of particularly charming rendezvous are listed in the recommendations below.

Many of Brussels' nightclubs/discotheques have been designed around a theme or boast an attention-grabbing feature to distinguish it from run of the mill establishments. **La Papaye,** in the Rue des Bouchers/Beenhouwersstraat, for example, offers its customers a jungle atmosphere: a Tarzan swings from the ceiling and a rhinoceros looms over the bar.

It is not only the dance floor which is exclusive at the **Happy Few** on the Avenue Louise/Louizalaan, but it is certainly as much of a talking-point as the club's glitzy clientele – transparent and made of glass, it forms part of an enormous aquarium.

Those whose taste for the aquatic is more extreme can submit themselves to the wide-eyed gaze of live crocodiles behind a glass partition at the **Crocodile Club** of the Royal Windsor Hotel in the Rue Duquesnoy/Duquesnoystraat. Further along the same street is the establishment known simply as **Le Garage**.

The **Cercueil** in the Rue des Haring/ Haringstraat caters for customers with a liking for the macabre: its tables are made from coffins and the drinks are served in skulls. More traditional is the perennially popular discotheque **Le Mirano** in the Chaussée de Louvain/ Leuvensesteenweg.

Amongst the city's best jazz clubs are the **Brussels Jazz Club** on the Grand' Place, the **Bierodrome** on the Place Fernand Cocq/Fernand Cocqplein, and

There are restaurants to suit everybody's taste in the Ilôt Sacré.

the **Chez Lagaffe** in the Rue de l'Epée/ Zwaardstraat.

Those who decide to start their evening pub tour early may well find themselves facing locked doors. As in most major cities in Europe, the majority of Brussels' clubs and discotheques do not open until 10 p.m..In the meantime, a stroll to the Place de Brouckère will help to pass the time. The square is one of the centres of the city's nightlife and a good place to meet up with friends and enjoy a beer; after dark it is brightly lit by the glaring neon signs around the periphery.

A word of warning for all nightclubbers: since in Belgium there are no rules governing the purity of beer, the brews on offer in Brussels' cafés, bars and pubs vary considerably.

Food first: Brussels is a bastion of gastronomy, as shown in the chapter "Brussels à la Carte". Some of the best restaurants are in the neighbourhood of the **Grand' Place** and the **Old Fishmarket** between the Quai Bois à Brûler/ Brandhoutkaai and the Quai aux Briques/Backsteenkaai. In general, the quality of the specialities on offer in the city's 1,800-plus restaurants is of an excellent standard. Belgian cuisine includes meat, fish and poultry dishes; typical examples are Brabant-style pheasant (with braised chicory) and beef stewed in Gueuze beer.

For wide-awake revellers, there are some 50 restaurants offering a wide range of specialities late at night. They include **Le Houchier** on the Place du Grand Sablon serving Slavic specialities to the sound of gipsy music, and, for those looking for a restaurant that can claim to be typically Belgian, the **Poechenelle** in Rue de la Samaritaine/ Samaritanessestraat.

And if you don't want a full meal when you emerge from a nightclub, head for a *frittüren* – a snack bar serving the ubiquitous chips with everything, especially mussels; every district has one and many of them stay open round the clock.

On tonight: the Big Kaai Bigband.

Anyone searching for famous sons and daughters of Brussels would do well to begin with a survey of the city's street names. Every other plaque and signpost that you come across on your tour of the town comemmorates a local celebrity of the past.

A leisurely stroll through the city centre may well start from the Place de Brouckère. This square recalls **Charles de Brouckère**, one of the fathers of the Belgian constitution of 1831. He later became the Minister of the Interior and the Minister of Defence; in addition, he was one of the founders of the Free University of Brussels and the Bank of Belgium. The list of De Brouckère's occupations is a long and varied one; at different points in his life it included university professor, a member of parliament, a city councillor and a magistrate. The reverential citizens of Brussels referred to him affectionately as the "Great Mayor".

Broad avenues fan out in all directions from the Place de Brouckère. The most famous thoroughfare in the entire city, the Boulevard Anspach, is named after **Jules Anspach**, who ruled Brussels in his capacity as mayor at the end of the last century. The city was in severe financial difficulties at the time; nonetheless Anspach was able to win the support of King Leopold I, a monarch known for his gargantuan building projects and ambitious plans for urban renovation.

Other names encountered here include those of Emile Jacqmain, Adolphe Max and Lemonnier. **Emile Jacqmain** was a member of the city education committee before World War I. Together with **Adolphe Max**, the mayor at the time, and the juror **Lemonnier**, he was arrested and deported by the Germans during the war. After their release in 1917 the three largest and finest avenues in the city were named after them.

The decision by the city council of the time was virtually unanimous; Adolphe Max himself was the only councillor who abstained from the vote.

After the 1830 Revolution and the foundation of the Belgian State, the Stock Exchange underwent a period of rapid expansion. The **Bishoffsheim** family, wealthy bankers from Mainz, settled in the capital of the newly-created state and founded a private bank there. The youngest son of the family, Jonathan, was a juror, senator and director of the National Bank; he played a decisive role in the public life of the city. In addition to his many other good works, he founded several schools, including one for girls – quite a rarity at the time. The people of Brussels subsequently honoured their benefactor by naming a street after him.

Jean Brouchoven, Count of Bergeyck, is one of the city's less well known sons. Yet he played a not insignificant role in the everyday lives of the capital's inhabitants. At the end of the 17th century he was senior treasurer in the service of the governor Maximilian of Bavaria. He had the remarkable idea of introducing progressive taxation rates. In those days craftsmen and traders were liable to pay a fixed sum each year, regardless of whether a tradesman sold a single item or 100.

The idea that taxation should be linked to turnover was a radical innovation in those days. Naturally, the young count's suggestion that tradespeople should be taxed according to this new principle was greeted with great enthusiasm by the governor. He was in severe financial difficulties at the time and could do with the extra cash it would raise.

Perhaps his enthusiasm wasn't shared by everyone in the country. The state took three centuries to decide to name one of the capital's street after the man who had boosted the public purse so ingeniously.

A question of identity: An account of the naming of the Rue Plétinckx is particularly interesting. According to one

Preceding pages: a pretty Brussels face. Below, another masterpiece.

explanation, the street was named after the worthy **M. Plétinckx** who, just before the turn of the century, worked as the director of the "Amigo" – not the luxury hotel that bears that name today, but the drying-out cells in the Town Hall prison nearby, known mockingly among 19th-century Brussels citizens as the "Hotel Plétinckx".

Jean d'Osta, a Brussels folk historian, who supplied much valuable information on local personalities for this chapter and who knows Brussels as if it were his own backyard, hopes that a memorial may one day be raised in memory of M. Plétinckx (he was awarded the freedom of the city in his lifetime). He denies, however, the veracity of this colourful explanation of the Rue Plétinckx's name and maintains that the street is named after a general who in 1830 crushed a popular revolt in the Lower City.

The first mayor of Brussels after the 1830 revolution was **Nicolas Rouppe**. The biography of this archetypal opportunist is truly remarkable. In 1786 he was a Doctor of Theology, he became a Jacobin during the French Revolution and in 1799 he was a *Commissaire du Directoire*. In 1830 he became mayor of Brussels for the first time. Even after the Revolution he was re-elected to this exalted position. In those days he was what is now known as a *Wendelin*, a "wryneck" or turncoat.

The overwhelming achievement of **Charles Buls** during his 20-year period as mayor of the city was to restore the city's market square, Grand' Place, to its former glory and magnificence. A side street in the vicinity bears the name of this famous son of the city, who died in 1899.

In the same street, on the right-hand side of the Town Hall, stands a statue of another famous inhabitant, **Evrard t'Serclases**. He freed the city from the tyranny of the Counts of Flanders in 1356. A local superstition claims that anyone who touches the statue's bronze hand will receive good luck for a year.

A portrait of the artist as an old man.

The tradition is a relatively new one. At one time the market traders had a monopoly on this source of good fortune, but during the past 50 years travel guides have notified a wider public about the statue's powers.

Nowadays hardly anyone would ever mention the names of the brothers **François** and **Jérôme Duquesnoy** were it not for the fact that the city owes one of them – which one is uncertain – the statue of the city's most famous "child" of all, **Manneken Pis**. Not far from the street named after the Duquesnoys lies the Rue de l'Etuve; it is here that the "Menneke", as he is known by local residents, has stood since 1469. (*Manneken* is the Dutch translation, and is therefore by no means popular with every resident.)

The full history of the capital's most famous son would occupy an entire book in itself. Menneke Pis has survived many trials and tribulations over the years: wars, kidnappings, wilful damage and all manner of official ceremonies. The little statue possesses over 300 outfits of clothing and folkloric costumes from all five continents; he has been mentioned in poems and songs. His story and significance have been dissected by researchers and scientists, including sociologists and even sexologists. Traders in the vicinity of the statue are particularly fond of the Manneken – they make a fortune out of him.

For the people of Brussels the little statue is a symbol of their determination to resist repression and their love of freedom. He is considered to embody all kinds of virtues, though not even his most ardent fans would claim he is in any way aristocratic. The citizens of Brussels see the little fellow ("*ketje*"), this son of the people, as cheeky, shameless, bold, fearless, cunning, inventive, mocking, rebellious and unbending. Above all, he has no compunction in showing his scorn for all oppressors, tyrants and despots.

The names of some less well-known but real Brussels heroes can be found in

Giant dolls in the August Maypole procession.

the names of the 19th-century houses in the Marolles: Bals, Bruxe, Bullinckx, Canivet, Defuisseau, Gerard, Jacobs, Peters, Puttemans, Ronsmans, Van Capenberg etc. They were known in the district by names such as Dikke Louis, Madame Fanny, Fintje and Léon. **Brueghel** lived here for a period, too, at 130, Rue Haute. Only one side street in the Marolles was named after the celebrated Brussels artist.

A far less famous painter was a somewhat droll Brussels personality: **Joseph Stevens** who specialised in painting dogs. His memory is also preserved by a street name.

A more controversial figure was the local architect **Joseph Poelaert**, whose most monumental work, the Palais de Justice, is impossible to overlook. Many local citizens are wont to describe the 19th-century builder as a megalomaniac. The Palais de Justice was certainly a mammoth project.

Poleart made himself particularly unpopular with the population of the Marolles because he built his "Palace of Justice" on the city's Execution Hill, which rises directly above the Marolles. The people of the district, who even today see themselves as the "original inhabitants" of the city, considered Poelaert a tyrant who wanted to drive them out of their homes. To this day, the word "Architek" is often used as a term of disparagement.

Illusions of grandeur: Madame **Albertine Fronsac**, who was better known to her many friends and admirers as "Titine", acquired a certain degree of fame in Brussels during the 1920s. She was a singer/actress who performed topical songs during the revues at the Alhambra, a venerably pompous theatre whose passing is still regretted by many local citizens. In 1959 she remained unshakeable in her conviction that the Place Albertine had been named after her. It had not, but the people in the cafés and brasseries around the "Monnaie" were quite happy to leave the ageing *chanteuse* to her illusions.

Another street at the heart of the city is named after **Auguste Orts**, a descendant of a famous old legal family in Brussels, who made his mark as university professor, member of parliament and juror.

Here the visitor will find traces of the most important theatre of the turn of the century, the "Olympia". It was the stage of the premiere of the most famous play in the Brussels folk repertory, *Le Mariage de Mademoiselle Beulemans* ("The Marriage of Miss Beulemans"). The work was translated into 10 languages and was performed by companies all over the world. The heroine's father, Mr Beulemans, is one of the most popular of Brussels folk heroes.

Those wanting to see living, breathing Brussels characters can meet **Paul van Kueken** in person in the Rue du Houblon. He is one of the multi-talented people characteristic of Old Brussels. He is a goldsmith, painter, humorist and chairman – or at least member – of various folk associations, including the

Organisation of Restaurateurs and Traders of the *Vismet* (Fishmarket). Nowadays, originals of the calibre of Van Kueken are a rarity.

The modern capital of today isn't very fertile ground for originality. Life moves too fast and, by and large, the citizens are too conservative, always keen to conform. For this reason, real individuals are seldom found outside the older districts.

Toone, the puppeteer who runs the marionette theatre cum restaurant Toon VII, and **Pol**, the landlord of the jazz club *Le Bierodrome*, are quite definitely members of a dying species. They are firm supporters of Brussels' traditions and festivals, such as that of the *Riesen*, the giant-sized, massive folkloric dolls, with names such as Antje, Mieke, Jefke and Rooske, which every year on 10 August are carried in procession through the streets of the old town to the site of a giant maypole.

Saintly rivals: The patron saint of all citizens of Brussels, great and small, is St Michael. But although it is his statue on the Town Hall that spreads protective wings over the city, his guardianship is not uncontested. St Gudula also has some claim to the title; the capital's principal church, for instance, was always referred to by local residents as St Gudula's, even though it was actually dedicated to St Gudula and St Michael.

But the virginal Gudula, alas, did not have the support of the church authorities: on investigation, Cardinal Suenens discovered that the Vatican held no record of the canonisation of Gudula and peremptorily decided to dedicate the cathedral to St Michael alone. However, he had not reckoned on the local citizens' loyalty to their St Gudula. They felt no real affection for the warrior archangel Michael, always portrayed dressed in armour and brandishing his sword. They loved instead the gentle Lady Gudula, a native of Brabant who remained chaste her whole life long. Thus the cathedral remains what it always was: "St Gudula's".

Left, mussels cooked with garlic and white wine, and eaten with chips, is a typical Brussels favourite. **Right**, roasted chestnuts are also popular.

BRUSSELS A LA CARTE

There is hardly another metropolis on the continent which can boast a denser concentration of top restaurants than Brussels. Its only rival is Paris; and some connoisseurs would dispute even this. Gastronomic critics rate the restaurants in Brussels very highly; their standards of food and service are considered exceptional. Discriminating restaurant-goers can expect to have all their demands met here.

Some gourmets maintain that the best chefs in France originally came from Belgium. It is certainly true that the country's cuisine, and in particular that of the capital itself, has a decidedly French accent.

International specialist gastronomic publications provide the latest reviews of the Belgian capital's restaurant scene. In addition, a team of experienced restaurant critics produces an annual guide entitled *Restaurants Gourmet*, obtainable from the local tourist office (TIB) in the Town Hall on the Grand' Place/Grote Markt. It provides an excellent and up-to-date introduction to the best eating establishments in Brussels. The critics employ a fleur-de-lis rating system to guide readers in their choice. A maximum of five fleurs-de-lis may be awarded to what they consider to be the most distinguished restaurants in Brussels.

In this city where culinary excellence is taken for granted it seems almost invidious to single out individual establishments for praise. The top restaurants in Brussels are world famous; and many of the gourmet places listed here are representative of other less famous establishments (*for further recommendations see also the index of restaurants in Travel Tips*).

Almost next door to each other in the vicinity of Koekelberg Basilika (Brussels, 1080) are a pair of celebrated restaurants bearing the names of their owner-chefs. **Bruneau**, owned by Jean-Pierre and Claire Bruneau (73–75 Avenue Broustin) is one of only three restaurants in the Brussels area to have been awarded the ultimate accolade – the coveted three Michelin stars. **Dupont**, run by Claude Dupont and his wife (46 Avenue Vital-Riethuisen), has two. The specialities on offer in both these restaurants vary according to season and reflect the chefs' daily visits to the local market: fresh game, fine poultry, vegetables and salads and herbs. Since neither restaurant is very large, would-be diners are advised to reserve a table well in advance.

Dine in style: If you want divine style as well as superb cuisine head for **Comme Chez Soi** (23 Place Rouppe). Here Pierre Wynants, its owner-chef serves three-star nouvelle cuisine specialities in an exquisite dining room with a belle-epoque atmosphere recalling the decorative style of Victor Horta, the famous Brussels architect of the 1920s and '30s.

Alternatively you might like to try **La Maison du Cygne** on the Grand' Place/ Grote Markt 9l lying at the very heart of the city. The entrance is discreetly tucked away in the Rue Charles Buls. It is a charming and elegant establishment and the perfect venue for a celebration dinner. To really make your meal an occasion, be sure to take an apéritif in the **Club Ommegang** beforehand. One impressed restaurant critic commented thus on his most recent visit to the restaurant: "To sum up, we should rejoice that establishments like this one still exist here in Europe – not casual meeting places for the jet set but the focal points of a well-established tradition of *les plaisirs de la table*."

At **L'Ecailler du Palais Royal** (18, Rue Bodenbroeck), René Falk and Attilio Basso are renowned for their exquisite seafood delicacies: nowhere is the fish fresher or more skilfully prepared than here.

Near the Bois de la Cambre stands the **Villa Lorraine** (75 Avenue du Vivier

Preceding pages: if you fancy some Belgian lobster, then head for La Table d'Or restaurant. **Left**, peace and quiet can be found in Café Falstaff.

d'Or), for many years a favourite gourmet rendezvous. The setting is immaculate. Among Freddy van de Casserie's specialities are the incomparable "Ecrivisses Villa Lorraine" – freshwater crayfish served with a sumptuous sauce of white wine and cream.

Pierre Romeyer serves particularly light, meticulously prepared dishes at his restaurant **Romeyer** (109 Chaussée de Groenendaal in Hoeilláart, 11 km/7 miles from Brussels). He has been awarded three Michelin stars – the highest mark of excellence – for his culinary achievements.

But it isn't just the food which makes a visit to his restaurant so memorable. There can be few more idyllic spots on a summer evening than the terrace in front of Romeyer overlooking its own gardens and private lake. Romeyer's philosophy, refreshingly self-effacing, is that a chef should adapt what he serves to meet the wishes of his customers, and not vice versa. The presentation, harmony of taste and variety of his specialities are equally highly commended. Of particular note are the home-made pâtisseries.

The outskirts of Brussels are also blessed with a number of first-class restaurants, including **De Bijgaarden** (20, I. Van Beverenstraat) in Grand-Bigard (7 km/4 miles northeast of the capital), **Le Trèfle à Quatre** in Genval (87, Avenue du Lac) and **Barbizon** in Jezus-Eik (95, Welriekendedreef).

Gastronomy on a budget: No city is complete without a wide-ranging choice of cafés, bistros and bars; Brussels is no exception. The district surrounding the Grand' Place/Grote Markt is particularly well endowed with places serving good food at inexpensive prices. In some of the narrow alleys hereabouts it seems as if every house has been converted into a restaurant of some kind. A typical example is Rue des Bouchers/Beenhouwersstraat where, in many cases, polished antique barrows and shelves laden with the ingredients of house specialities are placed in front

Waiting for hungry customers in the Ilôt Sacré.

of the restaurants to tempt passers-by. When business is slack, waiters and chefs often come out and stand in front of their restaurants to drum up trade. Don't be shy of accepting their invitations. Such fare is typically Belgian and reasonably priced.

The district as a whole is known as the city's "stomach". It is a fitting description, but you will find more than just places to eat. You will also find originality and a loving regard for centuries-old traditions.

One of the most atmospheric places to eat in town is **Toone VII** (located at Impasse Schuddevelt 6, Petite Rue des Bouchers) – an old inn containing a puppet theatre, which is reached via a claustrophobically narrow passageway between two houses. The theatre (go up the rickety stairs) stages performances of classical plays such as *Hamlet* and *Faust*, interspersed by personal comments on the plot by Toone, a true Brussels character. His remarks – frequently profound, sometimes witty –

lighten the tragic action on the stage. The puppet theatre/restaurant has been a feature of Brussels for several generations. Even foreign visitors who speak neither French nor the local dialect of the Belgian capital will find an evening here a delight.

The majority of bars and bistros cannot provide such original entertainment, but most of them offer at least a welcoming atmosphere. The décor, usually of a rustic nature and bearing the patina of age, radiates a relaxing ambience. The walls, stucco and beams of such place are invariably brown with generations of tobacco smoke.

In such a setting the city's local specialities taste particularly good. Typical of Brussels are poularde, and chicory – with minced beef, stuffed or rolled in ham. A variety of national dishes – Flemish *carbonade* or Mecheener asparagus – are nearly always available. They are all served with the national drink of Belgium: beer.

Like the French, the citizens of Brus-

Open-air dining is popular.

sels enjoy sitting at a table on the pavement in front of the restaurant or bar. Even in the sheltered, air-conditioned shopping galleries customers display a marked preference for outside tables. Here you will usually find coffee and a selection of tempting cakes and pastries on offer.

Elsewhere in the city, cafés-cum-pâtisseries tend to be thin on the ground. There are some excellent cake shops – **Wittamer**, on the Place du Grand Sablon, is one of the continent's best – but hardly any are attached to an attractive café of the type common in Germany or Austria. Occasionally you may come across a shabbily furnished room in a department store, where a cup of coffee and biscuits are served – or, if you are lucky, a so-called "Tearoom", where cakes and other sweet specialities are available.

The Boulevard du Midi/Zuidlaan is quite different. Here, in the **Café Strauss**, you can partake of excellent Black Forest cherry gâteau or an apple cake which tastes home-made in Berlin. German coffee is also served here. The owner, Gertrud Strauss, is actually a native of Germany.

Another excellent pâtisserie is in the Upper Town in the Avenue Louise/Louizalaan: **Nihoul** has a salon serving a wide variety of cakes, as well as a range of snacks and salads.

Within the Galerie du Sablon on the square of the same name you will not find a café as such; there is, however, an attractive restaurant: **Les Jardins du Sablon**. It is an ideal setting for recouping one's strength after the rigours of exploring the many interesting shops in this part of Brussels.

Recipes to try at home: Finally, for those who would like to try their hand at some of the specialities offered in the city's 1,300 restaurants, here is a selection of recipes:

Brussels-style chicory: Chicory is served as a vegetable, a salad or stewed with potatoes and onions, seasoned with lemon and nutmeg. Experienced

Below left, a smiling grocer. Below right, Chocolatier Neuhaus draws the sweet-toothed.

cooks recommend that when cooking chicory you should add half a lump of sugar in order to reduce the bitter taste. The vegetable will retain its attractive white colour if a few drops of lemon juice are added. **Brussels chicory with cheese and ham** (recipe below) is a particularly popular dish:

Ingredients: 1 kg chicory; one slice of cooked ham per plant; 50 g butter; 50 g flour; ½ litre liquid (chicory stock and milk); 100 g grated cheese; salt and pepper; breadcrumbs; a few knobs of extra butter.

Method: Wash the chicory thoroughly and boil it in lightly salted water; drain, reserving some of the stock. To make a sauce, melt the butter in a pan, and add the flour to make a roux. Cook for a few minutes, then gradually add the stock and milk. Thicken the sauce slightly over the heat, then stir in the grated cheese and season with salt and pepper.

Wrap each chicory plant in a slice of ham; lay the rolls side by side in an ovenproof dish. Cover with the cheese sauce, sprinkle with breadcrumbs and dot with knobs of butter. Bake in a preheated oven until well browned.

Brussels sprouts: The classic way of preparing sprouts is to boil them in salted water and then toss them in butter or pork dripping. They are also delicious when puréed in a blender and seasoned with a little nutmeg.

Brussels-style mussels: In Brussels, mussels are usually eaten with chips.

Ingredients: small piece of celeriac; one onion; a little finely-chopped parsley; approximately 1 kg mussels (clean them thoroughly in cold water and discard any which refuse to close when tapped); half a lemon.

Preparation: Finely chop the celeriac, onion and parsley. Fry gently in the butter in a covered pan for 10 minutes. Add the cleaned mussels, salt, pepper and the juice of half a lemon. Replace the lid and continue to cook gently for a further 10 minutes, until the mussels have opened. Serve immediately with

Moules et frites **as served in Bej den Boer.**

freshly-fried chips or French bread.

Brussels waffles: No meal is complete without a dessert and waffles are a perennially popular choice among the Belgians.

Ingredients: 1 kg flour; 250 g butter; 4 eggs; 50 g yeast; ½ litre water; ½ litre milk; ½ vanilla pod; 1 pinch salt.

Method: Warm the milk and water slightly. Melt the butter in a saucepan; add the egg yolks and, beating steadily, gradually mix in the warmed milk and water. Add the salt and the contents of the vanilla pod, and beat in the flour.

Dissolve the yeast in a little warm milk and stir into the dough. Allow to rise in a warm, draughtless place for 30 minutes. Shortly before the end of the rising period whisk the egg whites until they are white and fluffy. Fold into the risen dough. Bake the waffles one at a time in a preheated waffle iron. Serve hot with sugar, cream or jam.

To take home: Two other sweet specialities deserve a mention here: firstly, **pain à la Grecque** – "Greek bread". It has no connection at all with Greece; it was invented over 500 years ago by a Belgian monk living in an abbey located next to a ditch. At first it was known simply as "Bread from the ditch" (in Flemish: *Gracht*), but the French-speaking inhabitants gradually corrupted the name into "Grecque". Sold in virtually every baker's shop and pâtisserie in Brussels, the speciality is often heart-shaped. It can even be purchased in gift boxes.

The second sweet speciality worth looking out for are *speculoos*, the Belgian equivalent of the German s*pekulatius*, the popular spicy Christmas biscuits, but darker and available all the year round. At Christmas the *speculoos* are sold in the form of large figures in wooden moulds. These, however, are bought for decorative purposes rather than for eating A delicious variation on this type of biscuit, rectangular in shape and containing almonds, is **pain d'amandes** (almond bread). Bon appetit!

At Toone's you can enoy Belgian theatre as well as Belgian beer.

THE ANCIENT ART OF BREWING

A Latin inscription found on the gable of the "Maison des Brasseurs", the Brewers' House, overlooking Brussels' Grand' Place, translates as follows: "Thanks to St Arnold, the divine brew was created from the gifts of heaven and earth and human science."

The Benedictine monk commemorated by the inscription was responsible for spreading the art of brewing across most of Belgium. How a holy man acquired such expertise and felt it right to promulgate his discoveries has been the subject of conjecture. It is said that Arnold was trying to find out why prosperous citizens and noblemen had a considerably higher life expectancy than the common people. After studying the matter, he attributed the reason to the fact that the better-off were able to quench their thirst with beer, whilst those whom fate had treated less kindly had no choice but to resort to water, which was often contaminated by harmful bacteria.

The barrels in his home abbey of St Peter at Oudenburg, near Ostend, were always filled to the brim. Father Arnold exhorted his flock to avoid water and to drink instead beer (in moderation). Arnold was canonised after his death, and has been the patron saint of brewers ever since.

For centuries the art of brewing beer remained in the hands of the religious communities. Their craft, which enabled them to develop a continuous succession of new processes and flavours, spread as far as the court of Spain.

Today, Belgium has no fewer than 400 breweries scattered across the country. The experiments of the god-fearing recluses were developed further, and today the country produces more than 200 different kinds of beer; their colours range from light golden through every shade of brown to a deep reddish hue.

One of the most unusual beers is the *Lambic*. This also forms the basis for a number of other beers: the *Gueuze* (pronounced Göse), the *Faro*, the *Kriek* and the *Framboise*. These are yeastless beers where the fermentation occurs spontaneously. It is set into motion by bacteria which enter the liquid from the air. It is claimed that the necessary microbes exist nowhere except in the atmosphere of the capital. In the Gueuze Museum (*Musée de la Gueuze*) the visitor can observe the brewers at work as they process the raw ingredients in accordance with methods developed by their ancestors. (The museum is situated in the Rue Gheude/Gheudestraat; tel: 520 28 29; visits by appointment Monday-Saturday between 15 October and 15 May, or guided tours on Saturdays at 11 a.m., 2 p.m. and 3.30 p.m.)

A "young" beer must mature for three to six months and a "mature" one for two to three years. Fermentation takes place in both bottles and casks. The bottle method is used for so-called "Brussels Champagne". If cherries are added to the Lambic before the second fermentation, the resulting beer is known as *Kriek* (a Flemish word meaning cherry). *Framboise* results from the the addition of raspberries to the basic brew – 150 kg of fruit to 450 litres of beer.

Another variation is *Faro*, which is sweetened after fermentation with rock candy. Since beers of this type are subject to an uncontrolled fermentation, they may, like wine, taste different from one year to the next. Gueuze is only produced during cooler months; the outdoor temperatures are ideal between October and April.

An interesting type of beer is brewed in West Flanders. The Rodenbach Brewery stores 10 million litres in oak barrels. Brewed from winter and summer barley, best quality hops, caramel and malt, a dark brown full-bodied beer is manufactured and subsequently filled into champagne bottles. It is known as *Dobbelen Bruinen*. The *Goudenband* was nominated by the beer pundit Michael Jackson as the best brown ale in the world.

Most of the 12 million hectolitres of beer which leave the filling plants of Belgian breweries every year are destined for export. The country's pro-capita consumption is roughly on a par with that of Germany.

In Brussels there are more than 200 brands of beer to choose from.

THE GRAND' PLACE

The architectural climax of any sight-seeing tour of Brussels is undoubtedly the Grand' Place, the capital's market square where Gothic, Renaissance and baroque buildings are juxtaposed to such harmonious effect. It has been admired by visitors across the centuries, and attracted the attention of writers such as Victor Hugo to Jean Cocteau.

In French, the name for the market place is Grand' Place ("Great Square"); in Flemish it is known as the Grote Markt ("Great Market"). Facing each other across the square and occupying the two long sides are the Town Hall (Hôtel de Ville/Stadhuis) and the King's House (Maison du Roi). They are surrounded by baroque guildhalls with magnificent gables and sculptures. The facades of all the houses are of blackish-brown stone, against which the gilt ornamentation, figures, wrought iron and gables are beautifully contrasted.

As long ago as the 11th century, the market place – lying on a region of drained marshland – formed the focal point of Brussels. In those days, however, it consisted of a mere handful of wattle and daub huts in which the peasants and craftsmen used to gather. From the 12th century the town experienced a period of economic expansion; at the beginning of the 15th century, work began on the construction of the Town Hall on the south side of the square. This period marked the summit of the city's significance and economic prosperity. By means of its flourishing weaving industry, Brussels had gained wealth and status; the new Town Hall was to become a worthy symbol of this newly acquired importance.

The Town Hall: With its high belltower,

Preceding pages: the "stern" of the "Horn of Plenty" guildhall, the house of the river boatmen. **Left**, flower market on the Grand' Place.

the Town Hall of Brussels is one of the finest Gothic buildings still standing today. Like the church-like edifice adorning the main square in Bruges – also Gothic in style – it represents one of the most beautiful examples of Town-Hall architecture in a country famous for its *Hôtels de Ville*. (The town halls in Leuwen and Ghent were completed during a later period and exhibit Renaissance features.)

Its left wing is ascribed to the master builder Jacob Van Thiemen; it was completed in 1402. The right wing was added in 1444 by a craftsman whose name is unfortunately unknown to this day. The central tower, which is 96 metres (307 ft) high, was designed by Jan Van Ruysbrock. The lower rectangular section, incidentally, is not quite in the middle of the facade. According to legend, the builder threw himself from the top of the tower when he realised his mistake.

The base, which is four storeys high, is surmounted by an octagonal construction consisting of three storeys plus an openwork spire. This bears the massive gilt **Statue of St Michael**, one of the city's twin patron saints. It was cast in bronze by Martin Van Rode; a survivor of the fire of 1695, it is one of the oldest statues in the city. Visitors climbing the 400 steps to the top of the Town Hall tower will be rewarded by a spectacular view of the Grand' Place below and the entire city beyond.

The Great Fire of 1695 was an act of vengeance on the part of Louis XIV of France, who ordered Marshal de Villeroy to attack Brussels after the Belgians had fought against his armies in battle. On 13–14 April 1695 firebrands were shot on to the Grand' Place and its surroundings by cannons placed in front of the city walls. Most of the houses were destroyed; a total of 4,000 buildings within the city were burned to the ground.

The local citizens refused to be disconcerted, however; four years afterwards, they were concentrating all their energies on the rebuilding of the Grand'

The guildhalls recall the wealth of their creators.

Place, which was to be even more beautiful and magnificent than before.

Between 1708 and 1717, Cornelis Van Nerven built the section of the Town Hall between the Rue de l'Amigo/Vruntstraat and part of the Rue de la Tête d'Or/Guldenhoofstraat in the style of Louis XIV. It stands on the site of the second Weavers' Hall, which was built in 1353 and completely destroyed in the fire of 1695. It was reconstructed, and the Estates of Brabant used it up until the end of the Ancien Régime.

The facade of the Town Hall is decorated with numerous statues. These include several interesting specimens of 14th and 15th-century Brussels sculpture. Entering the courtyard, the visitor will notice two fountains. The one on the left, the work of Jan de Kinder (1714), represents the River Meuse; that on the right, created by Pierre-Denis Plumiers in 1715, symbolises the Scheldt.

The renovated Grand Staircase inside is adorned with busts of all the mayors of Brussels since 1830. The walls of the staircase are decorated with paintings by Count Jacques Lalaing dating from 1893 and known collectively as *The Glorification of Municipal Power*. The ceiling fresco is entitled *Castle Keep, Defended by All Powers of the Town against Plague, Famine and War*.

In times past it was usual for citizens to learn about the local byelaws by means of a formal proclamation from the balcony of the Town Hall. Another mural therefore depicts *To the Town and the World*, a municipal official reading a new regulation from the Town Hall tower. The main Council Chamber, today frequently referred to as the Gothic Hall, retains its original fittings. It was once used for official ceremonies. It was here that the Dukes of Brabant took their oath of allegiance, swearing that they would uphold and defend the rights and privileges of the city.

The last such dedication took place in this hall on 21 September 1815. In the presence of the entire council of the States General, William I took the oath of loyalty as King of the Netherlands. Originally the chamber was decorated with several paintings by Rogier van der Weyden; these were unfortunately destroyed during the bombardment of the city in 1695.

Originally appointed in the neoclassical style, the Council Chamber was redesigned in the Gothic idiom in 1868. Tapestries adorning the walls depict the city's principal crafts and the guilds which practised them. The wall hangings were created between 1875 and 1881 in Mechelen, in the workshops of Bracquenié. Former presidents of the municipal council are represented as gilt bronze statues in front of the columns. The windows illustrate the coats of arms of noble families of Brussels.

The wedding chamber in the Town Hall has been completely restored. The large mural by Cardon depicts, in the middle, the City of Brussels, presiding over marriage. On the left stands the Law and on the right, Justice. The coats

Flags are only displayed on official holidays.

of arms of the old guilds can be seen on the ceiling, recalling the fact that the heads of the nine corporations would have met here in council. These corporations were formed in 1421 from the assembly of craftsmen's guilds.

These corporations met in council with the representatives of the municipal authorities to determine – amongst other things – the affairs of the town.

At the far end of the chamber is a row of wooden statues. They represent famous local citizens of the 14th, 15th and 16th centuries, among them the artist Rogier van der Weyden and Ludwig van Bodeghem, the architect of the "Bread House". The statues were carved by the Goyers brothers in Leuven.

Many visitors are attracted to the Town Hall in order to see the so-called Brussels tapestries dating from the 16th, 17th and 18th centuries. Official guided tours include some of the offices of the mayor and jurors not normally on view to the public.

The King's House: The facade of the building facing the Town Hall is divided into three sections: two magnificent rows of guildhalls flank the central "King's House" (*Maison du Roi*). At the end of the 12th century the latter was the headquarters of the bakers of Brussels and was accordingly known as the *Broodhuis* ("Bread House"). Since, however, the bakers used it less and less frequently for the sale of their wares, it was abandoned during the course of time. In the 15th century it was rechristened '*t Hertogenhuis* (The Duke's House), since the ducal assizes were held here.

In about 1512 the entire building had to be demolished because the clay foundations gave way. The most distinguished architects of the time were called in for the reconstruction: Antoon Keldermans, Ludwig van Bodeghem and Heinrich van Prede. The building was rechristened yet again under Philip II, who had the royal assizes installed here. The new designation, *Pretorium Regium*, brought about the current name,

A detail of the house "L'Ermitage".

162

"King's House", since it was here that legal verdicts were pronounced in the name of the King of Spain.

Archduchess Isabella had the King's House rebuilt in stone during the 17th century, dedicating it to the Virgin Mary, whose statue can still be seen today. During the Marshal de Villeroy's attack on the city the building was almost destroyed. It was not until 1768 that the authorities decided on its reconstruction, sadly ignoring the original style.

After changing hands several times, in 1860 the King's House was purchased by the municipal authorities. They had it demolished and reconstructed in accordance with the original plans under the supervision of the architect Victor Jamar, who also used old etchings in his search for authenticity. A stone tablet in the entrance hall records that the project lasted from 1873 to 1896 – in other words, taking longer than the original building had done. The facade is of limestone and bluestone from Belgian quarries; the spire is of oak covered with slates. The weather vane bears a loaf of bread and a crown, thus symbolising the building's two names – the *Broodhuis* and the King's House.

In 1568 the celebrated Count Egmont and Count Horn, the two leaders of the revolt against the Catholic policies pursued by Philip II within the Spanish Netherlands, were held in the King's House before their execution on the Grand' Place. Lamoral Count of Egmont (1522–68), having distinguished himself in Charles V's military campaigns, had become dissatisfied with Spanish rule after being appointed stadtholder of Flanders in 1559.

Although his pleas for religious tolerance on behalf of the Protestants were to no avail he remained loyal to the crown, refusing to side with Prince William I of Orange and suppressing Calvinist uprisings; nonetheless, after the arrival of the Duke of Alva in 1567 he was arrested and convicted of high treason. In memory of the rebellion, statues of the two folk heroes were erected and origi-

Come here for your Brussels ace.

nally placed in front of the house; today they can be seen on the Place du Petit Sablon/Kleine Zavel.

In 1887 the City of Brussels transformed the King's House into the **Municipal Museum** (Musée Communal de la Ville de Bruxelles). Also known as the "Brussels Community Museum", amongst its most important exhibits – apart from the collections illustrating various aspects of the city's development and a selection of typical local decorative arts – is a series of 26 paintings donated by an Englishman, John Waterloo Wilson. These include the *Allegory of the United Provinces* by N. Verkolie, *Still Life with Food* by Willem Glaesz Heda and the *Portrait of a Clergyman* attributed to the painter Josse van Clece.

Two 16th-century Brussels tapestries also enrich the museum's collection: *The Wedding* by Pieter Brueghel the Elder and *The Legend of Notre Dame du Sablon*, probably the work of Barend van Orley.

One section displays Brussels ceramics from 1710 to 1845. The museum also contains the original sculptures from the Town Hall facade, renovated in 1840. The upper floor contains a Numismatic Collection, a Hall of Mirrors and a Lace Room.

The second floor of the museum houses – amongst other things – the costume collection of Manneken Pis (Garderobe de Manneke Pis/De Klerenuerzameling van Manneke Pis). The 300 items of clothing, costumes and uniforms would be sufficient to fill a museum in themselves.

The guildhalls: Buildings which also suffered badly during Marshal de Villeroy's bombardment of the city in 1695 were the guildhalls. From the High Middle Ages until the middle of the 19th century, the guilds functioned as craftsmen's associations within the city. Their houses surrounding the Grand' Place were originally built of wood.

After the destruction of the city, the prosperous craftsmen of Brussels wanted

Karl Marx once lived in "The Swan" house. Today the building houses a high-class restaurant.

rebuilding to take place as quickly as possible. They commissioned the best architects of the day. A basic unity of style can be attributed to the fact that several of the new buildings were designed by Guillaume de Bruyn and Antoine Pasterona.

During the 17th century, most architects were members of a guild; they were by trade either stonemasons, carpenters, painters or sculptors. Their original profession naturally influenced the style of building they favoured.

The most important function of the magnificent guildhalls was for the glorification of the guild concerned. Today, the name of each house recalls its former occupants.

Decide for yourself which house has the most beautiful gable.

The guildhalls were constructed in the Italian-Flemish baroque style. To the left of the Town Hall stands **L'Etoile** (The Star). This is the smallest of the guildhalls and one of the oldest buildings still standing on the Grand' Place. During the 13th century it served as an office building. In 1852 it was demolished to make way for a street-widening project, and reconstructed above an arcade in 1897.

Under the arcade stands a statue of Everard 't Serclaes, the Brussels folk hero. The figure's signs of wear are due to the custom of stroking its arm in passing in order to absorb some of the good luck it is supposed to endow. Everard 't Serclaes became famous for removing the flag which Louis de Maele, Count of Flanders, flew from the roof following his conquest of the Archduchy of Brabant in 1356. Everard was quickly arrested and tortured by the Lord of Gaasbeek. A priest rescued him and brought him, badly wounded, to The Star, whereupon the local populace, outraged by the event, destroyed Gaasbeek Castle.

Next door to The Star stands **Le Cygne** (The Swan). Rebuilt by a private citizen in 1698, from 1720 the house was the headquarters of the butchers' guild. Above the door is a carved swan with outspread wings; three statues above

the second floor portray Abundance, Agriculture and Slaughter.

The house is famous above all as the setting where Karl Marx and Friedrich Engels founded their "Workers' Association". This later became the Belgian Workers' Party and finally the Belgian Socialist Party. Today, the *Maison du Cygne* is the premises of one of the city's top restaurants.

Also forming part of this row of guild-halls is the **L'Arbre d'Or** (The Golden Tree). It was once owned by the Brewers' Guild; they in turn had taken it over from the weavers. The statue of Maximilian II Immanuel of Bavaria, governor of the Netherlands at the time of the French bombardment, was replaced in 1752 by a gilt equestrian statue of Charles of Lorraine. Three bas-reliefs between the storeys depict different aspects of the art of brewing: the vintage, the transport of the beer, and the hop harvest. Today the building contains the **Museum of Brewing**, displaying an old brewery with a complete collection of tools and implements. Visitors also have an opportunity to sample different types of Belgian beer.

The next guildhall is **La Rose** (The Rose), which was owned during the 15th century by the Van der Rosen family. The unadorned facade is typical of the burghers' houses of the end of the 17th century.

The last house before the Rue des Chapeliers/Hoedemmakersstraat is the **Mount Thabor** (Le Mont Thabor). Originally a private house, it is known today as the Three Colours (Aux Trois Couleurs).

The upper short side of the Grand' Place is occupied by a row of houses known as the **Maison des Ducs de Brabant** (House of the Dukes of Brabant). It consists of a group of six houses with a common front. Their names are **La Fortune** (Wealth), Le **Moulin à Vent** (The Windmill), **Pot d'Etain** (The Pewter Jug), **La Colline** (The Hill) and **La Bourse** (The Stock Exchange); they were built in 1698 by the architect Guillaume de Bruyn.

Just as the King's House was never the residence of a monarch, so no duke ever lived in the House of the Dukes of Brabant. The house was named for the busts of the dukes which adorn the capitals of the Ionic columns along the facade. From 1852, the French writer Victor Hugo lived in the Windmill after being exiled by Napoleon III.

Along the second long side of the square, past the corner of the Rue de la Colline/Heuvelstraat, stand three private houses dating from the 17th century. They are less elaborate in design than the rest of the houses surrounding the square. The first, **Le Cerf** (The Stag) is named after the emblem on the shield mounted above the door. Today this house is the home of a private club of the same name.

The next two houses, **Joseph** and **Anna**, share a common facade. They now contain a confectioner's shop where you can buy delicious traditional home-made chocolates.

A promising talent for the circus.

Next door stands **L'Ange** (The Angel). The lower section of the facade is adorned with Ionic columns and the upper section with Corinthian columns.

La Taupe (The Mole) and **La Chaloupe d'Or** (the Golden Sloop) once belonged to the Guild of Tailors. They were rebuilt with a shared facade following their destruction in 1695. Again the architect was Guillaume de Bruyn. Here, too, the columns are Ionic below and Corinthian above.

The door is guarded by a bust of St Barbe, the patron saint of tailors. Atop the gable is a statue of St Boniface.

Le Pigeon (The Pigeon) was formerly the Artists' Guildhall. The classical facade has Doric columns at street level, Ionic on the first and Corinthian on the second floors. Today the building is alive with birdsong, for the former guildhall houses a bird shop.

The last house before the King's House is **La Chambrette de l'Amman** (Official Rooms). The array of coats of arms on the facade has resulted in a second name, The Brabant Arms. The house containing the restaurant Maxim's also has a classical facade with three orders of columns.

The houses past the King's House – the **Helmet**, the **Peacock**, the **Little Fox**, the **Oak Tree**, **St Barbara** and the **Donkey** – reveal no specific classical elements. Today they house a number of restaurants.

The first house after the junction of the Rue au Beurre/Boterstraat, leading directly to the Stock Exchange, is the **King of Spain**. Since it was originally commissioned by the Bakers' Guild, the building is also known as the Bakers' Hall. The Bakers' Guild was one of the wealthiest corporations in the city. Their house, in the classical style, is thought to have been designed by the sculptor Jean Cosyn. A bust of Bishop Aubert, the patron of bakers, decorates the doorway. The inscription runs "Throughout his life, he was a saint remarkable for the compassion he showed to the poor."

A haven for geraniums.

Medallions depicting the Roman emperors Marcus Aurelius, Nerva, Decius and Trajan adorn the wall of the first floor. A bust of Charles II can be seen at second-storey level. On the balustrade above stand six statues of "Strength", "Grain", "Wind", "Fire", "Water" and "Prospects". An elegant golden figure standing on one leg can be seen atop an octagonal pedestal.

The next guildhall is known as **La Brouette** (The Wheelbarrow); it served as the meeting place of the city's tallow makers. The name of the architect of the Classical-style house is not known. The Corinthian columns on the third floor are roofed in by a gable, under which stands a statue of St Aegidius, the patron saint of tallow makers.

Le Sac (The Sack) is the guildhall of carpenters and coopers. The lower section of the building, which is Classical in style, escaped total destruction in 1695 and it was subsequently restored by a carpenter named Pastorana. Above the main entrance is the likeness of a man carrying a sack into which a second person is putting his hand.

The next house, **La Louve** (The She-wolf), was also only partly destroyed by the French attack. It was rebuilt in the Italo-Flemish style and subsequently acquired by the Guild of Archers. Several decorative elements on the facade at the height of the first floor allude to the art of archery. The balcony is decorated with cranks and quivers.

In front of each column on the second floor there is a statue, above which an inscription has been added. The house owes its name to the carved relief of the she-wolf with Romulus and Remus, the twin founders of Rome. The female statue on the far left is holding an open book; accompanied by an eagle, she represents Truth. The inscription reads "The pillar of the kingdom". The next figure is Falsehood. She is accompanied by a fox and is carrying a mask; her inscription reads "The nation's pitfalls". Then comes Peace, carrying a bundle and surrounded by doves, with the in-

Dressed for an occasion.

scription "The salvation of mankind". The statue on the extreme right represents Discord; since her inscription pronounces her to be "The ruin of the republic", she has wolves at her feet and bears a torch. Dominating all is a golden phoenix with outspread wings.

Le Cornet (The Horn of Plenty) was the house of the river boatmen; the gable, adorned with a medallion depicting Charles II of Spain, has the form of the stern of a galleon. Beneath the gallery is a row of fish-like sea-gods. The house's original name was The Mountain. It was rechristened by the bargees in 1434. After it was destroyed in 1695 the house was rebuilt in the Italo-Flemish style by the carpenter Pastorana. He designed the gable in the form of the stern of a ship. The facade is also adorned with a number of other items alluding to navigation.

The last house before the Rue de la Tête d'Or is **Le Renard** (The Fox). The architecture incorporates elements from several different styles. The fact that it originally belonged to the Haberdashers' Guild is clear from the subjects depicted on its facade: a stoneware merchant, a dyer's shop, a fabric shop and children preparing hides.

Five statues adorn the first floor: the central figure, personifying Justice, is blindfold, and bears a sword in one hand and scales in the other. The remaining statues symbolise Europe, Asia, Africa and America. At the height of the second floor stand four caryatids – Classical-style female figures in flowing robes which double as supporting pillars. A statue of St Nicholas, the patron saint of haberdashers, stands at the uppermost point of the facade.

As is usually the case in places which attract large numbers of tourists, the district surrounding the market place is well endowed with souvenir shops. Among the multitude of different items on sale, not all of which have much to recommend them, there are some good examples of the famous Brussels lace and fine crystalware.

wo men with view.

THE LOWER CITY

The centre of Brussels is characterised by the striking contrast between the Upper and Lower City. In the former you will find a good deal of the city's government and business infrastructure: the ministry offices, the parliament building, various official bodies and large insurance companies, for instance. The Flemish Old City, the so-called "Lower City" situated on the *Ilôt Sacré*, on the other hand, is one of the most lively districts in the capital, well known for its restaurants. The careful renovation and maintenance that has been lavished on the historic buildings of the area adds to its charm.

The Royal Decree of 1960 proclaimed that all rebuilding work should ensure that the historic facades of the buildings were retained. The city subsidises such projects with a 25 percent grant to help with the costs; this applies in particular to the Grand' Place.

Close to the Grand' Place is **Rue du Marché aux Herbes/Grasmarkt**, a narrow street housing a number of small shops and, at No. 61, the Tourist Information Office (TIP), where visitors can obtain theatre programmes, news of exhibitions, trades fairs and congresses as well as maps of the city.

Since most of the sites people want to visit are found within a relatively compact area, you are recommended to explore the city on foot, starting from the Grand' Place.

Famous landmark: Southwest of the Town Hall, at the junction of the Rue de l'Etuve/Stoofstraat and the Rue du Chêne/Eibstraat, stands the city's landmark, the celebrated **Manneken Pis** – a bronze fountain in the shape of a naked boy. On 13 August 1619 Jérôme Duquesnoy the Elder (*circa* 1570–1641) was

commissioned to produce the likeness. He was the head of a Brussels family of sculptors whose works were influenced by the style of Rubens (a contemporary) and whose son, François, was to achieve fame in Rome, working with Bernini on the famous baldachin in St Peter's, and in Naples, where his rendering of *putti* was greatly admired. The little bronze figure was to replace the statue on an earlier fountain.

It is one of the key landmarks in Brussels, as the cover to this guide testifies, and a source of inspiration to the souvenir manufacturers. The imitations of the little fellow vie with each other in tastelessness. The figure's likeness has been modelled in every possible substance; some of the copies are even larger than the original.

Manneken Pis is revered as the oldest and most celebrated citizen of Brussels. Also known as Petit Julien (Little Julian), the statue was originally merely one of the numerous fountains which provided the city with water. At some point, how-

ever, Manneken Pis progressed from being just a public fountain to become a legendary figure, probably owing its popularity to the countless stories surrounding its origins. Since no one knows for certain exactly where the statue came from, opinions vary as to which of the stories seems most likely. In any case, the little figure symbolises the local citizens' predilection for carping criticism, their cheekiness, courage and lack of respect – their so-called "ungovernable soul".

The best-known myth surrounding Manneken Pis's origins maintains that during the battle of Ransbeke the son of Duke Gottfried of Lorraine was hung in his cradle from an oak tree to give the soldiers courage. At some stage in the fighting he got out of his cradle unaided and was discovered urinating against the tree. He thus demonstrated his courage even as a child.

According to another legend, Manneken Pis is purported to have urinated on a bomb fuse, thus saving the Town

Chairs to look at...

Hall from terrorists who planned to destroy the building.

Yet another variation tells of the son of a Brussels nobleman who, at the age of five, cheekily left a procession in order to relieve himself. According to a variation on this tale, a wicked witch put a spell on the child because he dared to urinate against the wall of her house. She turned him to stone, thus condemming him to urinate for ever. Such legends are legion.

The statue escaped damage during the bombardment of the city in 1695, but it was stolen on a number of occasions after this. In 1745 it was captured by the British; and two years later the thieves were the French. But Manneken Pis was always recovered. By way of compensation for the French theft, Louis XV, who was in Brussels at the time, gave the statue a costume of precious gold brocade. The King had the culprits arrested and honoured Manneken Pis with the title "Knight of St Louis". His intention was to offer reparation for the lack of respect the French soldiers had shown the little statue.

In 1817 a newly released convict stole the statue, and when it was found it was in several pieces. These were used in the casting of the present bronze replica. On 6 December 1818 Manneken Pis was returned to its original site, where it can still be seen today.

On high days and holidays, the statue is dressed in costume. Many of its outfits reflect the various periods of history through which Manneken Pis has passed. On 6 April, for example, it wears the uniform of an American military policeman to recall the anniversary of the involvement of the United States in World War I. On 3 September every year Manneken Pis is dressed in the uniform of a sergeant of the Regiment of Welsh Guards to celebrate the liberation of Brussels in 1944; and on 15 September it is the turn of the uniform of a British Royal Air Force pilot – in remembrance of the Battle of Britain during World War II.

..and chairs o sit on.

In all, the statue possesses 345 uniforms and medals, all of which are stored in the Municipal Museum on the Grand' Place (most of the time he doesn't wear anything at all). Manneken Pis is without doubt the most famous site in the whole of Brussels.

Religion and capitalism: Leaving Manneken Pis and going down the Rue des Grands Carmes/Lievevrouwbroersstraat, the visitor soon arrives in front of **Notre-Dame-de-Bon-Secours/Onzelieve-Vrouw van Brjstand** (Our Lady of Succour). The church was built in 1664 by Jean Cortvriendt in the 17th-century Italian manner.

Another church in the vicinity, **Notre-Dame-aux-Riches-Claires/Rijkelklavenkerk**, dates from virtually the same period. It is the work of Luc Fayd'herbe (1617–1697), a pupil of Rubens known above all for his creation of colossal statues adorning the pillars of church naves. The ornate gables represent the typical Brussels interpretation of the Italian Renaissance.

Also near the Grand' Place, in the Rue Henri Maus/Henri Mausstraat, stands the Brussels **Stock Exchange** (La Bourse/de Beurs). This is the most important foreign exchange market in the country, before those of Antwerp, Ghent and Liège.

The Stock Exchange was founded on 8 July 1801. It changed locations several times after its original foundation in the former Augustinian monastery. When the city councillors became aware of the importance of such an institution they decided to erect a more imposing building on the site left vacant by the demolition of the "Récollets" monastery, which had had to make way for the new boulevard crossing the city from north to south. Léon Suys, one of the capital's most distinguished architects at the time, supervised the construction of the magnificent building between 1871 and 1873.

Built in handsome yellowish-beige stone, the massive exterior lends the Stock Exchange a fortress-like air. In **Hot snails on a cold day.**

particular, the broad staircase, over which two huge lions stand sentinel, lends the edifice a solid appearance. Rectangular in form, the facade is heavily ornamented and surmounted by a dome. The main entrance consists of a vast colonnade. Six Corinthian columns support a triangular tympanum decorated with a garland of fruits and flowers, above which sits a figure representing "Belgium".

Three magnificent portals lead to the inner halls of the Stock Exchange, which can be visited on weekdays between 11 a.m. and 2.30 p.m. Passing through an automatic double glass door, you will find yourself standing in an antechamber, from which you can observe the frenzied bustle of the stockbrokers behind a glass wall; visitors wanting to penetrate the "inner sanctum" may only do so by prior arrangement and as part of a guided tour. The sombre main halls are decorated with pillars, ornaments, statues and galleries which call to mind a place of worship rather than one of the hubs of the Brussels financial scene.

Before leaving the area the visitor should not fail to cast a glance inside the little **Church of St Nicholas** (l'Eglise Saint-Nicolas/Sint-Niklaaskerk). Dedicated to the patron saint of shopkeepers, the building has a colourful history reaching back to the earliest beginnings of the city. It was originally constructed as a market church during the 11th and 12th centuries, and rebuilt in the Gothic style in the course of the 14th and 15th centuries. Having suffered damage during the Wars of Religion which dominated the 16th century, as well as during the terrible bombardment of the city in 1695, the church was subsequently rebuilt apart from the tower, which was destroyed beyond repair.

The interior walls are lined with wood panelling and decorated with notable paintings. A Classical-style high altar, carved wooden confessionals and the pulpit date from the 18th century. The altar in the left aisle is adorned with a 15th-century Madonna. The pillar on the right-hand side of the choir supports a Spanish figure of Christ dating from the 16th century. A copper shrine in front of the pulpit recalls the martyrs of Gorcum, who were put to death in Brielle (near Rotterdam) in 1572 after suffering unspeakable torture at the hands of the Gueux. The painting of the *Virgin and Child Asleep* is attributed to the master Rubens.

Streetlife: Leading away from the Stock Exchange to left and right is the **Boulevard Anspach/Anspachlaan**, one of the city's busiest commercial thoroughfares. It is lined with specialist shops of every kind: department stores, fashion boutiques and cafés before which street musicians and traders with typical handcarts laden with mussels and snails ply their trade.

The avenue opens on to the spacious **Place de Brouckère/De Brouckèreplein**, where it meets the Boulevard Adolphe Max and the Boulevard Emile Jacqmain. The middle of the square used to be occupied by the **Anspach Monu-**

_unch-break.

ment, a 20-metre (64-ft) high fountain in memory of Jules Anspach, mayor of Brussels between 1863 and 1879 and the prime mover behind the construction of the avenues.

The capital's main boulevards cross the entire length of the Old City from the North Station (Gare du Nord) to the South Station (Gare du Midi). Today the Anspach Monument stands on the **Fishmarket** between the Quai aux Brigues/Bazsteenkaai and the Quai au Bois Brûlé/Brandhautkaai.

The glitter of the Place de Brouckère can best be observed at night, when the flickering of the brightly-coloured neon signs and the street lamps bathe the entire area in a flood of light. Numerous cinemas, snack bars and cafés enliven the square.

Not far away is the **Place Sainte-Catherine/Sint-Katelijneplein**, at the centre of which stands the church of the same name. It was built in about 1850 by Joseph Poelaert in the eclectic style, a blend of Romanesque, Gothic and Renaissance elements. **St Catherine's** occupies the site of the original church, which was destroyed in 1850. The old tower, known as the Tour Ste-Catherine/Katelijnetoren, remains, and still serves as belfry.

Within the triple-naved church, a painting of St Catherine by G. de Crayer hangs above the altar in the right aisle. In the left aisle stands the **Black Madonna** (Vierge Noire), dating from the 14th-15th century. The statue was originally carved from a light-coloured stone, but over the years it has become almost completely blackened.

Behind the church you will come across remains of the first city wall, dating from the 12th century: the **Black Tower** (Tour Noire/Zwarte Toren). The Place Ste-Catherine is another place to find street traders, their portable barrows laden with ready-to-eat delicacies such as oysters, mussels, snails and pickled herring.

Within easy reach of the square is the Rue du Cyprès/Cipresstraat, which leads **"Fasten bayonets!"**

to the **Church of St John the Baptist in the Beguine Convent** (St-Jean-Baptiste-au-Beguinage/Begijnhofkerk van Sint-Jan). The basilica, originally Gothic in style, was rebuilt during the 17th century and became one of the masterpieces of Belgian rococo architecture. Inside, the technique by which the baroque features were superimposed upon the original Gothic structure can still clearly be seen. The entablature, surmounting a line of arches, is particularly harmonious as it rests on a row of winged angels' heads. The Beguine community itself, which totalled 1,200 members in its heyday, was dissolved during the 19th century.

The well-known **Petite Rue des Bouchers/Kleene Beenhouversstraat** ("Little Butchers' Street") crosses the city centre on its way from the Stock Exchange to the Galeries Saint-Hubert and the Galeries Royales. The street, which is closed to traffic, is also known as the "Stomach of Brussels", as it is lined with good but cheap restaurants.

Street musicians serenade potential guests; universally popular are the stands offering fish and seafood.

A fun place to dine: In a narrow cul-de-sac leading off the Petite Rue des Bouchers lies the **Museum Toone**, one of the most famous marionette theatres in the world. The theatre first came to public notice in 1830 under Toone I, who invented the "Woltje", the Little Walloon, who is seen as the epitome of the typical Brussels street urchin and who has become an irreplaceable member of the cast. Dressed in a checked jacket and with his cap set at a jaunty angle, he acts as the narrator and speaks all the parts.

In 1911 a grim fate befell Toone III; he was discovered hanging dead between his puppets. Under José Géal, the seventh generation of the Toone dynasty, the marionette theatre experienced a new upsurge. In the 1960s he purchased an old house in the Schuddeveld Street and turned it into a puppet theatre cum restaurant. An antique pianola

Equipped for all weathers.

dominates the entrance; if you put a five-franc piece into the slot, it will tinkle old-fashioned songs. The tables and benches, together with the Gothic fireplace, give the restaurant a homely atmosphere. The traditional marionette theatre with a total of 50 seats is located up the stairs.

The Toone family's old-fashioned marionettes have been popular among Brussels citizens since 1815. Even today, the plays are performed in the local dialect, which originally evolved in the Marolles, the historic district at the heart of the old city. Here the Walloon and Flemish workers came together, creating a strange patois. Though based on the French language, it also includes a mixture of Flemish words and Spanish expressions adopted from the soldiers of the Duke of Alva. The dialect is used for every performance in the Toone theatre repertoire of 500 plays. (This shouldn't put you off; a knowledge of the dialect isn't a prerequisite for enjoying performances.)

Shopping in style: From the end of the bustling Petite Rue des Bouchers, it is only a stone's throw to the Royal **Galeries Saint-Hubert**. In 1830 the city, embracing its new role as the capital of the Kingdom of Belgium, dedicated the exclusive shopping arcades to its new King and Queen.

The glass-roofed streets, lined with shops, are divided into the **"Galerie du Roi"**, the **"Galerie de la Reine"**, and the **"Galerie des Princes"**. The galleries, which have a total length of 2,133 metres (6,998 ft), were designed in 1845 by the Brussels architect Jean-Pierre Cluysenaer, then only 26 years old. Once again, many stories are associated with its founding. A barber, for instance, is reputed to have slit his throat rather than consent to abandon his property to make way for the project.

King Leopold I laid the foundation stone on 6 May 1846. One year later, on 20 June 1847, the official opening of the galleries took place. The shopping arcade possesses four entrances – on the Rue des Bouchers, on the Rue du Marché aux Herbes/Grasmarkt, on the Rue de l'Ecuyer/Schildknaapstraat and on the Rue des Dominicains/Predikherenstraat. Lined with noble and elegant shops and boutiques, the Galeries Saint-Hubert is one of the oldest covered shopping streets in Europe.

Leaving by the northern exit of the Galerie du Roi, the visitor can cross the Rue de l'Ecuyer and reach the Place de la Monnaie/Muntplein, the focal point of which is the **Théâtre Royal de la Monnaie/Muntschouwburg**, the Brussels Opera House.

Belgium's first musical stage was elevated to the rank of National Opera (Opéra National) in 1963. The name of the square, and that of the theatre, are derived from the building which originally stood on this site – the Hôtel de la Monnaie (the National Mint), which was constructed here during the 15th century and which minted the coins for the Duchy of Brabant.

After the original building was de-

Waiting for customers.

molished in 1531, a spacious square was laid out here. Jean-Paul Bombarda, the Governor-General of the Netherlands, had the first theatre – with seating for an audience of 1,200 – built on the site in 1698. During its early years it enjoyed only modest success.

Then, the architect Damesne was commissioned to undertake a complete rebuilding programme. He planned a new edifice in the neoclassical style, surrounded by a roofed-in arcade. A triangular tympanum surmounted eight Ionic columns; it was decorated with a bas-relief depicting the *Harmony of Human Passions*. The new building was opened when construction work was complete in May 1819.

On 31 January 1855 a fire destroyed extensive sections of Damesne's building. Restoration work was completed by Poelaert within the space of just one year. The pillars and the bas-relief had escaped damage; the auditorium was considerably extended during the rebuilding. After its official opening by King Leopold I, the restored theatre was reserved exclusively for performances of opera and ballet.

Call to arms: Brussels opera house was the scene of one of the most important historic events in the city. It was here, on the night of 25 August 1830, that the Revolution which was to lead to the country's independence was actually triggered.

The opera *Masianello* (also known as *La Muette de Portici*), by Daniel François Esprit Auber and based on the Neapolitan Revolution of 1647, had been scheduled to be performed at the Opera some time previously. However, following unrest in the city, the authorities had felt it wise to postpone its run.

The première was finally held on 25 August before a packed house. Its effect on the audience was electrifying. As the opera progressed they became increasingly disturbed and when, in Act IV, the call to arms rang out, it could not be contained. With patriotic cries on their lips they streamed out of the auditorium

Extremely hard to resist.

towards the houses occupied by Dutch families, and then to the municipal park. The Revolution had begun.

The Théâtre de la Monnaie was not only the starting point for the Revolution, but also the setting for a succession of glittering premières. Many operas have received their first performance in the French language here. The Brussels Opera rates among the best opera houses in Europe.

One man's name is inextricably linked with this success: Maurice Huisman, who took over the direction of the Opera House in 1960 and who breathed new life into the theatrical world.

Furthermore, for many years the Brussels Opera House was the headquarters of the Twentieth-Century Ballet under Maurice Béjart. Whilst most French-speaking Belgian actors move to Paris in search of success in their profession, Maurice Béjart left the South of France for Brussels. He claimed that it offered him greater artistic freedom His principal contribution to the contemporary ballet scene was the infusion of a much more masculine approach to dancing. This contrasted starkly with the classical tradition, which was dominated by the feminine style.

Looking rather out-of-place opposite the magnificent old Opera House is the contemporary **Centre Monnaie**, housing numerous shops, assorted snack bars and one of the largest post offices in Brussels. Until 1965 the site was occupied by the 19th-century Hôtel des Postes – the main post office. The latter was demolished to make way for the Centre Monnaie as part of the complete remodelling of the district between the Place de Brouckère and the Place de la Monnaie.

Another popular shopping street, the **Rue Neuve**/Nieuwstraat, leads off the Place de la Monnaie. It is a bustling pedestrian area packed with modern stores, boutiques and a contemporary shopping complex, **"City 2"**. Tucked away amongst these modern palaces of Mammon is the baroque **Finistère**

Golden Mannekens for the grown-ups...

Church/Finisterakerk, built in 1708 and worth visiting for its elaborate interior decorations.

By taking a side street off the Rue Neuve the visitor will arrive at the **Place des Martyrs/Martelaarsplein**, which was formerly known as the Place Saint-Michel. Its symmetrical layout was devised by the architect Fisco in 1755. In the middle of the spacious square stands a monument by G. Geefs recalling the 450 heroes of the Revolution of 1830 who died fighting the Dutch. The crypt, in which these victims of the war of liberation were laid to rest, was consecrated on 4 October 1830 in the presence of government officials, the army and numerous Belgian patriots. The statue, *Belgia*, symbolises the newly-founded state.

To the cathedral: The area surrounding the Place des Martyrs is characterised by a number of empty houses in need of total renovation. Wooden shutters before the windows and holes in the roof seem incongruous only 20 metres away from the lively, popular shops of the Rue Neuve.

St Michael's Cathedral rises majestically on the hillside between the Upper and Lower City. It is an important example of the Brussels Gothic style. Previously occupying the site was the Carolingian baptistry dedicated to the Archangel Michael. After the relics of St Gudula were placed here in 1047 the two saints came to be regarded as the joint patrons of the church.

Although work was begun on the present cathedral at the beginning of the 13th century, it was not completed until the end of the 15th. The building thus exhibits a number of different architectural styles. The early 13th-century Romano-Gothic elements blend harmoniously with the ornamental style of the final flowering of Late Gothic during the 16th century. The dimensions are impressive: the main body of the cathedral, 108 metres (345 ft) long by 50 metres (160 ft) wide, is flanked by twin 69-metre (220-ft) towers. These domi-

...and Manneken lollies for the kids.

nate the entire exterior and never fail to impress visitors.

A staircase erected in 1861 leads to the triple doors of the cathedral. The nave impresses above all by its clarity of form, characterised by 12 round columns and ribbed vaulting. The pillars of the nave are formed by life-sized statues of the 12 apostles dating from the baroque era. They were carved by Jérôme Duquesnoy the Younger (Paul, Bartholomew, Thomas and Matthew), Luc Fayd'herbe (Simon), Jan van Milder (Philip and Andrew) and Tobias de Lelis (Peter and John).

A typically Belgian baroque wooden pulpit, carved in 1699 by Henri F. Verbruggen, portrays the banishment of Adam and Eve from Paradise. In 1937, excavations between the pulpit and the organ loft revealed the remains of foundations of a 12th-century Romanesque vestibule.

Situated too the left and the right of the high altar are three monumental tombs: two are dedicated to Duke Johann of Brabant and his wife, Margaret of York, who died in 1312 and 1322 respectively. The third is in memory of Archduke Ernst of Austria, who died in 1595; the brother of Emperor Rudolf II, he was also the Governor-General of the Netherlands.

The choir stalls originally stood in the Benedictine Abbey of Forest. The monastery was destroyed by fire in 1764 and closed completely in 1789.

Of particular note are the 17th-century tapestries. They were woven by **Van der Borght**, who appears to have drawn his inspiration from Rubens. They depict various scenes from the legend of the Miracle of the Sacrament. According to the story, in 1370 a group of Brussels Jews stole the Holy Sacrament and desecrated it with their fists in their synagogue. It is claimed that at this the Holy Christian Sacrament began to bleed, a phenomenon which was taken as proof of the guilt of the protagonists. They were all condemned to be burned at the stake.

Shades of autumn.

Although there is no documentary proof of the truth of this story, the theme was chosen as the subject of religious works of art on numerous occasions across the centuries. Nowadays the magnificent wall hangings are only displayed in the cathedral on special occasions (usually mid-July to mid-August).

The stained-glass windows above the High Altar represent important characters from European history: from left to right can be seen Maximilian of Burgundy, Philip the Handsome and Joanna of Castile, Charles V and his brother Ferdinand, Philip II with his first wife, Mary of Portugal, Duke Philibert of Savoy and Margaret of Austria.

The remarkable windows in the north and south transepts were designed by Barend van Orley in about 1300. The first shows Emperor Charles V and his wife, Isabella of Portugal, standing in front of the shrine containing the Holy Sacrament; also depicted are their patrons, Charlemagne and St Elizabeth. The window was commissioned by Charles V himself.

The second window portrays Louis II of Hungary and his wife, Mary of Hungary; they are kneeling in front of the Holy Trinity, accompanied by their patrons St Louis and Our Lady. Mary of Hungary, the sister of Charles V and Regent of the Netherlands, donated the stained-glass picture.

Other stained-glass pictures in the aisles date from the second half of the 19th century. They were executed by J.-B. Craponnier after drawings by Charles de Groux; they also portray episodes from the legend of the Miracle of the Sacrament.

The first two windows in the south aisle are gifts of the two Belgian monarchs, Leopold I and Leopold II, in memory of their royal consorts Louise-Marie and Marie Henriette. Also portrayed are the coats of arms of the ruling family of Saxe-Coburg and Orleans, as well as those of the Kingdom of Belgium and the House of Habsburg.

In the ambulatory there is a statue of the Virgin Mary by Artus Quellinus the Elder dating from 1645.

The **Chapel of the Miracle of the Holy Sacrament** often serves as the setting for chamber concerts, especially in August. The stained glass was a gift of Charles V and his family. Here, too, are scenes from the legend as well as portraits of the donors. The three left-hand windows were created by Barend van Orley; the sixth was the work of J.-B. Craponnier. In 1848 windows designed by him replaced numbers four and five, which had both been destroyed.

Behind the 19th-century alabaster altar lie the tombs of Albert, a Governor General, and his wife Isabella; they died in 1621 and 1633 respectively. Their portraits hang on the wall nearby; the paintings are copies of works by Peter Paul Rubens.

Behind the choir lies the **Chapel of St Mary Magdalene**, built in 1282 and remodelled in the baroque style in 1675. It contains a 16th-century statue of the Virgin with Child, which is thought to be the work of Konrad Meyt. The Italian alabaster altar stood originally in the Abbey of La Cambre, which was destroyed during World War I by invading German troops.

The Gothic-style **Chapel of Our Lady of Redemption** lies to the right of the choir. The 17th-century sketches for the stained-glass windows are attributed to van Thulden, a pupil of Rubens. They depict scenes from the life of the Virgin Mary, together with donors and their patron saints.

The Cathedral, dedicated to St Michael and St Gudula, the twin patron saints of Brussels, is the city's principal place of worship. For centuries it has been the setting for the country's great official ceremonies. In 1960 it was also the stage for the marriage of King Baudouin of Belgium and the Spanish Countess Fabiola Fernanda de Mora y Aragon. In 1962 the cathedral was officially named "St Michael's Cathedral" when it became the seat of the Archbishop of Mechelen.

CHATEAU ROYAL TO THE PALAIS CINQANTENAIRE

When the black, red and gold-striped flag is fluttering from the roof of the palace at Laeken, it is a sign to the citizens of Belgium that the royal couple is in residence.

The **Royal Palace** lies not in the centre of Brussels, but in the outlying district of Laeken, to the north. It was built by Montoyer during the second half of the 18th century; during the reign of Leopold II it was rebuilt in the style of Louis XVI.

Since it still serves as the private residence of the sovereign and his family, the palace is not open to the general public. The present building stands on the site of a former knight's castle which was purchased by the Governors General Marie-Christine and Albert of Saxe-Teck. It was here, in 1812, that Napoleon Bonaparte signed the declaration of war against Russia.

Exotic plants: The famous **Royal Greenhouses (Koninklijk Domein van Laeken)** occupy part of the palace gardens and contain an intriguing collection of plants. The series of 11 interlinked greenhouses were erected on the orders of Leopold II, a monarch with a considerable interest in architecture. The architect he chose for the project was Balat, whose ideas on the subject were revolutionary for the time.

Azaleas, geraniums and a host of exotic plants bloom in colourful profusion. King Baudouin and Queen Fabiola often receive their guests in the glasshouses, in particular in the adjoining winter garden. Once a year the greenhouses are opened to the public for two weeks (*see next chapter, page 197*).

The **Fountain of Neptune**, near the glasshouses, is a replica of the 16th-century original designed by the Flemish sculptor Jean de Bologne. The original fountain is in Italy, where it adorns the Piazza del Nettuno in Bologna.

The **Chinese Pavilion** and the **Japanese Tower** lend the park an exotic air. They were built for the World Exhibition in Paris in 1900. King Leopold II could not resist acquiring such interesting constructions for the garden of his residence. Originally planned to serve as a restaurant, today the pavilion houses a priceless collection of 17th and 18th-century oriental porcelain, displayed as part of a rotating exhibition. The exotic *objets d'art* are seen to good effect in a baroque interior.

The **Port of Brussels** extends right into the park at Laeken. It stretches from the Avenue du Port/Havenlaan to the Allée Verte/Groendreef. As early as 1434, the city had received from Duke Philip the Good the right to canalise the Senne, since the river was in grave danger of silting up. In 1477 a better solution was found to the problem: Mary of Burgundy gave permission for the construction of a lateral canal alongside the Senne, to link up with the Rupel near

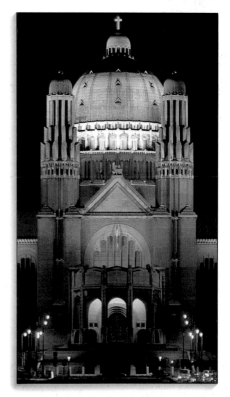

Preceding pages: the Triumphal Arch at the Parc du Cinquantenaire. Left, a smart Flemish lady. Right, the National Basilica.

Willebroek. During the following years three harbour basins were added in Brussels itself.

Between 1829 and 1836, the Willebroek Canal was deepened for the first time; after further work, plans were developed in 1902 for the construction of a sea canal. The outbreak of World War I delayed the execution of the scheme; the new channel was finally opened in 1922 to sea-going vessels with a draught of less than 5.80 metres (18 ft 6 inches). Today, the Port of Brussels has a direct link with the open sea; it also connects the capital with the industrial region of South Belgium via the Charleroi Canal. The city's waterways are used exclusively for the transport of goods.

The **Church of Our Lady of Laeken** stands at the junction of the Avenue de la Reine and the Avenue du Parc Royal. It was built by Poelaert in the neo-Gothic style on the orders of the first Queen of the Belgians, Louise-Marie. The sarcophagi of the country's deceased sovereigns lie in state in its crypt.

Also of interest in the church is a famous statue of the Virgin dating from the 13th century, and the early Gothic choir. A number of famous Belgian citizens are buried here, including the playwright Michel de Ghelderode, the architects Poelaert, Balat and Suys, and the violinist Charles de Bériot and his wife, who achieved fame under the name "La Malibran".

The tombs and chapels are decorated with numerous works of art, the most famous and impressive of which is undoubtedly the statue *The Thinker* by Auguste Rodin. The church is only open during services.

Home of the EC: Also within easy reach of the city centre is the **Europe Centre**. In 1958, when Brussels was chosen as the administrative headquarters of the European Community, the various offices of the different departments were initially housed in buildings scattered across the entire city. The present building was constructed between 1963 and

Europe in miniature under a giant atom.

1969 in accordance with plans drawn up by the architect de Westel.

Known as the **Palais Berlaymont**, the headquarters of the EC administration lies at the eastern end of the Rue de la Loi/Wetstraat, which runs from the city centre to the Parc du Cinquantaire. The officials moved in in 1967; at that time, the Community consisted of only six countries. After Denmark, Ireland and the United Kingdom joined in 1973, followed by Greece (1981) and Spain and Portugal (1986), the available space proved insufficient; a number of sections of the administration had to be housed elsewhere.

The highly conspicuous Palais Berlaymont, located at the Rond-Point Schuman, is shaped like a four-pointed star. Groups can tour the building by prior arrangement.

Near the European Community Headquarters lies the **Parc du Cinquantenaire**. It covers an area of 37 hectares (90 acres) and, as the name indicates, was created in 1880 as part of the celebrations marking the 50th anniversary of Belgian independence. Situated at the beginning of the Avenue de Tervuren, the park contains one of the largest museum complexes in Europe.

Around the periphery stand eight female statues symbolising the nine Belgian provinces. (The twin provinces of Flanders are represented by a single statue.) A **Triumphal Arch**, 60 metres wide (192 ft) and 45 metres high (144 ft) is visible from a distance. The openings in the colonnades on each side are 10 metres (32 ft) wide. The structure was designed by the architect Charles Girault. The four-horse chariot on top of the main arch is the work of the Belgian sculptor Thomas Vincotto; it portrays a victorious Belgium, confidently facing the future.

The **Palace of the 50th Anniversary Celebrations** lies surrounded by lawns; one wing houses the Royal Army Museum and Museum of Military History, as well as the Royal Museum of Art and History.

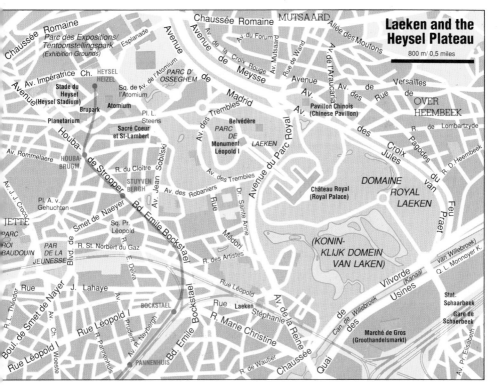

The **Royal Army Museum and Museum of Military History** display weapons, equipment and war posters from the last three centuries of Belgian history. Exhibits include sabres and cannon from the Brabant Revolution, as well as weapons used in both world wars. A separate section contains items tracing the history of the air force, including a display of some 100 aircraft dating from the early years of military flight (the *Nieuport*, a French aeroplane in use during World War I) to the British "classics" of World War II (the *Spitfire* and the *Hurricane*). The museum also includes a comprehensive library containing some 70,000 volumes on the history and technology of war, as well as documents and maps.

The **Museum of Art and History** provides the visitor with an impression of the diversity of world civilisations, from classical antiquity to the present day. The opening times vary on even and uneven days of the month.

Until 1929 the collections housed here, which had been assembled in 1880, were known as the Musée Cinquantenaire. The present department of antiquity displays Egyptian, Greek and Roman items as well as exhibits from the Near and Middle East.

The highlights of the museum are the famous 5th-century Apamea Mosaic from the Syrian town destroyed by the Persians in 612, and a bronze of the Roman emperor Septimius Severus. There are also sections where the visitor can investigate Belgian folk art and national archaeology. There are displays of handicrafts and interiors. Especially worth seeing are the sections covering Decorative Arts and Art Nouveau, and a department devoted to non-European civilisations. Of particular interest here is the 13th-century Civa Nataraja bronze from India, and a collection of painted Tibetan banners.

Disaster nearly struck the museum in 1946 when parts of the South Wing, in which the Department of Antiquities is housed, was burnt to the ground. Fortu-

Fountains at the old port.

nately it proved possible to rescue the priceless exhibits.

The museum has additional interest for scholars since it contains a specialist library of classical scientific works.

Classic cars: A further attraction within the Parc du Cinquantenaire is **Autoworld**, an impressive collection of vintage cars, within the Palais Mondial. The visitor can trace the development of the motor car from 1896 until the 1970s. Apart from the permanent displays, the automobile museum regularly holds special exhibitions. Its array of 450 top models from 12 different countries makes Autoworld the finest museum of its kind in the world. Apart from a large number of Belgian vehicles (for example, Rise, FN, Fondu, Hermes, Imperia, Miesse, Nagant and Minerva), the pride of the museum is the extensive display of veteran cars – many of them still in working order – from the **Ghislain Mahy Collection**.

Visitors wishing to move on to a higher plane – metaphorically speaking – should include a tour of the **Air and Space Museum**, also within the borders of the Parc du Cinquantenaire. The exhibition provides a summary of flight from its earliest beginnings until the present day.

Outer space: In the north of the metropolitan area, above the Parc du Cinquantenaire, lie the **Heysel Heights**, another popular green area in the city. This was the site for the 1935 World Exhibition. Afterwards the enormous halls which had been specially built were modernised for permanent use for trade fairs, exhibitions, shows, seminars and international congresses.

The park is dominated by the massive **Atomium**, 102 metres (326 ft) high and visible from much of the city (see chapter "The Atomium"). This model of an iron molecule, magnified 165 billion times, was designed by the engineer André Waterkeyn and erected for the 1958 World Exhibition. It was intended to symbolise the potential of Belgian industry.

n Laeken emetery: The Thinker y Auguste Rodin.

THE GLASS CITY

The Domain of Laeken was created under Marie-Christine and Albert of Saxe-Teck, the Governors General sent to rule the country on behalf of Emperor Joseph II of Austria. They looked around for a suitable site for a palace and in 1781 gained possession of the "Schoonenberg" in Laeken, a district just outside Brussels. Within the space of just three years their magnificent palace had been completed.

The two governors were well-known connoisseurs of art and acquired during their years of tenure a magnificent collection of paintings. It is claimed that the Archduke himself, a keen amateur architect, drew up the initial sketches for the palace and its extensive gardens. At the end of the 18th century the Domain of Laeken was considered to be one of the loveliest estates in the whole of Europe.

Austria did not have long to enjoy its new possessions, however. In 1794, France annexed Belgium. The Austrians left the country, transferring their works of art to a place of safety. They later formed the basis of the famous "Albertina" collection in Vienna, an exhibition of paintings and drawings which still bears the name of its founder, Archduke Albert.

The French forces of occupation intended to transform the palace into a public hospital. Although the scheme was never executed, the plans of the next purchaser, a surgeon, were fatal. He wanted to have the palace demolished and to sell the building material.

In 1804, Napoleon Bonaparte rescued the palace from total ruin – but not before some sections of the building had already been carted away. The palace became his residence until his defeat at Waterloo in 1815. The king of the Netherlands, William I of Orange-Nassau, became the next owner. He, too, had only a brief period to revel in the splendours of his new stately home, for a few years later, in 1830, the country became independent and Laeken became the residence of Leopold I, the King of Belgium.

The second King of Belgium, Leopold II, who reigned from 1865 to 1907, had a good understanding of architecture. His aim was to increase the international prestige of his country by means of brilliant and unusual schemes. One of his most successful projects was the development of Ostend into a seaside town. He was also responsible for the creation of the fine park at Tervuren. His most important and attractive scheme was his plan to develop the Domain of Laeken into a National Palace for international congresses. However, Leopold's death in 1909 and the outbreak of World War I shortly afterwards, meant that his ambitious project was never completed.

But a number of other significant new improvements were undertaken during his reign. The king had magnificent avenues built from the Domain to the capital; the palace itself was extended, and the park was embellished with a Chinese pavilion and a Japanese tower, relics of the World Exhibition of 1900. The crowning glory was the construction of the greenhouses.

This remarkable complex has remained virtually unchanged since it was first erected – a fact proved by a study of old photographs.

Leopold II's predecessors had toyed with more modest concepts. A Chinese tower with adjoining orangery had been built during the governorship of the Austrian archdukes. Napoleon, too, entertained grandiose plans for modern glasshouses – but these came to nothing as a result of his separation from the Empress Josephine. The orangery as it stands today was built on the instructions of William I of the Netherlands. Leopold I also had a number of greenhouses erected nearby to supply the palace with orchids and pineapples.

But the so-called "glass city", was

built at the behest of Leopold II. He commissioned one of the most important architects of the 19th century, **Alphonse Balat**, to execute his project. The resulting "city of glass" was to become an artistic masterpiece.

Balat made good use of recent technological innovations. During the second half of the 19th century, the techniques required to build metal-framed glass buildings had reached new heights of complexity and perfection, permitting the construction of fairy-tale palaces which combined a romantic enthusiasm for the exotic with a longing for unspoilt nature. The greenhouses represent one of the greatest and best-preserved forms of expression of this typical 19th-century phenomenon.

For the principal extension of the Domain of Laeken, Leopold II engaged the French architect Girault, who had achieved fame by virtue of his buildings for the World Exhibition in Paris. He was responsible for the spectacular "theatre" hothouse.

The Royal Greenhouses consist basically of the palm-tree plateau and the winter garden complex. The two sections are linked to each other by a large gallery. The palm-tree plateau is a playful succession of passages and galleries full of unexpected perspectives. The winter garden complex, however, is constructed according to a strict formal pattern. It consists of a row of large hothouses laid out along a central axis. The *pièce de résistance* is a dome-shaped hothouse which is 25 metres (80 ft) high and with a diameter of 60 metres (192 ft). All the greenhouses are interlinked and allow the visitor to stroll from one end to the other – a distance of 1 km.

The plants in the greenhouses are rare and precious, and harmonise perfectly with the architecture. Many species are of historical importance: most of the 44 species of orange tree in the orangery are more than 200 years old. Bananas and different varieties of palms grow between wall ferns, overshadowed by broad palmyra palms. Ferns and orchids

of indescribable beauty flourish beside camellias which are almost 200 years old, and which formed part of the hothouses' original 19th-century planting. Today they constitute the most valuable collection of their kind in the world.

At the end of the 1970s a face-lift for the "glass city" was embarked upon. The restoration work is now almost complete, and soon the entire complex will shine forth in its original glory once more, to the delight of the royal family and the millions of visitors alike.

It was the wish of Leopold II that the greenhouses should be opened to the general public once a year. For more than a century now, this tradition has been honoured. Each year, at the beginning of May, when thousands of flowers bloom in rainbow colours, the royal greenhouses are opened to the public. More than 100,000 visitors from all corners of the world come to stroll through the sunlit world of plants, enjoying the hospitality of King Baudouin and Queen Fabiola.

Orchids and ferns in the Diana hothouse.

THE ATOMIUM

The **Atomium**, a gigantic model of an iron molecule, can be seen from many districts of the city. It dominates the Heysel Plateau lying to the north of Brussels (Boulevard du Centenaire/Eeuwfeestlaan); access is easiest via the motorway ring.

Combined effort: The futuristic-looking monument, built for the 1958 World Exhibition, was originally designed to symbolise in concrete form the potential of Belgian industry. The decision to build the Atomium resulted from a co-operation agreement between the Belgium metal industry and the Commissioner General responsible for the overall planning of the World Exhibition. In November 1954 André Waterkeyn, a professional engineer and director of the Association of Metal-Working Industries, developed the plans for the unusual structure.

It was his idea to represent the concept of the atom, which forms the basis of all sciences concerned with investigating the constitution of matter. His ambition was to portray the processes which take place in the microcosm in monumental fashion.

With the opening date of the exhibition a strict deadline, it proved possible to construct the Atomium within a period of only four years. It was a huge success among the population. After the Exhibition, the City of Brussels placed a formal request that its new landmark should not be dismantled.

André Waterkeyn had chosen to represent an iron molecule, at a magnification of 165 billion times, as a symbol of the metal industry. In crystal chemistry, it is customary for the structure of crystals to be represented by spheres, whose central point indicates the central position of the atom within the network of crystals. The forces linking the atoms are represented by rods joining the spheres with each other.

The Atomium is based on this fundamental concept of a metal crystal. It consists of nine large spheres, represented in the basic constellation of a symmetrical three-dimensional system; each of the spheres is linked to the others by pipes measuring 3 metres (10 ft) in diameter.

All told, the Atomium is 102 metres (326 ft) high; each of the nine spheres or balls has a diameter of 18 metres (58 ft). Six of them can be visited by the public, who are transported from one sphere to the next by escalators – some of the longest in Europe at 35 metres (112 ft) and housed in the diagonal connecting pipes. The lift linking the bottom sphere with the top one is the fastest in Europe (it travels 5 metres/16 ft per second), enabling the visitor to ascend in only 23 seconds.

From the topmost sphere there is a spectacular view of the entire surrounding area. In the foreground are the buildings of the exhibition centre in the Parc du Cinquantenaire, and an amusement park (Brupark).

The **Brupark** contains – among other attractions – a "Mini Europe", featuring the continent's best-known monuments, constructed on a scale of 1:25; a cinema, with a total of 14 auditoriums; a tropical swimming pool and the Heysel Sports Stadium. After learning about the peaceful uses of atomic power in the lower sphere of the atomium, you can reward yourself by adjourning to the restaurant in the top sphere.

Night lights: The Atomium is a prominent landmark in Brussels, mainly because of its size, but also because of its gleaming aluminium coating. At night the nine spheres are illuminated by a succession of circular light fittings positioned about 1.5 metres apart. The lamps are switched on alternately by means of revolving switches, thus giving the impression that points of light are revolving around the spheres. The illumination is intended to illustrate the revolution of electrons around the centre of each atom of an iron molecule.

Left, impossible to miss: the Atomium.

SET TO BE CAPITAL OF EUROPE

Whenever the name Brussels crops up, it is usually in a discussion about milk quotas, butter mountains or farm prices. And any photographs of the city tend to feature lines of smiling European ministers attempting to conceal the differences aroused by conflicting national interests.

However, agricultural policy is not the only aspect of EC policy to be coordinated from Brussels; community exchange rates are also determined here, as is the defence policy of the Western nations. Brussels is the only place in the world which can boast three diplomatic corps: one at the royal court, one at the European Community, and one at NATO.

Brussels is the secret capital of Europe, a position it has held since the original European Economic Community set up its headquarters here in 1958. It may even become the capital of a future United States of Europe, a dream which will move closer to reality in 1993, when economic barriers within the community are removed. Brussels is already rehearsing for the role. Plans are being discussed for a "Europe City", the centre of which would be an enormous conference complex with space for about 600 delegates.

Brussels can produce a number of arguments to prove why it would be a suitable capital; geographically it lies at the heart of the continent, only 300 km (190 miles) from Paris, 244 km (150 miles) from Bonn, 233 km (145 miles) from London, and 232 km (144 miles) from Amsterdam. Belgium itself can also boast a long tradition of European history; in the past, before they became Belgians, its citizens were the subjects of Burgundy, Spain, Austria, France and the Netherlands.

Today's Belgians are first and foremost either Flemings or Walloons. Even in cosmopolitan Brussels the two communities still cultivate their idiosyncrasies; the age-old Romano-Germanic conflict dividing the city is demonstrated by the bilingual street signs.

All the contradictions which exist in Europe today are concentrated within the city boundaries. Some may feel this should disqualify Brussels from becoming the focal point of a united Europe; nonetheless, the citizens of Brussels have learned to live with the problem.

Virtually everyone living in Brussels speaks two languages – Flemish and French. Many also speak English or German. This fact has made life easier for foreigners coming to live here. Nowadays every fourth person in the city's population of over 1 million is a foreigner. An army of overseas diplomats, officials and businessmen lives in the 19 largely independent communities within the metropolitan area; Germans prefer the South or the Southeast, the Americans have created a "little Texas" in Waterloo, and the French, British and Italians prefer to live in the noble villas of the *quartiers élégants*.

Early supporters: The Belgians were amongst the first to support the European ideal. In 1921 the country took the initiative in establishing an economic union between Belgium and Luxembourg. In 1944, at their instigation, they were joined by the Netherlands. The economic union of the Benelux countries was born. Three years after the end of World War II, the West European Union was founded in Brussels. Originally a defensive alliance between Belgium, France, Luxembourg, the Netherlands and the United Kingdom, the group expanded seven years later to include Germany and Italy.

When the European Coal and Steel Union was formed – the next step along the road to a united Europe – Belgium played a losing hand. Brussels, although nominated as a possible headquarters, was rejected by the Belgians themselves, who favoured the iron-and-steel town of Liège. The third choice, which eventually won the day, was Luxembourg. At the end of the 1950s it was Brussels' turn once again. Since the founder countries of the EEC could not reach agreement on their new capital, the Common Market started out with three bases: Brussels, Luxembourg and Strasbourg.

Brussels, a city which the delegations had learned to appreciate during the preliminary negotiations under the chairmanship of former Belgian Prime Minister Henri Spaak, became the headquarters of the European Commission. This body monitors the implementation of resolutions and presents draft legislation to the Council of Ministers.

A further reason for choosing Brussels as headquarters of the EEC bureaucracy was the fact that the Belgian capital was in a better position to cope with the flood of new citizens than the other metropolises of Europe. Housing shortages were unknown; as a result of the building boom during the 1950s, there were many unoccupied flats.

Today, Brussels has become an expensive place in which to live, to the annoyance of many local citizens who earn less than the city's foreign businessmen and officials. On the plus side, many of them are now employed by the EC, NATO or one of the more than 800 other international associations and 1,300 multinational companies within the city – not to mention the landlords, restaurateurs and traders whose businesses flourish thanks to the high-income "guest workers".

In 1965, when the EEC, the European Coal and Steel Union and EURATOM (the European Atomic Energy Authority) joined together to form the European Community, the existing temporary arrangements were left in operation. This means that even today the EC continues to resemble a huge travelling circus. The Commission sits in Brussels, and – except in April, June and October – the ministers of all EC member nations meet here too.

During the other months the Council of Ministers meets in Luxembourg. The plenary sessions of the European Parliament take place in Strasbourg, whence

Europe's public servants get a special number plate.

most ministers hurry back to Brussels for committee meetings and parliamentary work. The Secretariat General has its headquarters in Luxembourg.

International commuters: What was intended as a temporary measure has become a permanent arrangement. Although it is the subject of constant complaint on the part of the members of the European Parliament, who have to commute constantly between Brussels and Strasbourg, the situation seems likely to die hard. It is evident that the best solution would be for the Parliament to move to Brussels, where its members already spend most of their time. So far, however, no decision has been reached as France and Luxembourg both fear they would then lose their sinecures.

The Commission moved some time ago from the Congress Centre where it was originally housed to the Palais Berlaymont on the Place Robert Schuman. The administrative building, designed in the shape of a star, is already bursting at the seams. A second office

block, the Charlemagne, was erected nearby, but here, too, space is rapidly becoming short. The original community of six nations has expanded to become 12. Denmark, Ireland and the United Kingdom joined in 1973, followed by Greece in 1981 and Spain and Portugal in 1986.

Today, almost 10,000 Eurocrats work for the Commission in Brussels, plus some 2,350 in Luxembourg and 2,600 elsewhere. Approximately one-fifth of the staff employed are translators and simultaneous interpreters.

The European Community has nine official languages. Each official document must be produced in Danish, Dutch, English, French, German, Greek, Italian, Portuguese and Spanish. In 1988 the translators produced some 900,000 pages of text. Quite an achievement, but one which presents no problem to the linguistically gifted citizens of Brussels. In a city in which two languages have always existed side by side, there is plenty of room for nine.

show solidarity.

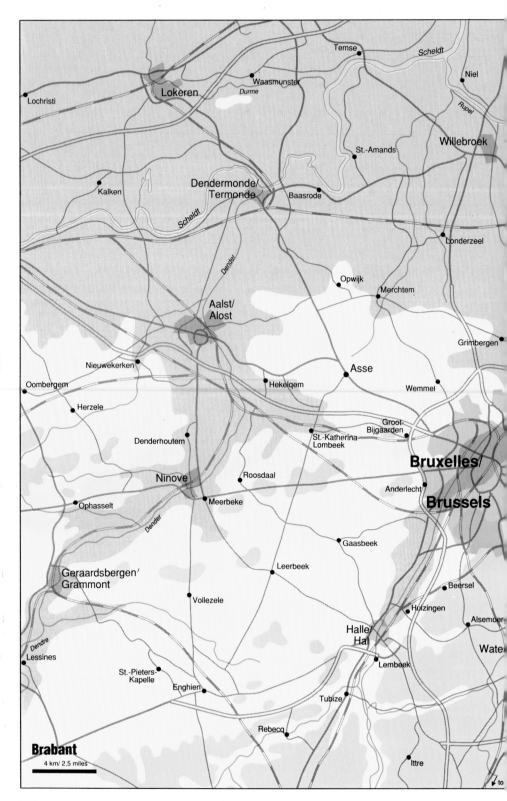

Lochristi

Lokeren

Waasmunster

Durme

Temse

Scheldt

Niel

Rupel

Willebroek

St.-Amands

Kalken

Dendermonde/
Termonde

Baasrode

Scheldt

Londerzeel

Dender

Opwijk

Merchtem

Aalst/
Alost

Grimbergen

Nieuwekerken

Asse

Oombergem

Hekelgem

Wemmel

Herzele

Groot-
Bijgaarden

Denderhoutem

St.-Katherina-
Lombeek

Bruxelles/

Ninove

Roosdaal

Anderlecht

Brussels

Ophasselt

Meerbeke

Dender

Gaasbeek

Geraardsbergen/
Grammont

Leerbeek

Beersel

Vollezele

Huizingen

Alsember

Lessines

Dendre

Halle/
Hal

Wate

St.-Pieters-
Kapelle

Lembeek

Enghien

Tubize

Rebecq

Brabant

Ittre

4 km/ 2,5 miles

to

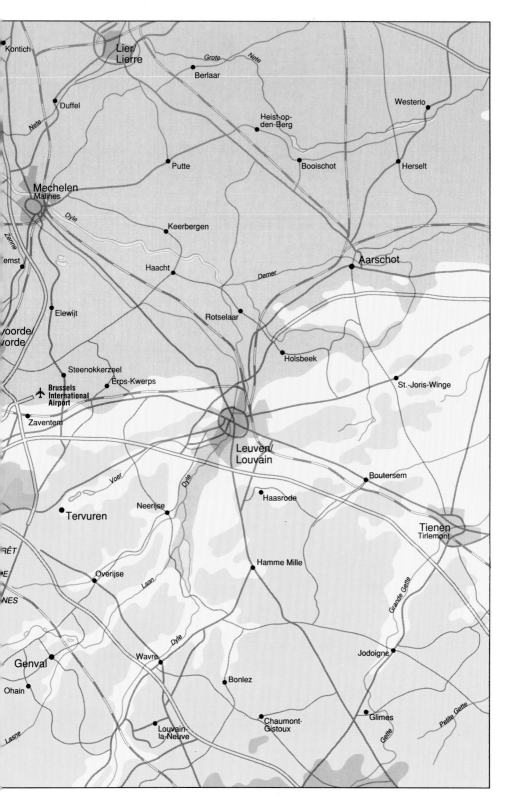

AROUND BRUSSELS

As even the shortest journey through the immediate environs of Brussels will take the traveller through both Flemish and French-speaking areas, a degree of flexibility is required for any exploration of the area around the capital.

The historic little town of **Tervuren** lies only a stone's throw to the southeast of Brussels. It can be reached by taking the Avenue de Tervuren/Tervurenlaan, a boulevard constructed by King Leopold II.

During the 17th and 18th centuries **Tervuren Park**, with an area of more than 200 hectares (500 acres), was the setting for many a glittering court ball. Even today, its manicured lawns, lakes, flowerbeds and ancient trees make it a favourite destination for excursions from the capital. Originally serving as a hunting lodge, the palace was rebuilt by Albert and Isabella at the beginning of the 17th century as a princely residence. It was demolished in 1781 upon the instructions of Emperor Joseph II; only **St Hubert's Chapel**, built in 1617, and the **Palace Stables**, dating from the 18th century, are still standing. Near the chapel you can rent boats for sailing on one of the larger lakes.

Encounter with Africa: Nowadays Tervuren is principally famous as the home of the **Royal Museum of Central Africa** (Musée Royal de l'Afrique Centrale/Koninklijk Museum voor Midden-Afrika). It lies on the edge of the spacious gardens, above the terraces. The core of the exhibition was provided by Leopold II's Congo Collection, displayed in a palatial neo-classical colonial villa designed in part by Henry van der Velde. The original collection grew so quickly that Leopold II commissioned the present building, a

Preceding pages: Leuven Town Hall is a masterpiece of Brabant Gothic. **Left,** you can get to Tervuren by tram.

dignified edifice in the style of Louis XVI, from the French architect Charles Girault. The entrance to the museum lies on the Chaussée de Louvain/ Leuvensesteenweg. On the opposite side of the road, a massive stone elephant points the way.

Inside, exhibits include Central African ivory carvings, dancers' masks, weapons, everyday tools, cult objects and sculptures . Focal point of the main gallery is an exhibition evoking everyday life in the area, emphasising the common elements found in all the local cultures. Another section covers the customs and traditions specific to the individual regions.

The most popular attraction in the museum is a huge pirogue – a boat carved from a single tree trunk – housed in the right wing. The zoological, geological, mineralogical and botanical sections provide a wealth of information about this region of the Dark Continent. Some sections of the building are devoted to displays of beetles, insects, snakes and birds. Children of all ages love the dioramas displaying stuffed crocodiles, antelopes, water buffaloes, rhinoceroses, zebras, lions, giraffes and elephants set in mock-ups of their natural habitats. They'll have to be tolerant of crowds, however: the museum attracts 250,000 visitors each year.

After visiting the museum, it's worth wandering round the town of Tervuren. The historic centre contains some fine examples of 18th and 19th-century townhouses, in particular those in the **Kasteelstraat**. The famous Art Nouveau architect Henry van der Velde lived in **Het Nieuwe Huis** (Albertlaan 3). It was built according to his own designs.

Capuchin monastery: If you are in need of a respite from museums and historic buildings, take a woodland stroll in the **Kapuzinenbos.** Leopold II had a little footpath laid between Tervuren and Jesus-Eik; it's a lovely route, skirting the domain of a former Capuchin monastery. An **Arboretum** was planted here in 1902, harbouring a collection of trees

The roof of Leuven's Town Hall.

from the temperate zones as well as a number of more exotic specimens. Grouped in sections according to their geographical origins – Europe, China and Japan – the main collection covers some 35 hectares (86 acres), whilst species from America extend across a further 65 hectares.

Medieval charm: The university town of **Leuven** (Louvain) lies some 25 km (16 miles) from Tervuren. Built on a succession of attractive terraces, the town has a pleasing aspect; its university, the oldest in the Netherlands, adds to its medieval character.

Leuven was founded as a trading settlement on the site of a fortress occupied by the Vikings, destroyed and later rebuilt by Count Lambert I during the 11th century. Thanks to its strategic position at the upstream navigable limit of the River Dyle and commanding the route linking the Rhine Valley region with the sea, it grew rapidly in importance. In the 12th century Leuven received its charter.

During the 12th and 13th centuries, its weaving industry made it one of the most important cloth manufacturing centres in Europe. Until the end of the 13th century it was the seat of the Counts of Leuven; in 1190 they were created Dukes of Brabant. The monasteries and churches still bear witness to their tremendous wealth.

In 1378 the guildsmen and peasants revolted against the ruling aristocracy; one of the nobles was killed by the mob as he attempted to flee. After reprisals at the hand of the Duke of Luxembourg, many of the weavers emigrated to England where the textile industries were beginning to thrive; the town itself, robbed of its raison d'être, ceded its dominant position to Brussels.

The brewing tradition established during the 18th century has been maintained until the present day, providing an interesting contrast to the remnants of medieval splendour.

The most famous sites in the town of Leuven are grouped round the market

place: the **Town Hall** (Stadhuis) and the 15th-century **Church of St Peter**.

The Town Hall was built by Mathieu de Layens between 1448 and 1463 for the ruling Duke of Burgundy, Philip the Good. The three-storey building has 10 pointed-arched windows per floor and six exquisitely carved octagonal turrets, making it a masterpiece of Brabant Gothic architecture. The niches in the facade not only house statues of famous local personalities, but also illustrate in relief themes in the Old and New Testaments. These reliefs were carved between 1852 and 1872. The facade suffered damage from lightning in 1890, but was subsequently restored to its original form.

Picture of justice: Within the Town Hall itself, visitors may tour the jury room, once furnished by paintings by Dieric Bouts, a famous artist who was a powerful influence on German 15th-century painting, who for a time lived and in 1475 died in Leuven.

Two of the works that used to grace the building are based on a legend of Gottfried of Viterbo, and were designed to serve as a model of fair judgement for the magistrates. One painting depicts the Emperor Otto, who ordered the execution of a nobleman because he was reputed to be in love with the empress. The second painting depicts the widow of the dead man proving by setting fire to herself that her husband was the victim of a calumny on the part of the empress. Upon hearing of her suicide, Otto is supposed to have had his wife burned at the stake (in fact, the historical Otto was never married). Dieric Bouts' pictures are now in the Royal Museum in Brussels.

Directly opposite the Town Hall stands the late Gothic **Church of St Peter** (St-Pieterskerk). The cruciform basilica with ambulatory and chapels was never finished because the foundations proved too unstable.

The exuberantly baroque pulpit, dating from 1742, is adorned with reliefs depicting Peter's denial and the conver-

The Royal Museum of Central Africa in Tervuren.

sion of St Norbert. Three arches completed in 1488 separate the choir from the nave. The church's most valuable treasures are two paintings by Dieric Bouts. The triptych illustrating the *Martyrdom of St Erasmus* is also of note.

The tabernacle is 12 metres (38 ft) high and contains the *Altar of the Last Supper*, in which the Apostles are shown gathered round a table, listening to the words of Christ. The figure of the latter is somewhat larger than those of the onlookers and is the only one looking out of the picture.

The **University** of Leuven has a venerable tradition. The "Studium Generale Louvaniense" was founded on 9 December 1425 by Pope Martin V at the request of Duke Jean IV of Brabant. The 12 teachers were summoned from Cologne and Paris.

Pope Adrian VI, Erasmus of Rotterdam and Justus Lipsius, who founded the discipline of classical and antiquarian studies, were all famous scholars with close links to the University of Leuven. The University printers produced the first Latin edition of Thomas More's *Utopia* (1516).

When the German troops invaded during World War I the entire archives, consisting of over 300,000 books, went up in flames. In May 1940 the new university library – a gift of the United States, and containing 1,000,000 books – was also destroyed.

For many years the University of Leuven was at the centre of the bitter feud between the Flemings and the Walloons. The problem was solved in 1962, when the Catholic university – founded in 1425 – was split into two sections: a Flemish section ("Katholieke Universität Leuven") and a French-speaking one: ("Université Catholique de Louvain").

When the language boundaries were decided by law, the French-speaking citizens of Leuven should theoretically have left the town. In 1969, however, **Louvain-la-Neuve** was built instead – "New Leuven". The division of the uni-

Colonial days recalled by a Congo couple.

versity into two halves was conducted in an equally bureaucratic manner. The books in the university library were shared out between the two universities by allotting those with an even catalogue number to the one, and the odd numbers to the other.

Everyday life in Louvain-la-Neuve is dominated by the university. As in Cambridge, the institution forms an essential part of urban life. With the preferences of residents foremost in mind, the town planner, Raymond Lemaire, set about designing an attractive, open place in which to live. Since the diameter from one side to the other is only about 2 km, it is perfectly feasible to commute between residential, study and leisure centres on foot. The town centre proper contains banks, shops, offices and the station, which forms part of the direct line from Luxembourg and Namur to Brussels.

The **Park Abbey** lies a short distance outside the town; it was founded in 1129 by Premonstratensian monks from Laon.

The character of the present building complex is dominated by the reconstruction work carried out between 1719 and 1730.

Tropical climes: In **Wavre**, some 25 km (16 miles) from Brussels, lies *Walibi*, the largest amusement park in Belgium. On admission, the visitor is transported into a fantasy world. Its tropical swimming pool draws the biggest crowds.

One of the most popular attractions in the entire province of Brabant – visited by approximately 1 million tourists from all over the world every year – is the battlefield of **Waterloo**, situated some 18 km (11 miles) from the capital. It was here that in June 1815 Napoleon suffered a crushing defeat at the hands of the united forces of Prussia and England. It led to his enforced abdication for the second time (*see the chapter The Battle of Waterloo, pages 39–43*).

The best view of the site on which the fighting took place can be gained from the famous "Lion's Hill", the *Butte du Lion*. The visitor must first climb the

A view from Leuven Town Hall.

226 steps to the top of the artificial mound. This was created in 1825 on the spot where the Prince of Orange was wounded whilst commanding an army of Dutch-Belgian troops. The hill takes its name from the cast-iron statue of a lion with its right forepaw placed symbolically on a globe. The statue, 4.5 metres (14 ft) long, 1.5 metres (5 ft) high and weighing 28,000 kg, was erected on a stone pedestal on the mound (soil scraped from the actual battlefield where thousands fell). At the foot of the hill there's a museum devoted to the battle.

The Belle Alliance, the inn in which Napoleon established his quarters, and the lodgings taken over by the Duke of Wellington are still standing. The village church dates from 1855; the numerous inscriptions on its walls recall the fallen multitudes.

Walking country: The region to the south of Brussels is ideal territory for taking extensive country walks. Nestling at the heart of this magnificent landscape lies the town of **Nivelles**, some 35 km (22 miles) from the capital. The town's history is closely linked to that of the **Abbey of St Gertrude**.

Founded in the 7th century, it is the oldest monastery in Belgium. According to legend, following the death of the Frankish ruler Pepin the Elder, his widow Itta retired with their daughter Gertrude to a villa on the hillside overlooking the Thines valley. After the death of her mother and after a declining marriage to Dagobert I, Gertrude founded the monastery, at the instigation of Amand, Bishop of Maastricht. She immediately set about ordering books from Rome and summoned monks from Ireland.

Nowadays, the abbey church is regarded as one of the finest Romanesque sacred buildings in Belgium. The present-day buildings were constructed in various phases from the 11th century onwards.

The porch is flanked by two small towers, the "Tour Madame" and the "Tour de Jean de Nivelles". Several explanations attempt to account for the

Every festival is attended by a brass band.

name of the former, including the theory that it derives from the fact that the abbess had to pass the tower on her way to the Collegiate Church. Others say that the name refers to the long list of abbesses who were in charge of the abbey from its founding in 645 until its secularisation in 1797.

The Tour de Jean de Nivelles contains a copper statue which has become a symbol of the town and which was donated by the Duke of Burgundy, Charles the Bold.

Sadly, after a fire in the church in 1940 only a handful of figures and fragments of architecture survived. There are a number of features worth seeing, however. Various reliefs depicting incidents in the life of Samson adorn the North Door, including a scene in which he is wreathed in garlands of flowers and fighting the lions; another in which Delilah is cutting his hair; and one in which he is blinded by the Philistines.

The South Portal of the church contains a statue of the Archangel Michael with outspread wings. The church consists of a main nave and two aisles, separated from each other by square and cruciform pillars.

The silver reliquary, containing the remains of St Gertrude, was crafted between 1272 and 1298 by Jacquemont de Nivelles and Colard de Duai, in accordance with a design by Jacques d'Anchin. Each year, on the Sunday following the Feast of St Michael, the bones of St Gertrude are carried in procession along a 12-km (8-mile) route through the town and its immediate surroundings. The tradition has been observed since the 12th century.

The village of Nivelles grew up around the abbey and developed into one of the country's most famous weaving towns. It prospered until well into the 17th century, but fell into economic eclipse after the Weavers' Uprising and subsequent emigration.

To the east of Nivelles, the visitor will soon arrive at the ruins of the **Cistercian Abbey of Villiers-la-Ville**, founded in

Leuven Town Hall in the days of yore.

1146 by St Bernard of Clairvaux (1090–1153). Under his guidance the order blossomed and became known as the Order of St Bernard.

The monastery was completely self-sufficient. The monks worked on the land, and the order's estates were soon extensive. During the Netherlands Wars of Independence against the Spanish, some sections of the building complex were destroyed. It was subsequently rebuilt, only to be dissolved under Austrian rule and finally destroyed once more by the French in 1794.

During the 19th century the ruins were sold piecemeal by a private investor. It was not until the 20th century that any interest was shown in the restoration of what remained of the buildings and sculptures, which by this time were in danger of total decay. Today all that is left are Romanesque sections of the earliest buildings and the pointed arches of the abbey church.

Flemish Brabant: Further to the West, 15 km (9 miles) south of Brussels, lies the pilgrimage town of **Halle**. The **Basilica of Our Lady**, formerly known as the Church of St Martin, contains a number of notable treasures. The building itself is a fine example of Brabant Gothic dating from the 14th century. The tower recalls the fortified towers of many Belgian town halls and weavers' halls. Inside, is an extensive collection of sculptures tracing the development of Belgian sculpture across the centuries.

Of particular note are the statue of the Madonna and Child by the West door and the series of Apostles in the choir above the arches. Above the high altar is a wooden statue of Our Lady; carved during the Middle Ages and thought by some to possess miraculous powers. Processions of pilgrims visit the statue of Our Lady at Whitsun and at the beginning of September each year.

In the **Chapelle de Trezgnies** stands an exquisite alabaster altar by Jehan Mone. A Renaissance work dating from 1522, it is adorned with carved reliefs depicting the seven sacraments and vari-

It's not so different today.

ous miniature statues. A marble memorial in the chapel recalls the Dauphin Joachim, a son of Louis XI of France, who died in 1420.

In nearby **Huizingen**, the extensive park covering an area of 91 hectares (225 acres) provides an excellent place for recreation. The magnificent gardens display over 1,200 species of flowers and plants.

From here it is worth making a short detour to the medieval moated castle of **Beersel**, which lies on the wooded green belt surrounding the city of Brussels. The castle has three massive 14th-century towers soaring high above the moat. The entire building was treated to major restoration in 1920.

Southwest of the capital, straddling both sides of the Charleroi Canal, is **Anderlecht**, a community forming part of the Greater Brussels Metropolitan Area. It is famous for its Gothic **Church of St Peter**, dating from the 15th century and boasting a belfry and magnificent frescoes.

In 1521 the famous humanist Erasmus of Rotterdam lived in Anderlecht for five months. The revolutionary philologist and critic vehemently attacked the malpractices of the Church, attempting at the same time to influence public opinion on the matter.

In memory of his stay in the little town, the house in which he lodged has been transformed into a museum. **Erasmus House**, once the property of Pierre Wichman, a canon and friend of Erasmus, occupies the east side of the square dedicated to Jan Dillen. The rooms, adorned with valuable paintings, still give a good idea of the original furnishings of the period. Erasmus's study still contains many of his possessions: his desk, his armchair, and even his inkwell and books. A reliquary holds his death mask and his private seal. The paintings are ascribed to the artists Quentin Metsys, Albrecht Dürer and Hans Holbein.

The North: The town of **Mechelen** is already within the province of Antwerp.

The Astronomical clock in Lier.

220

The Dyle (Dijle), a tributary of the Scheldt, splits into two before the gates of the town.

Mechelen's origins lie far back in history; excavations of pile dwellings have revealed that a small village existed here as long ago as Celtic times. An abbey was founded in 756 by St Rombout; but no further settlement developed until the 11th century.

The town experienced its Golden Age between 1507 and 1530 under the stadtholder Margaret of Austria, regent for the future Charles V. After her successor, Maria of Hungary, transferred her place of residence from Mechelen to Brussels, the town became an archbishopric in 1556 with a primate whose authority extended across the entire Netherlands.

Ring out the bells: The town is dominated by the 97-metre (310-ft) tower of the **Church of St Rombout**, named after the local saint who had founded the first abbey here during the 8th century. The church itself dates primarily from the 14th–15th centuries. The tower, whose construction was begun in 1452, was originally intended to reach a height of 168 metres (538 ft). However, in 1578 William of Orange had the stones reserved for its completion carried away for use in the building of the fortress of Willemstad on the Holandsch Diep.

Two **carillons** with 49 bells hang in the belfry. The ancient art of campanology was revived during this century in Mechelen by Jef Denijn. He established the only school of campanology in the world here. Carillon concerts take place on Monday evenings during the summer months.

The interior of the Church of St Rombout is baroque in style; the use of black, white and red marble indicate the town's former prosperity. A richly decorated choir blends with the three Gothic naves. The baroque high altar, in the shape of a Renaissance arch, is the work of the local sculptor Luc Fayd'herbe. Atop the arch stands the statue of St Rombout. Equally famous is the painting *The Crucifixion* by van Dyck. Twin tombs recall two famous princes of the church: Cardinal Granvelle, the first bishop of Mechelen, and Cardinal Mercier, who died in 1926, and in whose memory a funeral chapel of black marble was erected. Cardinal Mercier was the revered spiritual leader of the Belgian Resistance movement during World War I.

Today, Mechelen is a thriving industrial town in which agriculture nevertheless continues to play a significant role. It is still one of the country's leading spiritual centres.

One of the most important secular buildings of the town is the **Town Hall** on the **Grote Markt**. The latter is the setting for the courthouse as well as a number of Renaissance and baroque buildings. Forming part of the Town Hall complex – which today houses the municipal art collections – is the Weavers' Hall, which was modelled on the one in Bruges.

The **City Courts** were built between

Mass in the Beguine Convent in Lier.

1507 and 1529, which means they are some of the oldest Renaissance-style buildings in the country. They were originally built by Rombout Keldermans as a palace for Margaret of Austria, but later became the residence of Cardinal Granvelle. The Grand Diet convened here from 1616 until 1794. Also of note is **St John's Church**, dating from the 15th century and housing the famous altarpiece *The Adoration of the Magi* by Pieter Paul Rubens.

Mechelen once boasted no fewer than 12 gateways, of which only one – the twin-towered *Brusselpoort* (Brussels Gate) – remains today.

Novels and clocks: Fifteen km (9 miles) to the north, at the confluence of the Greater and Lesser Nete, lies **Lier** (Lierre). This town's main claim to fame lies in two famous sons: **Felix Timmermans** (1886–1947), the writer, and **Louis Zimmer**, the inventor of the astronomical clock.

Timmermans is one of the most significant Belgian folklore writers and painters. In his novels and stories he created a colourful, sometimes rather idealised picture, of life in Brabant – characterised by gentle humour and naive piety. Timmermans described Lier in many of his books and considered it to be the loveliest town in the country. His principal works include *Pallieter*, *The Child Jesus in Flanders*, and *The Gentle Hours of the Virgin Symforosa, the Beguin*.

The **Timmermans-Opsomer House** serves as a memorial to both Timmermans and the portraitist Baron Opsomer (1878–1967), who was also a native of the town.

Part of the ancient fortifications, the **Zimmer Tower**, still remain. The **Astronomical Clock** and the **Planetarium** were both the work of the clockmaker Louis Zimmer.

The clock itself is 4.5 metres (14 ft) high and represents the life's work of the master clockmaker. It was built into the tower in 1930 as a present to the town. Although only 13 dials are visible

Procession of Our Lady in picturesque Mechelen.

from outside, within the tower itself are a further 57 dials showing the time in every part of the world as well as numerous astronomical phenomena, including the phases of the moon and the course of the stars.

In the centre of the town lies the **Grote Markt**. Its principal building miraculously escaped damage during the German occupation of 1914. The **Town Hall** was built in 1740 in the rococo style, with no less than 3,600 windowpanes. Linked to the building is a Gothic belfry dating from 1369. In Lier, too, you can view a number of paintings by famous Dutch and Belgian masters. The **Museum Wuyts van Campen en Baron Caroly** houses works by Rubens, Teniers, Pieter Brueghel and van Dyck as well as contemporary pictures.

Near the market square is the late Gothic **Church of St Gummarus**, dating from the 15th and 16th centuries. The building has some fine stained-glass windows in the choir, depicting Emperor Maximilian of Habsburg and his wife, Mary of Burgundy. The window entitled *The Coronation of the Virgin* in the southern aisle recalls the style of Rogier van der Weyden. The triple-arched choir screen was executed in 1536 in accordance with the designs of F. Mynsheeren and J. Wischavens from Mechelen; it represents the evangelists and the fathers of the church.

Other interesting features include the baroque shrine of St Gummarus, by Dieric Somers, dating from 1682 and containing the relics of the town's patron saint, and the tower, which is 80 metres (256 ft) high and contains a carillon of 48 bells.

Maximilian's son, Philip the Handsome, and the Infanta of Spain, Joanna, the sultry daughter of Ferdinand of Aragon and Isabella of Castile, married in this church in 1496. It was an event of great historical significance, for it marked the beginning of the influence of Spain in the Southern Netherlands.

When Philip died in 1506 after only a year on the Spanish throne, and poor Joanna was deemed insane and kept in confinement by her father (hence her nickname Joanna the Mad), their son Charles only had to wait for his grandfather to die before succeeding as king of Spain. And thanks to the wheeling and dealing of his grandfather, when Maximilian finally passed away in 1519, at the age of 61, Charles was also crowned Holy Roman Emperor of German Nations.

The **Beguine Convent** in Lier is the best-preserved in Belgium. Passing through the entrance the visitor arrives in front of the convent church, an example of Flemish Renaissance architecture dating from the 17th century.

Whichever direction you choose to take, it is easy to escape the bustle of the capital. North, south, east or west - the province of Brabant is a treasure chest of unexpected pleasures. Idyllic little towns, fairy-tale castles and handsome churches all bear witness to the country's colourful history.

Mercator considers his projection on the Place du Petit Sablon.

GETTING THERE

BY AIR

Brussels' international airport, Zaventem, is situated about 14 km (8 miles) northeast of the city centre. It has a tourist information office in the arrival hall, (tel: 722 30 00), and international air services information is provided by Sabena, (tel: 511 90 30). Being a major European city and seat of the European government, Brussels is well served by international airlines. By air, Brussels is an hour from the European cities of Paris, London, Amsterdam and Frankfurt. Sabena, the Belgian airline, has particularly good links with Africa. For the United States, American Airlines flies daily to its gateway cities of Chicago and New York.

A fast and frequent train service (every 20 minutes) connects the airport with Brussels' main railway station. First and last trains are 5.39 a.m. and 11.46 p.m. The journey takes around 20 minutes.

International airline offices in Brussels:
American Airlines, Rue de Trone 98. Tel: 508 77 00.
British Airways, Rue Rogier. Tel: 217 74 00.
Lufthansa, Boulevard Anspach 1. Tel: 218 43 00.
Sabena, Rue Cardinal Mercier 35. Tel: 511 90 30.
Swissair, Place de Brouckère. Tel: 219 03 41.

BY ROAD

Belgium is criss-crossed by international motorways which have the advantage of being toll-free.

Distances to other European cities:
Amsterdam 232 km (144 miles), Paris 302 km (187 miles), Cologne 220 km (136 miles), Ostend 114 km (70 miles), Luxembourg 216 km (134 miles). Coach services from London are operated by Eurolines, London (tel: 071-730 0202). Hoverspeed (tel: 081-554 7061), also operate coach services from the UK to Belgian cities.

BY RAIL

The city's main rail stations are Brussels North (Nord) and Brussels South (Midi). Trains to Paris take 2 hours 27 minutes; to Cologne 2 hours 13 minutes; to Amsterdam 2 hours 25 minutes. In Brussels, rail information is available on tel: 219 28 80. P&O European Ferries in London, (tel: 071-834 2345), are a reliable source of information about boat trains to Brussels from the UK.

BY SEA

Ferry services between the UK and Belgium are operated by North Sea Ferries between Hull and Zeebrugge, tel: Hull 795141; by P&O European Ferries between Dover and Ostend, and Felixstowe and Zeebrugge, tel: 071-834 2345. P&O also operates a Jetfoil service between Dover and Ostend.

TRAVEL ESSENTIALS

VISAS & PASSPORTS

All visitors entering Belgium from countries which are members of the European Community or from Switzerland require a valid personal identity card or passport. Visitors from the United States, Australia, New Zealand, Japan and most other developed countries need only a valid passport; no visa is required. Children under the age of 16 must be in possession of a child's identity card/passport if their names have not been entered in one of their parents' cards.

Travellers bringing in cats or dogs are required to have an official certificate issued by a vet stating that their pet has been vaccinated against rabies. This vaccination must have taken place at least 30 days prior to arrival and be no more than 1 year old (in the case of cats, 6 months).

CUSTOMS

There is no limit as to the amount of foreign currency that can be brought into or taken out of Belgium.

Items for everyday use and those frequently transported by tourists, such as camera and sporting equipment, may be brought into the country duty-free. In addition to these, visitors over the age of 17 from European Community nations are permitted to bring the following items into Belgium duty-free: 300 cigarettes (or 150 cigarillos, 75 cigars or 400 grams of tobacco), 1.5 litres of liquor with an alcoholic content of more than 22 percent (or 3 litres of liquor with an alcoholic content of less than 22 percent, or 5 litres of wine or champagne). Duty-free as well are 1 kilo of coffee, 200 grams of tea, 75 grams of perfume (or 0.37 litres of Eau de Toilette), and gifts which do not exceed 15,800 Belgian Francs in total value.

MONEY MATTERS

The unit of currency in Belgium is the Belgian Franc, with 100 centimes to a franc. There are 100, 500, 1,000 and 5,000 franc notes and 50 centimes, 1, 5, 10, 20 and 50 franc coins in circulation.

Eurocheques can be exchanged for a maximum of 7,000 Belgian Francs per cheque.

As a rule, the exchange offices located in all large railway stations maintain longer hours than the banks.

Most international credit cards are accepted at larger hotels, in numerous gourmet restaurants, many shops and boutiques, some banks and at car rental agencies.

If you should lose your Eurocheque card, report the loss at once to your bank so that measures will be immediately taken to freeze your account. You should also report any lost credit cards at once to the security service in Brussels. They're open day and night and can be reached by dailling 539 15 02.

COMMUNICATIONS

TELEPHONE

The dialling code for Brussels is 02. Current calling rates can be found posted in all telephone booths; booths from which it is possible to make long-distance calls to other countries are marked with international flags. If you want to place a call outside Belgium, first dial 00, then the country code, and finally the number of the party you wish to contact (delete the zero in the area code).

TELEGRAMS

Telegrams can be sent by calling the number 1225, or through the reception at your hotel.

POSTAL SERVICES

The post office located at the South Railway Station is open every day around the clock. Other post offices are open between 9 a.m. and 5 p.m. and are closed on weekends as well as holidays.

NEWSPAPERS & MAGAZINES

Because Belgium is composed of three different language communities, you'll find numerous newspapers. The three most important French newspapers are the *Le Soir, La Libre Belgique* and *La Dernière Heure*. The three most widely distributed Dutch papers are the *Het Laatste Nieuws, De Standaars* and *De Morgen*. The most important German newspaper is the *Grenz-Echo*.

The weekly English language newspaper, *The Bulletin*, keeps the many thousand members of the international community in Brussels informed and up-to-date regarding what is going on in Belgium.

Foreign newspapers and magazines can be purchased at all larger bookshops located in the Brussels city centre.

RADIO & TELEVISION

Aside from the many local stations in Belgium, there are also some national radio stations: RTBF for Walloons, BRT for Flemings and the BRF for those who speak German. RTBF and BRT share the television monopoly; in addition to these channels, in practically all areas of the country it is possible to receive foreign stations if you have cable television.

EMERGENCIES

CHEMISTS

After regular business hours and during holidays you will find the name and address of the nearest chemist on night-duty posted at all chemists.

DOCTORS & HOSPITALS

Visitors from EC countries should obtain a form E111 before leaving home. This entitles them to some free treatment, but does not cover all eventualities. Treatment must be paid for and the cost recovered when you return home. All visitors are advised to take out private medical insurance.

EMERGENCY NUMBERS

In Greater Brussels the **Emergency Service** can be contacted day or night, tel: 479 18 18 and 648 80 00.
Accident aid and the **fire brigade**, tel: 100
Police, tel: 101
The **Red Cross**, tel: 649 50 10
Doctors on emergency call, tel: 479 18 18 and 648 80 00.

LOST & FOUND

There is a Lost & Found office at Brussels airport (Arrivals), tel: 720 91 13 or 722 39 40 (the Visitors' Hall).

For articles lost or left behind on a train, enquire at the nearest train station or at the Quartier Léopold Railway Station, Place du Luxembourg, tel: 218 60 50.

The Public Transportation Lost Property Office is located on Avenue Toison d'Or, tel: 513 23 94.

Lost items may also be reported to the police inspector's office in the respective city district (or community), or at the police headquarters at Rue du Marché au Charbon (in the city centre), tel: 517 96 11.

GETTING ACQUAINTED

GOVERNMENT & ECONOMY

In accordance with the constitution of 7 February 1831, Belgium is a constitutional monarchy passed down through the House of Saxe-Coburg. The legislative branch is composed of the senate and house of parliament, and members of both are elected every four years. The head of state is the monarch; since 1951 this has been King Baudouin.

The executive duties of the government are carried out by the prime minister and his cabinet. After more than 10 years the constitution was reformed in 1970–71 to guarantee autonomy to the country's Dutch, French and German cultural groups.

Brussels is the capital city of the Belgium kingdom and of the province known as Brabant. Due to the fact that the city is situated only a few kilometres north of the "language border" between Flanders (in the North) and French-speaking Belgium (in the South), it is officially bilingual. However, you'll find that in normal, everyday discourse French is by far the most common language used throughout Brussels.

Greater Brussels, the "Agglomération Bruxelloise", is composed of 19 different districts. Each district used to be a separate suburb; over time they have grown and expanded to create a single, built-up area.

Aside from the old part of the city, the districts in Brussels are Elsene, Etterbeek, Evere, Ganshoren, Jette, Koekelberg, Oudergem, Schaarbeek, Sint-Agatha-Berchem, Sint-Gillis, Sint-Jans-Molenbeek, Sint-Joostten-Node, Sint-Lambrechts-Woluwe, Ukkel, Vorst and Watermaal-Bosvoorde.

Brussels is the seat of the European Community Commission as well as of NATO. The city is regarded as an international place of high finance where over thousands of multinational enterprises maintain their headquarters. The majority of business operations are located in the old Flemish part of the city.

For hundreds of years, the textile industry has played an important role in Brussels; wool, upholstery fabrics and the world-famous "Brussels Lace" are all manufactured here. International metal, electrical and chemical concerns have also established themselves in the city.

GEOGRAPHY & CLIMATE

Brussels is situated upon several hills along the Senne, a small tributary of the Scheldt River. During the past century, the river has been completely built over within the centre of the city. The city centre lies at about 15 metres (50 ft) above sea level and the Forest and Duden Parks at about 100 metres (335 ft). Corresponding to its hilly character, Brussels falls naturally into two parts: the Upper and Lower Cities, the latter of which includes the old part of the town.

Belgium enjoys a temperate maritime climate with relatively cool summers and mild winters. In the summer, the average temperature is about 16°C (60°F), in the winter about 3°C (37°F).

WHAT TO WEAR

The people of Brussels are extremely fashion-conscious. Visitors wanting to make it past the doormen of upmarket bars, especially in the Upper City, should take care to don their most elegant clothes. But don't worry if you've left your best clothes at home; in most places you won't feel the least bit uncomfortable or conspicuous in everyday, casual attire.

TIME

Belgium is on Central European Standard Time. Daylight Savings Time lasts from the end of March until late-September (Central European Time plus 1 hour).

ELECTRICITY

The unit of electricity in Belgium is AC 220 volts.

SMOKING

Throughout Belgium smoking is absolutely prohibited in enclosed areas.

TIPPING

You're not obligated to leave a tip in Belgium. Nevertheless, at theatres and cinemas, for example, it is customary to pay a bit more in addition to the price of a programme. Tips are already included in the hotel room price, but here again it is usual to give the maid, doorman and porter a little something extra when you depart if you've stayed for more than a couple of nights. In public lavatories where you are not required to pay anything, it is usual to leave between 10 and 15 Belgian Francs.

BANKS

All banks in Belgium will exchange foreign money. Most open 9 a.m.–noon, and again from 2 p.m. to 4 p.m. Monday–Friday.

BUSINESS HOURS

There are no laws governing the closing times of shops in Belgium. Most businesses maintain hours between 9 a.m. and 6 p.m.; grocery stores often keep their doors open until 9 p.m. Some shops do close for a lunch break between noon and 2 p.m. On Fridays all stores and supermarkets in Brussels are open until 8 or 9 p.m. You'll also find a number of shops which are open around the clock, as well as on Sundays and holidays.

HOLIDAYS

1 January	New Year's Day
March/April	Easter Monday
1 May	Labour Day
May	Ascension Day
	Whit Monday
21 July	National Holiday
15 August	The Day of Mary's Ascension
1 November	All Saints' Day
11 November	Armistice Day
25 December	Christmas Day

If any of these holidays happen to fall on a Sunday, the following Monday is taken off.

GETTING ORIENTATED

Tervuren is only 13 km (8 miles) away from Brussels. It is well worth your while to pay a visit to Tervuren Park, Hubertus Chapel (dating from the 17th century), and especially the Royal Museum of Central Africa (Musée Royal de l'Afrique Centrale), which includes a collection of items from Belgium's past as a colonial power.

The university city **Louvain** (**Leuven**) is also just a short jaunt from Brussels. Be sure to take a stroll through the big market which takes place at the Town Hall (Hôtel de Ville) and St Peter's Church. The university was established in 1425.

Wavre, 25 km (16 miles) from Brussels, is not only a place where children have fun; adults also thoroughly enjoy "Walibi", Belgium's largest amusement park.

The most frequently visited tourist attraction in Brabant is the famous battlefield at **Waterloo**.

Nivelles is 35 km (22 miles) from Brussels. The Abbey of St Gertrude, founded in the 7th century, is situated here. Be sure to look for the "Jean de Nivelles' Tower" in Nivelles, where a famous copper figure sounds out the hour every hour.

A short excursion to the ruins of the Cistercian abbey of **Villers-la-Ville**, located east of Nivelles, is interesting; the abbey was established in the 12th century.

In the pilgrims' city **Halle** 15 km (9 miles) from Brussels, you will find a great variety of art treasures housed in the Notre Dame Basilica.

The abundance of parking places in **Huizingen** make it easy for visitors to leave their cars and step out for a relaxing walk. Not too far away you'll come across Beersel, a medieval moated castle. St Peter's Church (dating from the 15th century) and the House of Erasmus, both located in **Anderlecht**, also draw their share of visitors each year.

In **Mechelen**, north of Brussels, the Rombout Church has a 100-metre (330-ft) high tower and a famous carillon. The Town Hall (Hôtel de Ville) at the Grote Markt, Palace of Justice and Church of St John are all interesting places to visit.

The town of **Lier** is known mainly for two of its citizens: the author and painter Felix Timmermans, and Louis Zimmer, who constructed the first astronomical clock. The Timmermans-Opsomer House and the Zimmer Tower, the Town Hall (Hôtel de Ville), the Church of St Gommarus and the Wuyts van Campen-Caroly Museum are all worth visiting. Belgium's best-preserved Beguine Convent is located in Lier.

GETTING AROUND

The fact that Brussels lies at the centre of Belgium has a particular effect on traffic patterns throughout the country. A motorway runs around the centre of the city, enabling vehicles both access into as well as around the city. The following is a list of distances from Brussels to the most important Belgian cities: Antwerp 48 km (30 miles), Bruges 97 km (61 miles), Charleroi 61 km (38 miles), Ghent 55 km (34 miles), Liège 94 km (59 miles), Mechelen 27 km (17 miles), Mons 67 km (42 miles), Namur 63 km (39 miles), Ostend 114 km (71 miles) and Tournai 86 km (54 miles).

Brussels possesses a well-developed and extensive fast-train network, complimented by bus and tram routes. Timetables are available at the Reception Service, Rue du Marché aux Herbes (Grasmarkt) 61 and at the Tourist Information Office (TIB) in the Town

Hall. You can recognise fast-train stations by the "M" sign (a white "M" against a blue background; "M" stands for Metro). Bus stops are marked with red and white, tram stops with blue and white signs. At bus or tram stops sporting a sign that says *sur demande*, it's necessary to motion for the vehicle to halt and pick you up.

Further information and tickets for the National Belgian Railways (SNCB/NMBS), the Regional Railways (SNCV/MIVB) and for the Brussels Transport Services (STIB) are available in the booking hall at the South Railway Station (Gare du Midi).

Another place to get information and tickets for SNCV is at Rue de la Science 14. Tel: 230 03 30, for STIB on the 6th floor of the Galeries de la Toison d'Or. Tel: 513 30 64, as well as at the Metro Stations Porte de Namur, Rogier and Midi. Tickets can also be purchased in all larger Metro Stations, at numerous newspaper kiosks and in the Town Hall (TIB).

There are several different types of tickets issued, including single-journey tickets, multi-journey tickets which can be used for five or 10 rides, and a 24-hour ticket, good for the city centre.

If you are travelling to an outlying district, in addition to a regular ticket it is necessary to get a "Z" ticket. Transferring doesn't cost anything extra. Passengers caught riding without a valid ticket by the frequent, roaming control authorities are required to pay a hefty fine.

The Brussels Transport Service offers an array of interesting excursions to some of the more beautiful areas around Brussels. They are listed under the heading "Rose des Vents" and are conducted via metro, bus and tram.

AIRPORT

From the Zaventem Airport in Brussels it is possible to fly to various cities within the country. However, because of its relatively small dimensions, the customary and most efficient mode of transportation is the train.

BY RAIL

There are 4 railway stations in Brussels:
Gare du Nord (North Railway Station), Rue du Progrès.
Gare Central (Central Railway Station), located underground at the Boulevard de l'Impéatrice.
Gare du Midi (South Railway Station), Boulevard de l'Europe.
Gare du Luxembourg (Léopold Quarter Railway Station), Place du Luxembourg.

These railway stations are connected to one another by means of a fast-train network. For information regarding train schedules at all four railway stations in Brussels, tel: 219 26 40.

Reservations can be made in advance by calling 219 26 40 or 218 60 50.

Those wishing to transport their vehicle by train should contact Schaerbeek Railway Station, tel: 218 60 50.

BY BUS

There is a bus service operated by the European Railway Association and referred to as the "Europabus", running from various countries to Belgium during the summer months. It will deposit passengers at any of the larger cities in the country.

WATERWAYS

Brussels is situated on the Senne River. It is connected via the Brussels Sea Canal to Antwerp and by smaller canals to Charleroi. These waterways are primarily used for the transportation of goods and in terms of tourism are fairly insignificant.

TRAFFIC REGULATIONS

In Belgium the maximum speed limit in built-up areas is 60 kph (about 37 mph), and on country roads 90 kph (about 55 mph). On motorways and dual carriageways this limit rises to 120 kph (75 mph). The use of seatbelts is mandatory. In general, the rule "right before left" applies to most situations, meaning that the vehicle to your right usually has the right of way. It is illegal for children under the age of 12 to sit in the front passenger seat if there is room in the back seat. Motorcyclists and moped riders are obligated by law to wear helmets and parking is not permitted in places where the curb is marked with a yellow stripe.

Hazard triangles must be carried in the vehicle at all times. Trams always have the right of way. Foreigners caught defying traffic regulations are required to pay any fines incurred on the spot.

Most filling stations in Belgium offer unleaded petrol. (Just ask for Loodvrij or Essence sans plomb.)

Breakdown services:
Touring Secours. Tel: 233 22 11
RACB. Tel: 736 59 59
VAB. Tel: 219 28 80

TAXIS

Taxis can be ordered from the central dispatch service of the following companies:
ATR. Tel: 242 22 22.
Autolux. Tel: 512 31 23.
Taxis Orange. Tel: 513 62 00.
Taxis Verts. Tel: 511 22 44.

WHERE TO STAY

HOTELS

Visitors to Brussels will find a large selection of hotel accommodation in every price range. Many of the larger hotels offer special bargain rates for weekend stays. In the official hotel guide you'll find a complete list, including addresses and prices, of the 120 or so hotels in the city. This guide is available at the Reception Service, Rue du Marché aux Herbes (Grasmarkt) 61, and in the Town Hall (TIB). It is also possible to book accommodation here. Hotels are obligated to post their room rates at the reception desk and are permitted to charge only these prices on your final bill.

The TIB Accommodation Service and BRT (Belgian Tourist Reservations) will gladly book a hotel room for you. It is also possible to reserve a hotel room at the last minute. They can be contacted at Postbus 41, B-1000 Brussels 23. Tel: 230 50 29. Telex 65 888 btr b.

THE BEST HOTELS

Amigo, Rue de l'Amigo. Tel: 511 59 10
183 rooms; luxury-class hotel.
Brussels Hilton, Boulevard de Waterloo 38. Tel: 513 88 77
373 rooms; a luxury-class hotel with 4 restaurants, a bar and conference facilities. All rooms have a view of the city and a park.
Sheraton, Place Rogier. Tel: 219 34 00
476 rooms; a luxury-class hotel with 2 restaurants, a piano lounge, swimming pool, sunbathing terrace and fitness studio. Rooms contain a colour television and telephone; there is a breakfast buffet each morning.
Président World Trade Center, Boulevard E. Jacqmain. Tel: 217 20 20
305 rooms; a brand-new luxury-class hotel with conference facilities. All rooms have a mini-bar, colour television set, radio, telephone, sauna and solarium.
Hotel Metropole, Place de Brouckère 31. Tel: 218 02 20
410 rooms; a luxury-class hotel rich in tradition. It has a restaurant, bar and fitness floor. All rooms come with a colour TV, telephone and mini-bar; a breakfast buffet is offered each morning.
Pullman Astoria, Rue Royale 103. Tel: 217 62 90
112 rooms; a comfortable hotel with its own restaurant and piano lounge. Each room has a colour TV, mini-bar, radio and telephone.

ADDITIONAL LUXURY CLASS HOTELS

Arcade Stephanie, Avenue Louise 91. Tel: 539 02 40 (142 rooms).
Château du Lac, Genval, Avenue du Lac 87. Tel: 735 00 00 (38 rooms).
Hyatt Regency Brussels, Rue Royale 250. Tel: 217 12 34 (315 rooms).
Jolly Hotel Atlanta, Boulevard Adolphe Max 7. Tel: 217 01 20 (244 rooms).
Royal Windsor Hotel, Rue Duquesnoy 5. Tel: 511 42 15 (292 rooms).
Tagawa, Avenue Louise 321. Tel: 640 80 29 (77 rooms).

GOOD HOTELS

Queen Anne, Boulevard Emile Jacqmain. Tel: 217 16 00
57 rooms; located close to the Grand' Place.

Rooms each have a colour television and telephone; there is a breakfast buffet offered each morning.

Albert I, Place Rogier 20. Tel: 217 22 50
253 rooms; a luxurious hotel located not far from the North Railway Station, with conference facilities and a tavern. Rooms come with a mini-bar and colour TV; there is a breakfast buffet served daily.

Arenberg, Rue d'Assaut 15. Tel: 711 07 70
158 rooms; near the Central Railway Station. Rooms with bathroom/shower/WC.

Avia, Boulevard d'Anvers. Tel: 217 55 88
33 rooms. Offers special group rates.

Chambord, Rue de Namur 82. Tel: 513 41 19
69 rooms; a comfortable hotel with a piano lounge. All rooms have a bathroom/WC, telephone, colour television and mini-bar; some have a balcony.

Diplomat, Rue Jean Stas 32. Tel: 537 42 50
68 rooms; a modern hotel located in the midst of the elegant shopping area along the Avenue Louise. Rooms with bathroom/ shower/WC.

Ramada, Chaussée de Charleroi 38. Tel: 538 90 14
202 rooms; all rooms have colour TV, mini-bar, telephone and air-conditioning.

Siru, Place Rogier. Tel: 217 75 80
101 rooms; a newer hotel situated not far from the North Railway Station with restaurant and conference facilities. The rooms have been furnished and decorated by different artists and have either a bathroom/WC, or shower/WC, telephone, radio and colour television.

Holiday Inn Brussels Airport, Diegem, Holidaystraat 7. Tel: 720 58 65 (288 rooms).
Novotel Brussels Airport, Diegem, Olmenstraat 1. Tel: 720 58 30 (160 rooms).

REASONABLY PRICED HOTELS

Arcades, Rue des Bouchers 36. Tel: 511 28 76 (17 rooms).
Belmont, Rue du Marché 17. Tel: 217 47 03 (30 rooms).
Derby, Avenue de Tervuren 24. Tel: 733 08 19 (28 rooms).
Des Esperonnes, Rue des Esperonnes 1. Tel: 513 53 66 (12 rooms).
Du Congrès, Rue du Congrès 42. Tel: 217 18 90 (37 rooms).
Gascogne, Boulevard Adolphe Max 137. Tel: 217 69 62 (18 rooms).

Grande Cloche, Place Rouppe. Tel: 512 61 40 (45 rooms).
Ruche Bourse, Rue Grétry 1. Tel: 218 58 87 (16 rooms).
Sainte Catherine, Rue Joseph Plateau 2. Tel: 513 76 20 (234 rooms).
Sabor d'Or, Boulevard d'Anvers 5. Tel: 217 69 48 (40 rooms).
Van Belle, Chaussée de Bergense Mons 39. Tel: 521 35 15 (137 rooms).
Vendome, Boulevard Adolphe Max 98. Tel: 218 00 70 (92 rooms).

CAMPGROUNDS

There are no campgrounds in Brussels itself. However, the following three sites are located in places quite near the city:

Huizingen, 13 km (8 miles) south of Brussels, Provinciaal Domein 6. Tel: 380 14 93.
Neerijse, 20 km (13 miles) east of Brussels, Kamstraat 46. Tel: 016/47 76 36.
Wezembeek-Oppem, 10 km (6 miles) east of Brussels. Warandeberg. Tel: 152/782 10 09.

YOUTH HOSTELS

Breughel Youth Hostel, Heilige Greeststraat 2, 1000 Brussels. Tel: 511 04 36.
Accommodation for Young People, Acotra, Rue de la Montagne 38, 1000 Brussels. Tel: 513 44 80 and 513 44 89.
Maison International des Etudiants (International Students' Hostel), Chaussée de Wavre 205, 1000 Brussels. Tel: 648 85 29.

FOOD DIGEST

The people of Belgium have the reputation of possessing especially fine tastebuds and this fact is attested to by the large number of excellent restaurants, particularly in Brussels. (You'll find numerous establishments which specialise in French cuisine.) The "Gourmet" dining guide is available at the

Tourist Information Centre (TIB); this booklet contains a list of restaurants along with their addresses, hours, prices and particular house specialities. Belgians usually have their lunch sometime between noon and 2 or 3 p.m.; dinner is customarily eaten at any time between 6 p.m. and midnight.

Brussels is especially well-known for its fresh mussels, oysters and lobster. Fish dishes made from sole, cod and turbot are prepared in a variety of tasty ways. Belgian chicory is also quite renowned, frequently in the form of a kind of casserole. Two more delicious dishes which can be recommended are red cabbage prepared in the Flemish style and asparagus from Mechelen.

Beer – and there are well over 200 different kinds to choose from! – is the beverage most typically consumed in Belgium. However, the wine, primarily imported from France, is also recommended.

By the way, a "café" is not necessarily the place to find a cup of coffee. Generally speaking, a café refers to a pub where you can get a relatively inexpensive bite to eat – for example, a bowl of soup, a sandwich or a piece of home-made quiche. Coffee and tea are served in special tea rooms (Salon de Thé, Cafeteria). In the city centre along the boulevards around the opera house and stock exchange, as well as around the Grand' Place, there are numerous places to sit down and enjoy a waffle, slice of pie or cake, or a cold drink. In addition to these eateries, all larger hotels in the city serve various beverages and snacks.

FIRST-CLASS RESTAURANTS

La Truffe Noire, Boulevard de la Cambre, 1050 Brussels. Tel: 640 44 22. Open: noon–2 p.m. and 7 p.m.–midnight.

Bruneau, Avenue Broustin 73, 1080 Brussels. Tel: 427 69 78. Open: noon–1.45 p.m. and 7 p.m.–9.45 p.m. Closed: Tuesday evening and Wednesday.

Claude Dupont, Avenue Vital Riethuisen 46, 1080 Brussels. Tel: 427 54 50. Open: noon–2.30 p.m. and 7 p.m.–9.30 p.m. Closed: Monday and Tuesday.

La Maison du Cygne, Rue Charles Buls 2 (at the Grand' Place). Tel: 511 82 44.. Open: 12.15 p.m.–2.30 p.m. and 7 p.m.–10.30 p.m. Closed: Saturday afternoon and Sunday.

Les 4 Saisons (located in the Royal Windsor Hotel), Rue de l'Homme Chrétien 2, 1000 Brussels. Tel: 511 42 15. Open: noon–2 p.m. and 7 p.m.–12.30 a.m.

Villa Lorraine, Avenue du Vivier d'Oie 75, 1180 Brussels. Tel: 374 31 63 or 374 25 87. Open: noon–3 p.m. and 6 p.m.–9.30 p.m. Closed: Sunday.

L'Ecallier du Palais Royal, Rue Bodenbroeck 18–20, 1000 Brussels (at the Place du Sablon). Tel: 512 87 51 or 511 99 50.. Open: noon-2.30 p.m. and 7 p.m.–11 p.m. Closed: on Sunday and holidays.

Romeyer, Chaussée de Groenendael 109, 1990 Hoeilaart. Tel: 657 05 81. Open: noon–3 p.m. and 7 p.m.–10 p.m. Closed: on Sunday evening and Monday.

Comme Chez Soi, Place Rouppe 23. Tel: 512 29 2. Art Nouveau decor; the speciality here is oysters served with chicory.

GOOD RESTAURANTS

Chez Flo, Rue au Beurre 25. Tel: 512 31 52. Entertainment, 120 seats; the specialty here is burbot served with vegetables.

La Belle Maraîchere, Place Ste-Catherine. Country-style decor; the speciality is seafood.

Chez Léon, Rue des Bouchers. Tel: 513 08 48. The speciality is seafood.

L'Ecailler du Palais Royal, Rue Bodenbroek 18–20. Tel: 512 87 51. Elegant decor, seating for 65; specialities are fish and seafood.

La Maison de Thailande, Rue Middelbourg 22. Tel: 672 26 57. Luxurious decor, seating for 35; Thai specialities.

Le Mouton d'Or, Petite Rue des Bouchers 21. Tel: 511 88 39. Country-style decor; the specialities here are salt-water fish dishes.

Mamma Mia, Rue Antoine Dansaert 158. Tel: 512 36 76. Country-style decor, seating for 80; Italian cuisine.

Le Paon, Grand Place 35. Tel: 513 35 82. The building dates back to the 17th century, seating for 100; the speciality here is rabbit.

Le Paradoxe, Chaussée d'Ixelles 329. Tel: 649 89 81. With a piano lounge, seating for 100; vegetarian dishes are the speciality here.

La Rose, Rue du Marché aux Herbes 97. Tel: 512 52 66. Country-style decor, seating for 60; the specialities are rabbit and sole.

La Vieux Saint-Martin, Place du Grand Sablon 38. Tel: 512 64 76. Country-style decor, seating for 75; specialises in steak.

BISTROS

L'Archiduc, Rue Antoine Dansaert 6. Tel: 512 06 52.

La Bécasse, Rue de Tabora 11. Tel: 512 13 95.

Fallstaff, Rue Henri Maus 25. Tel: 511 98 77.

La Fleur en Papier Doré, Rue des Alexiens 53. Tel: 511 16 59.

A l'Image de Notre Dame, Rue du Marché aux Herbes 6. Tel: 511 13 96.

La Mort Subite, Rue Montagne aux Herbes Potagères 7. Tel: 513 13 18.

De Ultieme Hallucinatie, Rue Royale 316, 1210 Brussels. Tel: 217 06 14.

HOTEL RESTAURANTS

The following excellent hotel restaurants are highly recommended to all gourmets:

Ambassade Hotel
Arenberg Hotel
Astoria Hotel: the "Palais Royal"
Bedford Hotel
Hilton Hotel: "En Plein Ciel" and the "Café d'Egmont"
Hyatt Regency Hotel: "Hugo's Rotisserie"
Metropole Hotel: "Z'Alban Chambon"
Novotel Hotel: "Novotel Grill"
Ramada Hotel: "Le Bouquet"
Royal Windsor Hotel: "Les Quatre Saisons"
Sheraton Hotel: "Comte de Flandres" and "Le Pavillon"

CULTURE PLUS

The daily newspapers contain information about entertainment in Brussels. Visitors can reserve tickets for the opera, concerts and theatre productions at the Brussels Tourist Information Centre (TIB).

In Brussels there are theatres which perform dramatic pieces in both the French and Dutch languages. Most of the important concerts take place in the Palais de Beaux Arts. Opera and ballet productions are performed at the Théâtre Royale de la Monnaie (the National Opera House), the most famous stage in Brussels. Puppet shows played out in the Brussels dialect have been performed at the Toone Puppet Theatre since 1830.

THEATRES

Beursschouwburg, Rue Auguste Orts. Tel: 513 82 90.

Centre Bruegel, Rue Haute 243. Tel: 511 04 09.

Communauté Française, Passage 44. Tel: 218 25 99.

Espace Sygne, Rue du Maelbeek 3. Tel: 217 63 95.

Halles de Schaerbeek, Rue Royale 22a. Tel: 218 00 31.

Jeune Théâtre de l'ULB, Av. Paul Héger 22. Tel: 640 69 27.

Kamertoneel, Place de la Chapelle 8. Tel: 511 80 75.

Maison du Spectacle de la Bellone, Rue de Flandre 146. Tel: 513 33 33.

Nouveau Théâtre I, Rue de Viaduc 122. Tel: 640 84 37.

Nouveau Théâtre II, Place des Martyrs 22. Tel: 640 84 37.

Théâtre Molière, Galerie de la Porte de Namur 22. Tel: 513 58 00.

Théâtre National, Centre Rogier. Tel: 217 03 03.

Théâtre Poème, Rue d'Ecosse 30. Tel: 538 63 57.

Théâtre Royal des Galeries, Galerie du Roi. Tel: 512 04 07.

Théâtre Royal du Parc, Rue de la Loi 3. Tel: 511 41 47.

Théâtre Toone VII, Petite Rue des Bouchers 21. Tel: 511 71 37.

Théâtre de la Balsamine, Avenue F. Marchall 1. Tel: 733 23 02.

MUSIC & BALLET

Théâtre Royal de la Monnaie, Place de la Monnaie. Tel: 218 12 02.

Cirque Royal, Rue de l'Enseignement 81. Tel: 218 20 15.

Ancienne Belgique, Boulevard Anspach 114. Tel: 512 59 86.

Forest National, Avenue du Globe 36. Tel: 345 90 50.

Halles de Schaerbeek, Rue Royale Ste-Marie 31. Tel: 219 07 58.

Palais des Beaux-Arts, Rue Ravenstein 23. Tel: 512 50 45.

MUSEUMS

A wide variety of art objects originating in numerous different epochs are housed in over 70 museums in Brussels. Most museums are open daily except Monday, from 10 a.m.–5 p.m. and offer reduced entrance fees to groups, children, senior citizens, etc.

The following is a list of some of the more important museums:

Atomium, Boulevard de Centenaire. This museum was built on the occasion of the 1958 World Exhibition and symbolises an atom in the form of an iron crystal molecule, enlarged 165 billion times in a cubically-centred system. The exhibit displays the development of nuclear energy. Hours: 9.30 a.m.–6 p.m. daily; the sphere with a view is open daily from 1 May–31 August, 9.30 a.m.–10 p.m.

Autoworld, Parc du Cinquantenaire, Palais Mondial. The vehicles on display here date from between about 1886 and 1960. Hours: 10 a.m.–5 p.m. daily 1 November–31 March; 10 a.m.–6 p.m. daily 1 April–31 October.

The Beer Museum (Musée de la Gueuze), Rue Gheude 56. Gueuze beer is brewed here from a special recipe which has been handed down through the ages from generation to generation. Hours: 11 a.m.–2 p.m. and by appointment Saturday, from 15 October–15 May.

The Museum of Brewing, Grand' Place 10. Real brewing as it was done in the 17th century. The history, theory and techniques of beer brewing in Belgium. Hours: 10 a.m.–noon and 2 p.m.–5 p.m. Monday–Friday, 10 a.m.–noon Saturday.

The Brueghel Museum, Rue Haute. House of Pieter Brueghel the Elder, containing a display of paintings, documents and keepsakes of this famous painter who died in Brussels. Hours: 2 p.m.–6 p.m. Wednesday–Saturday.

Charlier House (Musée Charlier), St.-Josse, Avenue des Arts 16. The villa of internationally known Art Nouveau-style architect Victor Horta, furnished with silver,

furniture, etc. In the house are also paintings by Ensor and Meunier, among others. Hours: 1 p.m.–5 p.m. Monday–Friday.

Comics Museum (**Centre Belge de la Bande Dissinée**), Rue des Sables 20. A wonderfully funny museum located in a renovated house designed by Horta. Fun and enjoyment for both the young and the young at heart. Hours: 10 a.m.–6 p.m. Tuesday–Sunday.

The Railway Museum (**Musée du Chemin de Fer Belge**), Gare du Nord (North Railway Station), Rue du Progrès 76. An exhibit of Belgian trains. Hours: 9 a.m.–4.30 p.m. Monday–Friday.

The Fire Brigade Museum (**Musée du Feu**), Rue Simons 23. Hours: 10 a.m.–4 p.m. each weekend from May–October.

The Flemish Folklore Museum (**Musée de la Vie Flamande à Bruxelles**), Rue des Poissoniers 13. The Flemish tradition in Brussels. Hours: 9 a.m.–4.30 p.m. Monday–Friday.

Local Museum of the City of Brussels (**Musée Communal**), Grand' Place. There are exhibits of the historical and archaeological development of the city, collections of porcelain and stoneware as well as Manneken Pis' clothing closet. Hours: 10 a.m.–12.30 p.m. and 1.30 p.m.–5 p.m. Monday–Friday. The museum closes at 4 p.m. between 1 October–31 March.

The Woluwe St Lambert Local Museum (**Musée Communal de Woluwe-St Lambert**), Woluwe-St-Lambert, Rue de la Charette 40. Hours: 9 a.m.–noon and 2 p.m.–5 p.m. Monday–Friday.

The Horta Museum (**Musée Horta**), Rue Américaine. The former house and office of the famous Art Nouveau-style architect Victor Horta containing an exhibit of photographs of his most well-known architectural feats. Hours: 2 p.m.–5 p.m. Tuesday–Saturday.

The Museum of Musical Instruments (**Musée Instrumental**), Place du Petit Sablon 17. Here there are over 5,000 musical instruments collected from every country in the world and all periods in history. Hours: 2.30 p.m.–4.30 p.m. Tuesday, Thursday, Saturday, 2 p.m.–4 p.m. Wednesday, and 10.30 a.m.–12.30 p.m. Sunday.

The International Press Museum, Chaussée de Louvain 696. A nearly overwhelming collection of over 150,000 magazines from all over the world and from just about every era. Hours: 9 a.m.–noon and 2 p.m.–5 p.m. Monday–Friday. Closed: 15 July–31 July.

The Children's Museum (Musée des Enfants), Ixelles, Rue du Bourgmestre 15. An altogether fascinating museum for children. Hours: 2.30 p.m.–5.30 p.m. Wednesday, Saturday and Sunday.

The Museum of the Cinema (Musée du Cinéma), Hortastraat 9. Includes an extensive collection of equipment from the era of silent films. Hours: 5.50 p.m.–10.30 p.m. daily and by appointment.

The Royal Army and Military History Museum (Musée Royal de l'Armée et d'Histoire Militaire), Parc du Cinquantenaire. Weapons and armaments from the 7th to the 18th centuries. In the aviation section there's an exhibit of the history of military aviation and of parachuting from 1912 to the present day. Hours: 9 a.m.–noon and 1 p.m.–4 p.m. Tuesday–Sunday.

The Royal Museum of Fine Arts (Musée Royaux des Beaux-Arts), Rue de la Régence 3 and Place Royale 1. One of the most famous museums in the world with an emphasis on paintings, graphics and sculpture dating from the 15th, 16th and 17th centuries. Art treasures from the 20th century (the entrance is at Place Royale), in the Musée d'Art Moderne, can be viewed from 10 a.m.–1 p.m. and 2 p.m.–5 p.m. Tuesday–Sunday. The other part of the museum (the entrance is on the Rue de la Régence), the Musée d'Arts Anciens, is open 1 p.m.–7.30 p.m. Tuesday–Friday and 10 a.m.–5 p.m. Saturday and Sunday.

The Royal Museum of Art and History (Musée Royaux d'Art et d'Histoire), Parc du Cinquantenaire. Works from Roman, Greek and Egyptian antiquity; relics from the Roman and Frankish eras in Belgium. Hours: 9.30 a.m.–12.30 p.m. and 1.30 p.m.–4.45 p.m. Tuesday–Friday and 9.30 a.m.–3.30 p.m. Saturday and Sunday. Different sections are open alternately on odd and even days.

The Royal Institute of Natural Sciences (Institut Royal des Sciences Naturelles de Belgique), Rue Vautier 29. Unusual collections of minerals, fossils and skeletons provide an insight into mineralogy, zoology and prehistory in Belgium. Hours: 9.30 a.m.–4.45 p.m. daily.

The Royal Museum of Central Africa (Musée Royal de l'Afrique Centrale), Chaussée de Louvain 13. An exhibit of African culture. Hours: 9 a.m.–5.30 p.m.; between 16 October–15 March 10 a.m.–4.30 p.m.

The Organ Museum (Musée d'Orgues de Kermesse), Schaerbeek, Rue Waelhem 104. There are a number of lovely, original kermis organs here to admire. Hours: by appointment only. Tel: 241 27 91.

The Post Museum (Musée des Postes et Télécommunications), Place du Grand Sablon. An extensive collection of stamps from Belgium as well as from other countries. In addition to this, the entire, general evolution of the post and telecommunication systems is explained in conjunction with a display of various telecommunications equipment. Hours: 10 a.m.–4 p.m. Tuesday–Saturday, 10 a.m.–12.30 p.m. Sunday.

The Brussels Town Hall (Hôtel de Ville), Grand' Place. Visitors can view the reception rooms and offices of the councillors. The walls of these chambers are hung with priceless woven tapestries from Brussels, dating from the 16th, 17th and 18th centuries. Hours: 9.30 a.m.–5 p.m. Tuesday–Friday, 10 a.m.–4 p.m. Sunday. Visitors are obliged to join a tour.

The Toy Museum (Musée du Jouet), Anspach-Center, Boulevard Anspach 36. Hours: 10 a.m.–6 p.m. daily.

The Toone Theatre Museum (Musée du Théâtre Toone VII), Petite Rue des Bouchers. On the third floor of the famous Toone Marionette Theatre there is an assortment of old puppets, posters and manuscripts relating to the history of the theatre. Hours: open during theatre intermissions.

The Wax Museum (Musée de Cire), Place de la Monnaie. Life-sized wax figures commemorating 2,000 years of history. Hours: 10 a.m.–6 p.m. daily.

The Resistance Museum (Musée de la Résistance), Anderlecht, Rue Van Lint 14. Exhibits depicting the Belgian resistance against the occupying forces of both World War I and II. Hours: 9 a.m.–noon and 1 p.m.–4 p.m. Tuesday–Thursday.

Wiertz Museum (Musée Wiertz), Ixelles, Rue Vautier 62. A fascinating glimpse into the studio and paintings of the Romantic artist Antoine Wiertz. Hours: 10 a.m.–6 p.m. Tuesday–Sunday.

BOOKSHOPS

Librairie de Rome, Avenue Louise 50. Hours: 9 a.m.–8 p.m. Also open on Sunday; books and magazines.
Librairie Internationale, Boulevard Adolphe Max 99. Open 24 hours a day; books and magazines.
Librairie Japonaise, Rue du Fossé aux Loups 28. Also open on Sunday; books and magazines.
Librairie 44, Passage 44. Books and magazines.

LIBRARIES

The Albert I Royal Library, Monts des Arts. Here you'll find a selection of diverse manuscripts, prints and book covers which afford a good overview of the history of books from antiquity up until the present time. Hours: 2 p.m.–5 p.m. Monday, Wednesday, Saturday.
Bibliotheca Wittockiana, Rue Bernel 21. Tel: 770 53 33.
Bibliothèque du Parlament, Palais de la Nation, Place de la Nation. Tel: 519 81 11.
Bibliothèque Régionale de Woluwe-Saint-Lambert, Rue Saint-Henri 62. Tel: 735 28 24.
Bibliothèque Publiques Communales d'Uccle, Uccle Centre, Rue du Doyenné 84. Tel: 345 86 00.
Bibliothèque de l'Université Libre de Bruxelles, Avenue F. Roosevelt 50. Tel: 642 23 84.

CINEMAS

Moviegoers will find the greatest concentration of cinemas in two different areas: in the Lower City, between the Place Rogier and the Place de la Bourse, and in the Upper City near the Porte de Namur and the Avenue de la Toison d'Or.

Many films are shown in the original. Usually French movies do not have subtitles, but English ones always do.

FESTIVALS & EXHIBITS

The following events take place at the same time each year:

JANUARY

Automobile Exhibition (Autosalon), every two years
Film Festival (at the Congress Palace)

FEBRUARY

Carnival (in the city centre)
Antique Fair (at the Palace of Fine Arts)

MARCH

Belgian Indoor Tennis Championships (in the Exhibition Park)
The Holiday, Tourism and Leisure Time Fair
The International Book Fair (at the International Rogier Centre)

APRIL

Son et Lumière at the Grand' Place

MAY

Open door at the Royal Greenhouses in Laeken
The Queen Elisabeth International Music Competition (in the Palace of Fine Arts), every two years
Foire Commerciale (Trades Fair)
Petro-Mobile-Oldtimer-Rallye
The International Comic Festival

JUNE

The 20 km Brussels Run
Reconstruction of the Battle of Waterloo
European Festival

JULY

Ommegang (Grand' Place). Originally a religious procession dating back to the 14th century, today a carnival-like parade.
National Holiday (21 July, celebrated with festivities in the park)
Foire du Midi (a large, annual market which takes place at the South Railway Station)

AUGUST

Erection of the *Meiboom* (Grand' Place) **"Tree of Joy"**, accompanied by procession.

The Brosella Folk and Jazz Festival (Théatre de Verdure)

The Flower Carpet (Grand' Place), every two years

The International Carillon Competition in Mechelen

SEPTEMBER

The Eddy Merckx Grand Prix (La Cambre Forest)

The Brussels Marathon

The Brueghel Festival Days

The Food Fair and Eureka Hobby Fair (Exhibition Park)

Ommegang (Grand' Place)

NOVEMBER

Brussels International Show Jumping Competition (Exhibition Park)

DECEMBER

The Christmas Market(Zavel)

The Crib and Christmas Tree Display (Grand' Place)

CONFERENCES

The Brussels Tourist Information Association (TIB), Hôtel de Ville (Town Hall), Grand' Place. Tel: 513 89 4. Maintains a special service called "Service Congrès", which will provide interested parties with pertinent information regarding conference facilities.

Information regarding conferences themselves is available from the "Bruxelles-Congrès", a department of the Brussels International Conference Centre, Parc des Expositions, Place de Belgique. Tel: 478 48 60.

You can get in touch with the International Press Centre, Boulevard Charlemagne 1. Tel: 736 80 15.

The National Congress Service, Brussels Convention Centre, Coudenberg 3, can be reached by telephoning 513 41 30, and the Expo Rogier Centre, Rue du Progrès 32. Tel: 218 50 91.

NIGHTLIFE

Night spots in Brussels change hands frequently and are often only in existence for a short time. Because of this, it's wise to phone before you set your heart on spending the evening at a certain place, just to make sure that when you get there, you won't find the door locked and the place dark.

The bars and discos located in the Lower City are on the whole more relaxed and enjoyable than those in the Upper City. Prices at places in the latter are generally a good deal more expensive, and the clientele pays much more attention to dressing stylishly.

Discos rarely open their doors much before 10 p.m. A few of the more unusual discos are the **Happy Few** (Avenue Louise 19), where fish swim under the transparent dance floor, and the **Crocodile Club** (Royal Windsor Hotel), where live crocodiles keep an eye on dancers from behind glass. **Le Garage** (Rue Desguerroy 16) and **Le Morano** (Chaussée de Louvain 38) are also quite popular.

BARS

Canne à Sucre, Rue des Pigeons 12.
Cap de Nuit, Place de la Vieille Halle aux Blés 28.
Président Club W.T.C., Boulevard E. Jacqmain 180.
Vol de Nuit, Rue du Magistrat 33.
Wine Bar, Rue des Pigeons 9.

RESTAURANTS

La Grande Porte, Rue Notre-Seigneur 9. Open: until 2 a.m. during the week and until 4 a.m. on the weekend.
Mok Ma Zwet, Rue des Carmélites. Open: until 2 a.m. during the week and until 3 a.m. Friday and Saturday.
Le Mozart, Chaussée d'Alsemberg. Open: until 5 a.m. during the week and until 6 a.m.

on the weekend. Closed: Monday and Sunday.

La Roue d'Or, Rue des Chapeliers. Open: until midnight. Closed: Sunday.

SHOPPING

There are numerous areas in Brussels where you can shop to your heart's content. In the Lower City you'll find fine shops at the Place de Brouckère, the Place de la Monnaie, along the Boulevard Anspach (predominantly fashion boutiques), in the modern shopping complex "City 2", located on Rue Neuve, in the "Passage du Nord" and the "Galerie du Commerce". The Rue au Beurre and Rue du Midi are also two well-known shopping beats; along the latter there are quite a few music stores.

Some of the absolutely best places to go window shopping are in the glass-roofed arcades, for instance in the famous "St Hubert", which was constructed in 1847 and is one of the oldest, glass-roofed department stores in all of Europe.

Fancy shops with internationally recognised names are concentrated in the Upper City around the Place Louise and along the Avenue Louise, Porte de Namur and Chaussée d'Ixelles. The noblest and most elegant arcades are located in the Upper City as well. You'll find both the "Galerie Espace Louise" and the "Galerie Louise" at the Place Louise; the "Galeries de la Toison" and the "Galerie d'Ixelles" are located at Porte de Namur.

Brussels is known for its fine chocolate, crystalware, weapons, diamonds and, last but certainly not least, the world-famous Brussels Lace. You'll find souvenir shops just about everywhere tourists tend to visit: around the Grand' Place, by the Manneken Pis, near the stock exchange and opera house.

Foreigners enjoy the advantage of being able to purchase items without paying additional tax.

There are several different markets in Brussels also well worth visiting. Take a stroll through the Flower and Bird Market (Sunday mornings at the Grand' Place Grote Markt), the Flea Market (operating daily at the Place du Jeu de Balle), or the Antique Market (taking place on weekends at the Place du Sablon).

SPORTS

The most popular sport in Belgium is cycling. You'll find avid cyclists everywhere, despite the fact that traffic in Brussels is relatively chaotic and drivers more or less inconsiderate. Bicycle racing also enjoys wide-spread popularity – as evidenced by the sheer number of spectators who come out to cheer.

SPECTATOR

SOCCER

Heizel Stadium, Marathonlaan 135, 1020 Brussels.
Royal Belgian Football Association, Wetstraat 43, 1040 Brussels.
Racing White Daring de Molenbeek, Charles Malisstraat 61, 1080 Brussels.
Royal Union Saint-Gilloise, Brussels-esteenweg 223, 1190 Brussels.
Sporting Club Anderlechtois, Thé Verbeecklaan 2 (Park Astrid), 1070 Brussels.

HORSE RACING

Boitsfort, Terhulpsesteenweg 51, 1170 Brussels.
Groenendael, Sint-Jansberglaan 4, Hoeilaart.
Sterrebeek, Avenue du Roy de Bliquylaan 43.

PARTICIPANT

There are sporting and recreational centres located in all the different districts of Greater Brussels, where non-members will find plenty of opportunities to work up a sweat. The selection of available activities runs the gamut from bowling to ice-skating, soccer, golf, mini-golf, roller-skating, tennis, swimming and squash. Avid cycling fans can rent bicycles all over the country.

In the park "Le Bois de la Cambre" there is a large lake where you can rent a rowing boat.

ICE-SKATING RINKS

Poseidon, Dapperenlaan 4. Tel: 762 16 33.
Vorst Nationaal, Globelaan 36. Tel: 377 41 67.

GOLF

Brussels Golf School and Training Center, Ter Hulpsesteenweg 53A, 1170 Brussels.
Royal Golf Club of Belgium, Route de la Marache 19, 1328 Ohain.

SPORTS CENTRES

Heizel, Marathonlaan 135. Tel: 479 36 54
Neder-over-Heembeek, Korte Groenweg 99. Tel: 267 96 33.
Omnisport, Lombardsijdestraat 130. Tel: 268 00 43.
Sint-Pieters-Woluwe, Salomélaan 2. Tel: 762 12 75.
Soignes-Wald, Schallerlaan 50. Tel: 660 12 82.
Woluwe, Mounierlaan 87. Tel: 762 85 22.
Zuidpaleis, Rogier van der Weydenstraat. Tel: 513 39 77.

SWIMMING POOLS

Anderlecht, Lijsterstraat 51. Tel: 523 11 65.
Bosvoorde, L. Wienerlaan 60. Tel: 673 39 29.
Brussels, Reebokstraat 28. Tel: 511 24 68.
Elsene, Zwemkunststraat 8-10. Tel: 511 90 84.
Etterbeek, Veldstraat 71. Tel: 640 38 38.
Evere, Oud-Strijderslaan 260. Tel: 242 50 55.
Ganshoren, Fabiolaplein 10. Tel: 427 31 91.

Heizel, Oceadium. Tel: 478 49 44.
Laeken, Kerkveldstraat 73-89. Tel: 425 57 12.
Molenbeek, Van Kalckstraat 93. Tel: 522 08 03.
Neder-over-Heembeek, Lombardsijdestraat 130. Tel: 268 00 43.
Schaarbeek, Neptunium, Jerusalemstraat 56. Tel: 512 72 08.
Sint-Gillis, Wipstraat 38. Tel: 539 06 15.
Sint-Joost, Sint-Franciscusstraat 23-27. Tel: 217 39 41.
Sint-Lambrechts-Woluwe, Dapperenlaan 2. Tel: 771 76 89.
Sint-Pieters-Woluwe, Salomélaan 2. Tel: 762 12 75.
Ukkel, De Frésquare 1. Tel: 374 90 04.

LANGUAGE

FRENCH

GENERAL TERMS

Good day	*Bonjour*
Good evening	*Bonsoir*
Goodbye	*Au revoir*
I	*je*
me	*moi*
we	*nous*
yes	*oui*
no	*non*
please	*s'il vous plaît*
thank you	*merci*
excuse me	*pardon*
where	*où*
when	*quand*
how long?	*combien de temps?*

TIME

today	*aujourd'hui*
yesterday	*hier*
tomorrow	*demain*
day	*jour*
week	*semaine*

month	*mois*
year	*année*
Monday	*lundi*
Tuesday	*mardi*
Wednesday	*mercredi*
Thursday	*jeudi*
Friday	*vendredi*
Saturday	*samedi*
Sunday	*dimanche*

OPPOSITES

left/right	*à gauche/à droite*
open/close	*ouvert/fermé*
big/little	*grand/petit*
cheap/expensive	*bon marché/cher*
early/late	*de bonne heure/tard*
old/new	*vieux/nouveau*
cold/hot	*froid/chaud*

NUMBERS

0	*zéro*	
1	*un/une*	
2	*deux*	
3	*trois*	
4	*quatre*	
5	*cinq*	
6	*six*	
7	*sept*	
8	*huit*	
9	*neuf*	
10	*dix*	
11	*onze*	
12	*douze*	
13	*treize*	
14	*quatorze*	
15	*quinze*	
16	*seize*	
17	*dix-sept*	
18	*dix-huit*	
19	*dix-neuf*	
20	*vingt*	
30	*trente*	
40	*quarante*	
50	*cinquante*	
60	*soixante*	
70	*soixante-dix*	*(belg. septant)*
80	*quatre-vingt*	*(belg. huitant)*
90	*quatre-vingt-dix*	*(belg. nonant)*
100	*cent*	
200	*deux cents*	
500	*cinq cents*	
1000	*mille*	

NOUNS

railway station	*gare*
airport	*aéroport*
mail office	*poste*
mailbox	*boîte aux lettres*
stamps	*timbre-poste*
police	*police*
bank	*banque*
chemist's	*pharmacie*
petrol station	*station-service*
supermarket	*supermarché*
hairdresser's	*coiffeur*
hospital	*hôpital*
doctor	*médecin*

SHORT SENTENCES

What's your name?
Comment appelez-vous?

I don't understand
Je ne comprends pas!

Do you speak English?
Parlez-vous anglais?

How much does that cost?
Combien ça coute?

DUTCH

GENERAL TERMS

Good morning	*Goedemorgen*
Good day	*Goedendag*
Good evening	*Goedenavond*
Good-bye	*Tot ziens*
I	*ik*
we	*wij*
yes	*ja*
no	*nee*
please	*alstublieft*
thank you	*dank u wel*
excuse me	*pardon*
where	*waar*
when	*wanneer*
how	*hoe*
how long?	*hoelang?*
how much?	*hoeveel?*

TIME

today	vandaag
yesterday	gisteren
tomorrow	morgen
day	dag
week	week
month	maand
year	jaar
Monday	maandag
Tuesday	dinsdag
Wednesday	woensdag
Thursday	donderdag
Friday	vrijdag
Saturday	zaterdag
Sunday	zondag

OPPOSITES

left/right	links/rechts
open/closed	open/gesloten
big/little	groot/klein
cheap/expensive	goedkoop/duur
early/late	vroeg/laat
old/new	oud/nieuw
cold/hot	koud/heet

NUMBERS

0	nul
1	één
2	twee
3	drie
4	vier
5	vijf
6	zes
7	zeven
8	acht
9	negen
10	tien
11	elf
12	twaalf
13	dertien
14	veertien
15	vijfteen
16	zestien
17	zeventien
18	achttien
19	negentien
20	twintig
30	dertig
40	veertig
50	vijftig
60	zestig
70	zeventig
80	tachtig
90	negentig
100	honderd
200	tweehonderd
500	vijfhonderd
1000	duizend

NOUNS

railway station	station
airport	vliegveld
post office	postkantoor
postbox	brievenbus
stamps	postzegel
police	politie
bank	bank
chemist's	apotheek
petrol station	tank station
supermarket	supermarkt
hairdresser's	kappa
hospital	ziekenhuis
doctor	arts

SHORT SENTENCES

What's your name?
Hoe heet u?

I don't understand
Ik versta u nit!

Do you speak English?
Spreekt u Engels?

How much does that cost?
Wat kost dat?

FURTHER READING

Hugo Claus, *The Sorrow of Belgium*.
The story of a boy growing up in Nazi-occupied Flanders.

Michael Glover, *A New Guide to the Battlefiled of Northern France and the Low Country*.

A. de Meeiis, *History of the Belgians*.
Colourful and wide-ranging history of the Belgians.

Gregory Martin, *Bruegel*.
Introduction to the works of Pieter Bruegel.

Alastair Smart, *The Renaissance and Mannerism Outside Italy*.

Theo Aronson, *Defiant Dynasty: The Coburgs of Belgium*.
Gossipy history of the kins of the House of Saxe-Coburg-Gotha from 1831 to 1950.

John Gunter, *Twelve Cities*.
Includes a lively if dated essay on the temperament of Brussels and its citizens.

E.H. Kossman, *The Low Countries: 1780–1940*.
Thorough history.

USEFUL ADDRESSES

OUTSIDE THE REGION

Denmark
Det Officielle Belgiske Turistbureau
Vester Farimagsgade 7–9
1606 Kopenhagen V
Tel: 12 47 77/12 30 27. Telex 22 941.

France
Office Belge de Tourisme
21, Boulevard des Capucines
75002 Paris
Tel: 1/47 42 41 18
Telex 214726 tourbel f.

Germany
Belgisches Verkehrsamt
Berliner Allee 47
4000 Düsseldorf
Tel: 0211/32 60 08
Telex 8588260 beva d.

Great Britain
Belgian Tourist Office
Premier House, Gayton Road
Harrow
Tel: 081-861 3300
Telex 296358 – Pretsel 29029.

Holland
Belgisch Verkeersbureau
Herengracht 435–437
1017 BR Amsterdam
Tel: 020/25 12 51
Telex 13452 belto.

Italy
Ufficio Belga per il Turismo
Piazza Velasqua 5
20122 Milano
Tel: 286 05 66.

Japan
Belgian National Tourist Office
Tameike Tokyu Bldg 9 F 1–14
Akasaka 1-chome, Minato-ku Tokyo
Tel: 586 70 41/2
Telex T23 81 – cgt.tyo

Sweden
Belgiska Turistbyra
Box 19520
10432 Stockholm 19
Tel: 34 15 75/31 41 19
Telex 13 812.

USA
Belgian Tourist Office
745, Fifth Avenue
New York 10151
Tel: 212/758 81 30
Telex 237933 bntour.

BRUSSELS

It is possible to book a hotel room anywhere in Belgium by calling one of the following numbers (if calling from outside Belgium, dial the international code followed by 32, and omit the zero from the Brussels code):

Belgium Tourist Reservations
Postfach 41
1000 Brussels 23
Tel: 02/230 50 29
Telex: 65 888 BTR B.

Vlaams Commissariaat-Generaal voor Toerisme
Grasmarkt/Rue du Marché aux Herbes 61
1000 Brussels
Tel: 02/513 90 90
Telex 63245 BBRU B. Fax 02/513 88 03.

Office de Promotion du Tourisme de la Communauté Française de Belgique
Rue du Marché aux Herbes/Grasmarkt 61
1000 Brussels
Tel: 02/518 12 11
Telex 26816 OPTOUR B.

BORDER INFORMATION

Information is available at the following border crossings:
The border on the E 10 (Breda – Antwerp – Brussels)
The border on the E 5 (Aachen Liège – Brussels)
The border on the E 10 (Paris – Valenciennes – Mons – Brussels)
At the National Zaventem Airport (in the main arrival hall)

CITY TOURS

Sightseeing Tours, Rue de la Colline 8. Tel: 513 77 44.
Arau, Rue Henri Maus 37. Tel: 513 47 61.
Arcadia, Avenue de Tervuren 289. Tel: 358 61 11.
Association du Patrimoine Artistique, Rue aux Laines 20. Tel: 512 34 21.
Bavard, Galeries du Centre, Rue des Fripiers 15. Tel: 512 54 11.
Brukselbinnenstebuiten, Rue L. Lepage 9. Tel: 511 78 83.
Panorama Tours, Rue du Marché aux Herbes 105. Tel: 513 61 54.

AUTOMOBILE CLUBS

Royal Automobile Club de Belgique (RACB), Rue d'Arlons 53, 1000 Brussels. Tel: 230 08 10 and 736 59 59.
Touringclub Royal de Belgique (TCB), Rue de la Loi 44–46, 1000 Brussels. Tel: 233 22 11, 513 82 40 and 512 78 90.
Vlaamse Automobilistenbond (VAB), Jacqmain 126, 1000 Brussels. Tel: 219 32 44.

CHAMBER OF COMMERCE

International Chamber of Commerce/ Chambre de Commerce Internationale, Rue Sols 8. Tel: 512 65 41.
Brussels Chamber of Commerce/ Chambre de Commerce de Bruxelles, Avenue Louise 500. Tel: 648 50 02.
Swiss Chamber of Commerce/Chambre de Commerce Suisse, Rue du Congrès 1. Tel: 217 55 43.

EUROPEAN COMMUNITY OFFICES

The building housing the European Community offices is located at Robert-Schumann-Platz. You'll find the EC Council of Ministers at Rue de la Loi 100. Tel: 234 61 11. The EC Commission also has its seat in the Rue de la Loi, No. 200. Tel: 235 11 11. You can register for a guided tour by calling one of the above numbers.

DIPLOMATIC MISSIONS

Great Britain
Rue Joseph II 28
Etterbeck
Tel: 217 90 00

USA
Boulevard de Regent 27
Tel: 513 3830

Canada
Avenue de Telvarel 2
Tel: 735 60 40

Australia
Avenue des Arts 52
Tel: 213 05 00

Ireland
Rue du Luxembourg 19
Tel: 513 66 33

ART/PHOTO CREDITS

INDEX